MW01199074

The Poets' Encyclopedia *is available in hardbound, paperbound and magazine editions.*

First Edition

The Poets' Encyclopedia, *as an issue of* Unmuzzled Ox, *was made possible by grants from the National Endowment for the Arts and the New York State Council on the Arts.* Unmuzzled Ox *is edited by Michael Andre and Erika Rothenberg, and is located at 105 Hudson Street, New York N.Y. 10013.*

Hardbound ISBN 0-934450-02-1
Paperbound ISBN 0-934450-03-X
Magazine US ISSN 0049-5557

PRINTED
IN
U.S.A.

THE POETS'
Encyclopedia

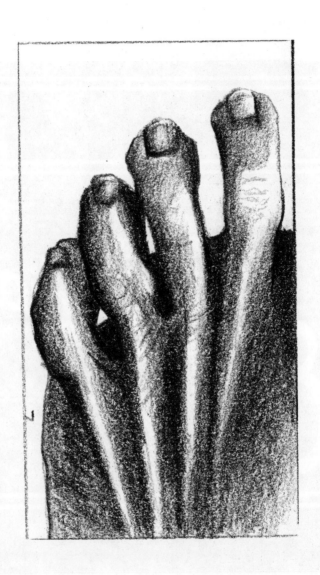

See "Giant," page ix   —Marisol

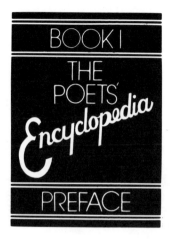

BOOK I

THE POETS' Encyclopedia

PREFACE

As the author's chair was empty, we sat in it, assuming all authority. Poets are the best authors. And here their business is to examine, not the individual, but the species, to remark general properties and large appearances. Audacious! The Poets imagine all knowledge; and thus their Encyclopedia contains everything worth knowing or imagining. Everything? The poet, of course, does not number the streaks of the tulip, or describe the different shades of the verdure of the forest. Everything is seen as a part of the Whole.

ALCOHOL

We were thinking about abstractions, and as it happens we were brunching with **Marisol** and **Arakawa** and **Madeleine Gins,** slugging back the tequila, and **Robert Creeley** said, "This sure gets in your blood."

"I stay pretty staid if the level of alcohol in my blood is less than 0.05%," said **Tom Shannon.** "I don't tend to turn sprightly until the level rises to 0.1%, and I don't get courageous until the level reaches 0.2%. Raising the level to 0.3% can make me dangerous, and raising it again to 0.4% has made me delerious. By the time the concentration of alcohol in my blood reaches 0.5%, I am generally drunk. Afterwards if the concentration reached 0.6% I would probably seem dead drunk, and if it reached 0.7% I would without doubt die."

We all nodded assent.

"You should put that in the poets' encyclopedia," Madeleine said.

"What's that?" I said.

DAVE'S CORNER

The next morning **Phil Corner** and I had the identical breakfast at Dave's Corner, a 24-hour truck stop. In the Sixties **Alison Knowles** ate the same lunch every day at the same place, and Phil, having lunch there with Alison, pointed out that this *habit* was a *piece*. Phil and I were commemorating that lunch in an effort to jar us into a collaboration.

"It'd take us years just to do Volume A" I told Phil, speaking of Madeleine's idea.

"I'd do 'armony" said Phil—who is not only, like Alison, a Fluxus performer, but a composer.

"It couldn't just be about the arts," I said.

"I'd do army" he said.

UNMUZZLED OX OCARINA ORCHESTRA

That night the ocarina group met, as usual, over the Ear Inn. Between pieces, **Charles Morrow**, another composer, made up three three-word definitions. That advanced matters but didn't help matters, i.e. it showed that poets, artists and musicians all had *ideas* but that, at Charles' rate, the Encyclopedia would need ten years or 1200 contributors.

"I wrote a book called *The Domesday Dictionary*," said **Armand Schwerner**, a poet who double tongues a wild ocarina, baby. "It's been out-of-print fifteen years but judging from the newspapers I think its time has come again. The definitions from physics and psychology—and poetry—would flesh out your Encyclopedia." Ti-toot, ti-toot.

Unmuzzled Ox Ocarina Orchestra! An ox muzzle, according

to Joseph Quinn, is made best of a heavy iron frame covered with chicken wire, it fits over the head of the ox with a strap over the horns and keeps the ox from eating. "Without a muzzle," Joe says, "an ox will eat all the time and do nothing else. A horse can be checked up, but not an ox."

Joe Quinn believes the ox is the solution to the energy crisis. He's written a book to prove it—as if I needed convincing! But on this matter of the muzzle he differs significantly from Deuteronomy: "Thou shalt not muzzle the ox who treadeth out the corn." Paul, in a later testament, questioned whether Moses wrote this for its relevance to agriculture or for its meaning in our lives. Paul said: "For our sakes, no doubt, this is written; that he that ploweth should plow in hope; and that he that thresheth in hope should be partaker of his hope."

HOPE

Corn? Did Moses have corn? I referred Paul's remarks to **Daniel Berrigan** and Moses' to **David Rosenberg**. Daniel said that there used to be a coffee shop at Cornell named Unmuzzled Ox, and he ate there frequently, but never corn. David would only say that Joe Quinn's practise was not kosher.

THEORY OF TITTLEBATS

A casual observer, adds the secretary, to whose notes I am indebted for the following account—a casual observer might possibly have remarked nothing extraordinary in the bald head and circular spectacles which were intently turned towards his (Rosenberg's) face during the making of the above jokes; to those who knew the gigantic brain of **T.W. Fretter** was working beneath that forehead, and that the beaming eyes of Fretter were twinkling behind those glasses the sight was indeed an interesting one. There sat the man who had traced to their source the mighty ponds of Hampstead and agitated the scientific world with his Theory of Tittlebats, as calm and unmoved as the deep waters of the one on a frosty day or as a solitary specimen of the other in the inmost recesses of an earthen jar. And how much more interesting did the spectacle become when, starting into full life and animation, as a simultaneous call of "Fretter" burst from his followers, that illustrious man slowly mounted into the Windsor chair, on which he had been previously seated, and addressed the club which he had founded. What a study for an artist did that exciting scene present! The eloquent Fretter, with one hand gracefully concealed behind his coattails and the other waving in air to assist his glowing declamation; his elevated position revealing those tights and gaiters, which worn by an ordinary man might have passed without observation, but which when Fretter clothed them—if we may use the expression—inspired voluntary awe and respect; surrounded by the men who had volunteered to share the perils of his travels, and who were destined to participate in the glories of his discoveries. On the right hand sat **Mr Dick Higgins**, the too-susceptible Higgins, who to the wisdom and experience of maturer years superadded the enthusiasm and ardour of a boy, in the most interesting and pardonable of human weaknesses: love. On the left of his great leader sat the poetic **Mr Michael Brownstein**, and near him again the sporting **Mr Russell Edson**, the former poetically enveloped in a mysterious blue cloak with a canine-skin collar, and the latter communicating additional lustre to a new green shooting-coat, plaid neckerchief, and closely fitted drabs.

THE EIGHTIES

"Robert Bly," began Fretter, "has combined Imagism and Surrealism to produce (his magazines) *The Fifties, The Sixties* and *The Seventies.* In the greatest modern poetry, Bly says, 'Everything is said by image, and nothing by direct statement.' Bly favors the 'deep image'—a kind of particularism. **Allen Ginsberg** has sung, literally, his praise of particulars, Jerome Rothenberg actually first used the term 'deep image'; it is the accepted hippy literary dogma.

"But the modesty of thirty years of examples pains us," continued Fretter. "In shunning the general, they have forgotten the universal. Robert Bly writes of the blood but does not know the chemistry of the blood. When we slipped in a quote from Samuel Johson in the beginning of *The Poets' Encyclopedia*—the poet is concerned "not with the individual, but the species'—we violated this dogma. *The Poets' Encyclopedia* violates this dogma. It is a literary upstart.

CONCEPTUAL ART

"However thought is not altogether a novelty in the art world, as **Donald Kuspit** emphasizes in his entry 'Conceptual Art.' Indeed, as we put the Encyclopedia together, talking about it or sending invitations to any artist who interested us, we noticed a majority of those who responded could have been called, although they themselves may not care for the term, Conceptual Artists: Arakawa, **Les Levine, General Idea, John Baldessari, Vitaly Komar** (though perhaps not **Alexandr Melamid), Ray Johnson, Christo, Chris Burden, Carolee Schneemann, Walter de Maria.**" Fretter paused, that the club would appreciate the weight of his list, then with a slightly cutting tone cited two last facts, evidently decisive. "**Mr Timothy Baum** then pointed out that Bly in fact misinterprets the Surrealists, that they were most prone to generalize; and **Ms Ursule Molinaro** found as final proof the *Dictionaire Abrigé du Surrealisme,* working up for our *Encyclopedia* imitations of some thirty entries!"

PORTION OF THE HYPERBOLE OF THE FOOT [OX]

The castration of a young bull by nomads in Anatolia after about 8,000 B.C. was doubtless a superstitious and barbarous sacrifice. But it produced an ox, which was the first draught animal. With that beast, the nomads could settle down, cultivate the soil and themselves, and start writing.

Before words there were pictures, and a "first" picture was the ox. The Assyrian glyph for ox became the Egyptian hieroglyph for ox, which went through Talmudic, Arabian, Greek, and Hebrew to become our letter "A." In English we can keep sight of the primacy of the ox, since it has been given in letters the two most universal abstract symbols: the circle and the cross, the whole and the denial. The wholeness of the bull was sacrificed, cancelled.

CONCLUSION OF AN EXAGGERATED ANIMAL [GIANT]

Much of the writing in the *Encyclopedia* is language-oriented; that is, the language is used not only as a tool of description but as the object of that description as well. The first entry is "About" by **James Sherry**, the last is "Zyxt" by **Ron Silliman.** Robert Creeley starts with etymology, finding first clues in the history of language. An encyclopedia lops off as a dictionary. **Gary Snyder** begins—and ends—with etymology—wittily. A dictionary condenses into an issue of a magazine. What is this, then—the giant's toe, shrunken?

Let us think about the giant's toe. Will he be back to get it? Auspicious to all who long for further grandiosities! **Bulent Ecevit** has become prime minister of Turkey again. (He is a poet; who is the last painter to head a country? Adolf Hitler?) Only **Rene Levesque** of our other contributors heads a state; and Levesque's entry was, like all our autobiographical entries, taped. Using the appendix thoughtfully, you can answer remaining questions and fill your days with meaning. Do I hear a distant heavy tread shaking the mountains? This concludes my contributors' notes, they're far too brief, omitting everyone (save Fretter) of importance, a mere line strung between polemical and narrative twigs. But, you hear? here it comes, limping and crashing, thrashing, tearing the trees. Like me, e-vacuate your old abodes. Hear it come!

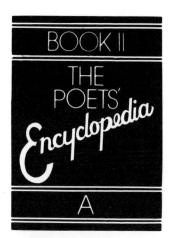

BOOK II
THE POETS' *Encyclopedia*
A

ABOUT

This is about about, until now a subject reference, point of interest or city all roads converged upon. This is about about; to say what it's about and to be about it on all sides, around its house, in circuit, around the outside, here and there, approximately, almost, also includes a reversed position, in rotation, colloquially, near, in the vicinity, all round, in the neighborhood, not far from, on the verge of as a gerund (about being), concerning, but no longer "the subject" or what it's "about", more in the original sense of outside. It is the indexed subject, a space of nouns, persons in action, the words that pertain to their vicinity and intention or set them off by opposition. Space is made for a subject by delineating around it. The subject is what's left over: Not the thing, but what's about it.

Such non-referential and abstract modes express characteristics; for example, beauty is about ends, the spaces between our points of view, that is, about the corruption that fosters it—a possibility not out of line with traditional notions of transience. This is presented as an alternative to narrative creation, clothes that do not fit or are artified to appear to fit. The emperor's new clothes concealed nothing, and one can see now he is naked.

—James Sherry

ABSOLUTE, THE

French fried ice cream.

—Michael Brownstein

ABYSS STRUCTURE
See Self-Reflexivity

ACADEMIC
Same thing as acne, something which grows on the body surface and leaves ugly marks long after the initial symptoms have been gotten rid of.

—Les Levine

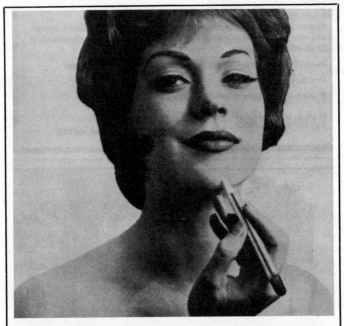

GET RID OF UNWANTED HAIR

ACNE
See Academic

ACTION

When the form and effect of a pursuit could not have been predicted from the variables of its context, the pursuit is said to have been an *action*. In this, actions differ from *behavior*. Behavior is consistent with the variables of its context and is more or less predictable; it can be studied and controlled; it can be reproduced in machines; it supplies constancy to the environment. Actions connote deeds; they produce innovation, and, in concert, revolution. That actions vanish under observation—they are total victims of the reflexive phenomenon—is one reason why innovation becomes habit, and revolutions are lost.

—Armand Schwerner & Donald M. Kaplan

Action is the nearest thing to oblivion. It leaves no impression on the soul, somewhat like happiness, which likewise passes in a vague state through the memory and leaves no mark.

—Carl Rakosi

ACTIVE

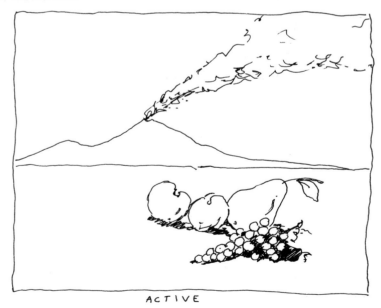

ACTIVE

—Brian Buczak

ADDRESS

I'm no poet (since 1935) and can't rhyme for ENCY-CLOPEDIA. But can define *address* as being place where I am. Left Florida long time ago and now get mail in Arizona. Thanks.

Best wishes,
—Erskine Caldwell

P.O. Box 4550/Hopi Station
Scottsdale, Arizona 85258

AEROPLANE

A man wants an aeroplane to like him. He doesn't like it, but he wants it to like him. The aeroplane doesn't.

He says to the aeroplane, like me.

The aeroplane doesn't; and likes him even less than it might have had he not pushed himself on it.

Like me, screams the man, you rotten king of the poopers!

The aeroplane considers him one of those mentally defective things that constantly go outside their category to find other things to like them, because their own category doesn't.

Well, I don't like you neither, you kinky thingumajig! you snotty despicable! you rum-crazy dummy! you shit-faced carrot! you applesauced whacker! you collie dog without a nose! you sugarplummed dowager!

Meanwhile, the aeroplane has fallen asleep.

The man was screaming, wake up, you carpet tack! you ticklish custard; wake up when I talk, you clever sap!

The aeroplane just doesn't think it worth waking up to hear this particular category's particular sounds, no matter the flattery intended in this particular category's peculiar sounds...

—Russell Edson

4

AESTHETIC

Same thing as anesthetic, something to put you to sleep.

—Les Levine

See Academic

AESTHETICS

That branch of religion which is concerned with the unseen or unperceivable mysteries of the arts: a specialty of Central Europeans, but an unmentionable topic in North America.

—Dick Higgins

ALARMA!

At the time I lived in Mexico, the leading scandal magazine was *Alarma!* It was very popular and I saw it being read everywhere. I never looked at such magazines in the United States, but for some reason I did in Mexico. Partly it was because they were prominently displayed and the lurid photos caught my eye. Looking at *Alarma!* was also a one-minute Spanish lesson. I never held a copy in my hand or got beyond the front page. But I always paused at the magazine stands, most often on the busy streetcorners of Mexico City, to look at the arresting photos and read the headlines and captions.

Alarma! and its imitator *Alerta* often featured morgue photographs of murder victims, juxtaposed with photos of the living murderers. They also juxtaposed photos of people when they were alive with photos of their dead faces. Suicides of young people were a favorite subject, especially those who had hanged themselves. I still remember a poignant photo of a teenage girl who had stepped out of her shoes first.

A typical headline in *Alarma!* was "Fourteen Murders in Huasteca." One time I saw a photo of a wistful-looking little man; then the caption said that he had killed five of his six children with a machete. Another headline was "He Kills His Old Wife to Be with a Young Girl," with photos of the three of them. A gang-rape story was headlined "The Night Ends in Misery for the Romantic Señorita."

I was interested in the comments, denunciations, and moral judgements that often followed the headlines in *Alarma!,* such as: The Scoundrels!....Depraved!....A Madman!....The Beasts!....Horrible!....An Outrage!....The Vultures!....A Monster!....Incredible!

I remember a story about Mexican soldiers who were searching passengers on a rural bus, looking for weapons being smuggled to guerrillas. The outraged headline read "Soldiers Touch Women in Their Intimate Parts!" For me, reading this in Spanish *(Partes Intimas)* on a busy streetcorner in Mexico City, it was unreal. The most memorable headline of all in *Alarma!* was this: "He Screws His Daughter's Dead Body, Then Lends It to a Friend!"

—Kenneth Gangemi

ALBERTFINE, THE

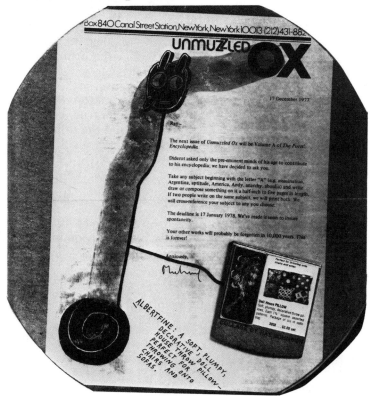

Box 840 Canal Street Station, New York, New York 10013 (212) 431-882

UNMUZZLED OX

17 December 1977

Ray—

The next issue of *Unmuzzled Ox* will be Volume A of *The Poets' Encyclopedia*.

Diderot asked only the pre-eminent minds of his age to contribute to his encyclopedia; we have decided to ask you.

Take any subject beginning with the letter "A" (e.g. assasination, Argentina, aptitude, America, Andy, anarchy, aboulia) and write, draw or compose something on it a half-inch to five pages in length. If two people write on the same subject, we will print both. We will cross-reference your subject to any you choose.

The deadline is 17 January 1978. We've made it soon to insure spontaneity.

Your other works will probably be forgotten in 10,000 years. This is forever!

Anxiously,

ALBERTFINE: A SOFT, PLUMPY, DECORATIVE THROW DOLL. HOUSE THROW PILLOW. PERFECT FOR THROWING ONTO CHAIRS AND SOFAS.

—Ray Johnson

ALIMENTARY

"Alimentary, my dear Watson!" was the initial form of Sherlock Holmes' admonition to his colleague and co-worker, Dr. Watson. In the latter part of the nineteenth century, where piano legs were draped to avoid the suggestion of nudity, this was thought to be too apparent a reference to the nether part of said canal so, on the suggestion of his editors, Holmes' creator, Sir Arthur Conan Doyle, altered his statement to what has become one of the most quoted single lines in all fiction:"Elementary, my dear Watson!" This half-rhyme allusion to the word from the original line was sufficient to alert prurient *cognoscenti* the world over to the real meaning of this passage: "Watson, you anus!" (This of course reverts, in the vulgate, to "Watson, you asshole!")[1] The joke was doubly on Sir Arthur's editor, a former American schoolmaster who understandably (but mistakenly) associated "elementary" with "primary school" rather than the "four elements" to which Sir Arthur was referring. These are, naturally, earth, fire, water, and air—or wind, a conventional metonymy of the era, which cleverly masks Sir Arthur's true intent: "Break wind, Watson!" Only too late did the unfortunate editor realize that Holmes was admonishing his dear friend to "fart," an action characteristic of Sir Arthur's favorite part of the body, the nether (or "hind") section of the *alimentary* canal.

—**Jane DeLynn**

[1] Whether and how this sheds light on Holmes' relations with his one-time and apparently platonic roommate is unfortunately beyond the scope of this inquiry.

AMATEUR ARTIST
An artist whose ideas are still alive and changing, hence unacceptable.

—**Dick Higgins**

AMBIGUOUS
Something that is too big for its boots.

See Permanence   —**Les Levine**

AMERICAN ART
What middle class dropouts make for upper class sponsors when they aren't too busy posing as socialists.

—Dick Higgins

AMPERSAND

Ampersand

—Hannah Weiner

ANAL INTERCOURSE
Dimitri's cock was the instrument perfectly shaped to penetrate without pain. The head tended towards a point, aided by the closed foreskin which slid back only a fraction of an inch to expose little more than the hole in the head. Dimitri knew the technique: lubricate the asshole with saliva, knead with the finger's tip; after more saliva is applied, rub and tease the anal opening to excite a pleasurable feeling, spit on the head of your prick, do not insert more than half the glans at first, spread buttock cheeks with both hands—or, better, enlist the service of your partner for this—then with slow, working up to accelerated, motions move the entire head forward and backwards, taking care not to extract it entirely. 'Now you do it,' say to your partner, and hold still while he thrusts backwards with his ass. Once your prick is in beyond the head, leave it to him (or her) to make all the movements. As your prick grows larger, thrust further, and have your partner pinned firmly down, for it is at this junction that he may feel some pain due to the maximum stretching of the sphincter, and, when you are in still further, the prick comes in contact with the end of the colon where it curves into the rectum. It is precisely at this curvature that both pain and pleasure will be pronounced, the pain turning more and more into pleasure the more the recipient approaches orgasm. Maximum pleasure will be felt by him at the Turning Point rather than in the head of his prick. This is known as an anal orgasm. Dimitri was an expert at inducing such

9

pleasure and it was the first time Greene had experienced it. The fact that Dimitri shot his load at the same time that Greene came made the union perfect. If Dimitri's orgasm had been delayed after Greene ejaculated, the pleasure of being fucked would have vanished, and only a disagreeable sensation would remain, of something being bruised. All wars are sex wars. Those with the most explosive balls win. You can't sneeze with a cunt but an asshole can spit back.

—Charles Henri Ford

BRAINARD-73

See Sex

—Joe Brainard

ANDY

Andy Warhol did a cover and picture portfolio for *Kulchur 13* in 1964. He did my portrait in 1966. In 1967 I published a collaboration between him and Gerard Malanga, called *Screen Tests.* He gave me a gift of 10 Marilyn silk screens in 1968. Now I don't see much of Andy anymore.

—Lita Hornick

Andy's feet, Victor Hugo's body, Photograph: Jimmy de Sana

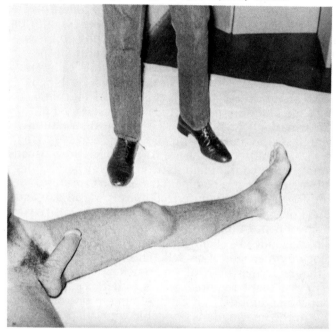

ANESTHETIC

An anesthetic, which comes at times as Gas, at times as Liquid but always as a Drug, is the very opposite of an esthetic which comes solely as choice and is always an acknowledgement of pain. The anesthetic and the aesthetic have battled for time immemorial for domination of the mind. The anesthetic has always come at the time of an excess of esthetic and has always produced new reasons for the next esthetic.

The greatest anesthetic ever assembled is the United States of America. Its political, social and economic structures are at the service of an anesthetic impulse: the elimination of pain at all cost, the so-called "pursuit of happiness." This Nation-Drug has produced a human mutation here, a person who is individually ruthless and tribally dedicated to the art of abstraction, to the annihilation of particulars. The rituals of this society consist in a squeezing upward of energy toward an obscure repository of spirituality *which never overflows* thereby giving rise to the perfectly plausible assumption that this energy *feeds something or someone up there.* American culture is a commentary on a future inspiration which *hasn't paid a red cent yet.* America has no present, it is a huge investment in a Future nothing is known about except that it is *exact,* like a machine. Under the sanction of exactitude, it has stamped out its imagination. North America is the most structurally oriented society in the world and it has found myriad ways to instantly comprehend form. Forms are grasped at once, while content and its attending mysteries does not exist except as a commentary on the capture of form, for which a computerized hunt is waged day and night. For a nation, an experience composed entirely in the act of capturing form, is an enormous spiritual drain, it is indeed a shameless exhibit of the rape of biology by mechanical models. This rape and its pain are the modern esthetic of America.

The anesthetic required by this esthetic cannot be produced communally, it can be found in one place only: in the imaginations of people who can populate the world with Imaginary Beings (*q.v.*).

Fortunately, these people are omni-present. Conventionally, there aren't many of them. But if counted with their Creations, the statistics skyrocket. These people, in disguises, under cover, pro personae, are to be found at *every capture of form.* In fact, their presence slowly permeates the essence of the hunt until the hunt comes to a standstill. The Century Insurance Man, with his rifle pointed dreamily in the air, is a statue. He cannot move. America is going through the motions. It is at this moment, when the world is at a standstill, that we have a paradoxical commitment of faith to an esthetic which propagandises

the anesthetic. But the moment passes, and the under-
belly of the wheel shows up.

—Andrei Codrescu

ANOMIE

(Gk. a—*without, hence, not; and* Nomikos, *customary).*
*Non*adjustment, as opposed to *mal*adjustment. The latter
implies a determined but repeatedly ineffectual effort
at getting on in one's environment. The former *(anomie)*
also involves not getting on in one's environment but
without the determination or the effort to do so. Hence,
anomic individuals are the eccentrics, the hermits, those
bizaare but "harmless" characters who go about their
business entirely "out of things," indifferent to groups,
to culture, to events current in the community. They are
found, in cities, living peculiar and isolated lives on the
borders of, rather than in, neighborhoods. They usually
give the impression of being maintained by strange sources
of income. Actually, most anomics are supported and
looked after by patient and resigned relatives.
   Anomie is thought to result when an individual has
been brought up strictly and narrowly to survive in a highly particular social structure, which somehow changes.
Thus, the aged, whose lives do span social change, are
especially prone to anomie; likewise numerous members
of those populations exposed to sudden social revolution
or extreme environmental alteration as by natural or man-
made disasters.   **—Armand Schwerner & Donald M. Kaplan**

ANSWER

an apple asked an
asp in Athens
do angels have
assholes?

the asp ate the
apple
a la carte
and went back to
reading
Aeschylus.

—Charles Bukowski

13

ANT

...referred to by entomologists as a relative of the bee who has not set foot in Paris.

—Peter Kostakis

ANTIMATTER

One of the plausibilities of a physics which has succeeded in discovering both more and less than it can account for.

Thus, the observations and mathematics of the currently numerous subatomic particles require the view that matter resides at two energy levels: a plus level and a minus level. Matter at the plus level composes that universe whose existence has always been apparent. Matter at the minus level also exists, but its existence, in respect to matter at the plus level, is only potential. On statistically concrete occasions a particle of matter at the minus level is struck by a vagrant ray of some kind, say, a cosmic ray, and the particle thereby acquires sufficient energy to materialize at the plus level. At this instant, a counterpart at the plus level may drop out of existence into the vacated energy hole, or a collison may occur between the materialized particle and a counterpart and both simply disappear in a wink of energy.

The likelihood of a cancellation of the cosmos in one swoop is small, according to the mathematics that separates the two levels of matter.

—Armand Schwerner & Donald M. Kaplan

See August 6, 1945

ANTI-WORLD

A place where thousands hear and see your participation, and free enterprise finds its moment of meaning. As in, "The paper bag rustled. Two women inside were talking."

—Michael Brownstein

ANXIETY

A painful sense of impending dread available only to a creature whose mentality has evolved sufficiently to entertain three prerequisite notions: *freedom of choice, the future,* and *the unknown.* It differs from *fear,* wherein

the danger is actual and external. In anxiety, the danger
is internal (psychological) and only imminent.
—**Armand Schwerner & Donald M. Kaplan**

ANYTHING

When the anything enters the bathroom, it
immediately throws the Vera towels
into the tub. When anything sits down,

it realizes the Vera towels are yellow,
orange, sticky, dirty, wet, "que porkeria,"
anything whispers into its bag, remorse

dribbling from anything's hot pants. When
anything is my last wife, I am never able
to locate it. It is a tackle-box full of fluff.

I can't even put this stupid anything away.
Her bones are filled with the ah-ah disease.
Try & burn that as if it was a simple bag

of worms killing the apple tree. My son
is being turned into another anything
by a bunch of Russian turnips. My son,

the anything of their accountant's desire.
My son's eyes are full of anything but
tears, fear, or loss. I dry myself

with anything that is left over.

—**Terry Stokes**

APPRENTICE

I began life in a house of tiny people; the tallest, my
grandpa, without his elevator shoes, stood a full five feet
tall. Immigrants from Czarist Russia, none of my people
understood my passion for American sports and the depth
of my disappointment when because of my small stature I
failed at one after another. I had been a good student at
Detroit's Roosevelt Elementary School, but Webster's

Collegiate Dictionary—second prize in a school-wide spelling bee—was not the kind of prize I sought.

At age thirteen I took a job at Wolfe Sanitary Wiping Cloth Company. Ed Wolfe, the owner, took a liking to me, and the following year he asked me to be a driver and general handyman for his wife Lottie. In racing circles, I soon discovered, she was known as "Lucky Lottie," a hardy woman who smoked constantly, drank but never got drunk, and took up horses when her doctor advised her to find a diversion to ease her heart trouble. At that time she was owner of an enormous stable of horses trained by Stan Lipiek, who'd had more winners the previous year than any other trainer in North America. Stan was an ex-jockey who bought suits by the half-dozen in outlandish colors, peach, apple, pear, and had the nerve to wear them on or off the track. It was Stan who first suggested to me that I enroll in the Apprentice Jockey Program at the Detroit Racing Association, the largest program of its kind.

The first year of riding was the most glorious of my life. I was still under five feet, and I had no trouble making the weight. Stan gave me mounts, and before I was fifteen I'd broken my maiden in a $1,000 claiming race on a 12-1 shot named Phastbuck. I went South that winter to ride first in Maryland and then at the Fairgrounds in New Orleans. I began to smoke and occasionally drink. I carried myself with a slightly muted swagger, and one night a week I played poker with the other riders, often finishing long after dawn, flat broke, but happy and proud.

Back in Detroit that spring, I began to experience my first weight problems. I was fifteen now and suddenly 5'4" With my 7½ pound apprentice allowance I had to come in at under 105, and this was proving harder and harder. My fellow jockey, Johnny LaTurco, had a passion for chocolate doughnuts, which he bought by the dozen and offered freely to all of us. One greasy doughnut, and I was over my limit. In May I had to spend a week without mounts, starving and sweating to get the pounds off. Even without food it seemed I was growing: my hands looked larger, my face lengthened and saddened, my shoulder bones stretched the purple striped fuchsia silks of Lucky Lottie to the bursting point.

Stan began giving me better mounts, and in June I won going away on his marvel of a filly, Shout About, at

8-1. Sensing this was my last season, I was riding suddenly
with an abandon and fury I never dreamed were mine. In
The Woodward Mile I brought Son of Tara from 17 lengths
off the pace, through the pack on the backstretch and surging for the lead at the head of the stretch. I heard Tony Bianco, on Derby Dieppe, shouting, "Hold him back, Jew boy!"
but I went on to win by a head. After the race in the jockey
room, no one spoke to me, and I felt a sudden chill along
my back as I changed for the 8th race. "I told you, Jew boy,"
Bianco muttered staring into the locker beside mine. It had
been a boat race. Wise Moss was down to 3-1 with all that
"smart" money, but no one had bothered to tell the kid on
the 22-1 shot. In the next race I was bumped coming out of
the gate and knocked four times against the rail. I was lucky
to finish.

    Two nights later the first call came. "Hold her back if
you wanna keep your right hand." And the phone went dead.
The same call came the next night and the next. Stan was
running Shout About in the Michigan Mile that coming Saturday; it was the premier race of the season, and she would
be in against the class of the Midwest: Air Sailor, 3rd in the
Kentucky Derby, Night Crawler, track record holder at 6

17

furlongs. With her filly allowance of 6 pounds and her lack of stakes experience, she would come in at 105 or less. She had a chance; Stan thought so and so did someone else. Each night when the call came, I thought of the heavy-set one-armed man who yelled at me as I rode Son of Tara into the winner's circle, "Nice ride, Sammy, nice ride!" He hadn't been smiling. On Friday night I took the phone off the hook, and at 12:30 a telegram came: "A loss for a hand" was all it said. I hadn't been sleeping.

The next day Lucky Lottie was decked out in her own fuchsia colors, with a big purple stripe across her rear. She had a fist full of $100 win tickets, and she shouted out in her breathy voice, "Do it for Lottie, Philly boy!" Stan gave me a leg up and said, "Stay outside, out of trouble." It was too late for that. Luckily, I was in 7th position, and I let her break slowly. At the end of the 2nd furlong she was in 5th, just outside of Sarah Lorraine. On the backstretch I could feel her letting it out, and I pulled her into 4th just behind a laboring Wise Moss. Air Sailor was 3 lengths ahead as we entered the final turn, and I could feel my game filly's desire to go out and get him. I held the reins with all I had and faked the whip as we entered the stretch. Still, I passed Grey Days, and there was only half a length between me and Air Sailor, but I refused to let her go. I could feel the heart going out of her as we crossed the finish line. She knew she could have caught him. "Turn in your silks," Stan said when I brought her back. "You don't ride me any more." I couldn't look at either him or Lottie. I don't know what they were feeling, but whatever it was they had a right to it.

—Philip Levine

ARBUTUS

(hallowed be thy
name is love

shallow grave

in soil or mud

(a calloused hand
not west but ever
large enough
to see

18

TRAILING ARBUTUS. *Epigæa repens.*

a grove of trees
the barest shade
of pink

another country
of the north
where poplars grow

& in the dark
of winter
a fullness
in the heart

mysterious lovers
in the park

—David Wilk

ARCHAEOLOGY

First the reduction to a past of a culture which was, until
then, a present and, above all, a future, by another culture,
together with associated misunderstandings (such as El-
dorado & all that). Then, after centuries of silence and
burial of all remembrance of that past: its painstaking re-
construction once more into a present and a future by the
conqueror for the benefit, of course, of all mankind.

—Nathaniel Tarn

See Of

19

ARMONY

The way that things belong to each other with the "harm" removed.

—Philip Corner

ARMY

Being surrounded by khaki for so long and clad in khaki, I can see a peculiar quality of the color khaki, that it does not blend with anything.

In normal life dressing is "fastidious" or "casual" according to the varying amounts of accumulated time preparation imbedded in the fabric along with the starch. The criteria are inapplicable at an army inspection because the most slovenly participant (will be reprimanded for such) surpasses by far the fussiness usually and ever met with. It invites a fleeting comparison with clothingstore mannequins—we suddenly recognize inanimate immaculateness as the chosen ideal: dummy as the (still) living.

The worthy man is too individual to be led, and too generous to command.

> We are here..........
> To help our allies..........
> Resist agression..........
> Prove to men everywhere..........
> Preserve that heritage..........
> Of freedom..........
> Inherited from our honored forebears..........
> Share with all people..........
> Blessing of liberty..........
> Preserving..........
> Mutual cooperation of free nations..........

I hate the military
as much as I could
hate any enemy
So whom should I fight
against?

> There is a life which is khaki-clad and marches
> in step. And is not a life at all.

I do not remember precisely exactly what I was not doing—somewhat absent-minded in the vicinity of a preparation

one per regiment

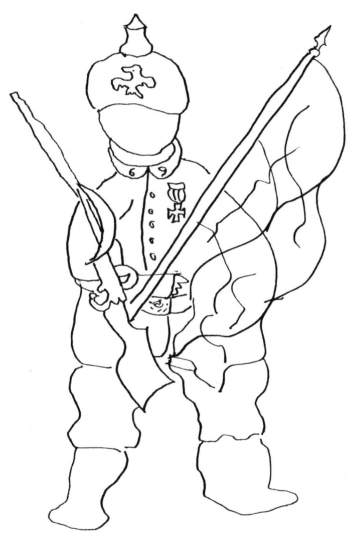

the surrender man carries the white flag

—William Cply

21

for guard duty. Not looking really, seeing them inspecting the weapons, those men not able to afford being absent-minded, but interested too, as I. Certainly not more prepared with their somewhat involvement than I for the SHOT.

Someone had left the cartridge in the chamber and cleaning the rifle before the inspecting officer it was shot off. Such a spur to purpose. Heads jerked round, some kind of quick quick appropriate action—surprise, indignation, someone even hit the dirt, the commander leaping for that weapon, the soldier too dismayed to resist its being taken...

How striking, this concern for safety's sake. How laudable absolutely to assure since after all you know how dangerous a loaded rifle can be, especially a round carried unknowingly god! just think of...should be...what if carelessness such as this...

I was thinking of a similar man in action.

How concerned they are that you are killed in the approved way.

Unfortunate man, losing out on the first step to valor. What might have been a medal will be a court-martial. Severe too. Yet the sound of a shot is as appalling in every place. The potential of the undischarged weapon is ready for anyone to handle; (someone will)

> !officers and men..........
>> "I prefer to be a man."
> When the commander gives his "men—MEN, I'm
>> proud of you!"
>>> (that familiar tradition-dad line)

> auditory stimulus projected on
>> wood figure standing
> ...and who would suspect that one of those
> protuberances could be guilty of thought?..........

Is an army post expressly made so that the deprivation of the freedom to leave it is the most terrible threat?
Snipping the lawn's edge straight and straighter...
no little grass allowed to grow over

—Philip Corner

ART

Art has gotten a bad press from intellectuals who are often (only) articulating their own thwarted creativity. Plato spoke of artistic inspiration as madness & &, tho he conceded that this contains veritably divine & healthful elements, banished its exponents from the ideal state. Freud bracketed it with other ludic & philosophic manifestations as "anal eroticism" which, coming from him, is an unpleasant & dismissive term. And thus are the Philistines, always potentially with us, provided with extra encouragement to revile art as a public scapegoat—notably in insular Britain, victim at the time of writing (January 1978), to various socio-economic strains. My reaffirmation of its value incorporates a riposte to the recent non-definition by an influential Scottish commentator, Fyfe Robertson: who branded last summer's first 'Hayward Annual' exhibition of innovative painting, sculpture & performance art nothing more nor less than a "Phart" in the public eye...

[My closing citation is filched from the pen of Our Vater, which art in Heaven: the ultra cunninglinguish (I mean, oral) artifisher James Joyce.]

> The Republic and The Laws of Plato
> dropped the arts like a hot potato,
> missing out on the Arse Poetica
> you too might look up and into, Herr Doktor
> —there's a lot more to it than banal erotica.
> And there's no real reason art should bring to mind
> a puritanical retreat from the human behind
> —nor yet, auld Robbie, this piddling grind
> about phoney or noisome breaks in the wind
>   Farts and belches come in twos
> like the Christians and the Jews—
> but *if* it come, Art is *not*   unnatural
> (no more   than they are
> but often—) more like leaves
> to the tree of life

ART . . . IS

> —not "phart"—or
> art is not all fart—till
> art is not at all fart, then
> art is not at all far—&
> art is not at all f—
> art is not at a
> art is not a
> art is no
> art is n
> art is
> art
> —
> a
> ,

        . . . art is not fat
            art is not thin
            art is well fed
            in the loony bin . . . . . .

        Art is yes—och—aye—i e,
    is poster-peelings, a way
    of seeing, sometimes a mess
    —call that messy art,
    but why add fuel (have a heart)
    to the massive dreary anti-art chart
    of the Great Municipal Public dustcart
    which would much rather junk it as rubbish[1] or "Phart"
    than have to wake up and actually start
    thinking, enjoying—playing a part
    and working at it, drat it

        . . . to find
    aah!—Art
    thou
    with it
    now? Then rejoyce—dada lives
    and mama, baba live—playing, praying
    in good voice . . .
                . . . *Loud,*
                    heap miseries upon us
                    yet entwine our arts
                    with laughters low
                    —Michael Horowitz

    [1]*Garbage* in America

ART COLLECTOR (BIG)
A commodities investor specializing in futures on culture,
usually for tax advantages.

—Dick Higgins

ART COLLECTOR (SMALL)
A fan of the fashion industry trying to make money in hard-
ware when what he knows is shoes.

—Dick Higgins

24

ART EDUCATOR

An artist emeritus, usually one who receives foundation grants for his annual sabbatical.

—**Dick Higgins**

ART MUSEUM

A building where The Same Old Work is shown in radically innovative contexts. A subsidized market for art galleries.

—**Dick Higgins**

THE BOY WHO BREATHED ON THE GLASS IN THE BRITISH MUSEUM.

An Ante-Bellum Tragedy.

ARTOO-D2

"Who's that cute little computer in Star Wars?" I asked David.

"Artoo-D2," he said in a flat voice.

"Is he a good guy or a bad guy?" I was trying to figure out how to talk to an eight year old.

"Good guy." He ran to the corner and waited for me to catch up with him. I didn't know if I should run or walk so I sort of skipped.

"Finally," he reproached me when I got there. We passed an appliance store. There was a round vacuum cleaner in the window.

"Looks like Artoo-D2," David remarked.

"My friend said she's in love with Artoo," I laughed. "Can you imagine anything so weird?"

He walked away from me and pointed to the street sign above. "What street is Star Wars on?"

I didn't know what to say so said nothing.

"I saw Star Wars five times," David then told me. He began to sing the melody of the theme song and snap his fingers.

I had waited on line two hours to get in to see Star Wars. The girl ahead of me fainted and was carried out by the theatre manager . They revived her near the refreshment stand with Coca-Cola. By the time I got to my seat, I was so exhausted that I slept through most of the movie.

"I only saw Star Wars once," I told him. "I missed a lot of it because I fell asleep." I made some snorting sounds like snores.

"Are you kidding?" David shook his head. "Dummy."

He was right. I was a dummy. Suddenly he was in a big hurry to get home. Everytime I tried to catch up with him, he would walk a little faster.

—Ellen Kahaner

ART OPENING

A wake for the artist's virginity, at which the artist's friends and colleagues voice their preconceptions of his work and inventory who is there.

—Dick Higgins

ART WORLD

1. THE POPULAR ART AND THE REAL ART

Sometimes on a really hot summer's day, gently stirring masses of arts can be seen clustered on the sunny side of their hillock for an hour's siesta. But such a sight is exceptional. It is for their industry and their constant, often apparently aimless, bustling to and fro that the arts are renowned. Pliny noted that they continued to work throughout the night in summer, when the moon was at its fullest and brightest. Aelian compared the complicated arrangements of their galleries with the famous labyrinths of Crete. For centuries it was really believed that a species of desert art mined gold. But Saint Jerome and also Solomon saw the arts in another light, as unusual societies in which all work together with none superior to another and where no individual has private property but everything belongs to everyone.

Those students who have only studied the arts in a laboratory and do not know their behavior in the field tend to regard them as stereotyped creatures of little learning. Those who have watched them under natural conditions over many years are convinced that some element of reason is present in their behavior. The fact is, it really doesn't matter. Is reason such a great gift? The slightest touch of stimulus or instinct or memory, the welling up of immense desires upon the faintest chord of a patterned tune, the nervous quiver of life at full stretch bring to the arts a finely honed response to artish things. These are the characteristics of the art world as near as can be put in human terms.

II. ART HISTORY

Two-hundred million years ago, the pre-art wandered the plains and swamps of central Asia. Little is known about it, but undoubtedly it was a predator. Gradually the climate became warmer, flowers and insects began to flourish and the pre-art, male and female, bred in ever-increasing numbers as the sun shone. Arts preserved in amber are as complex in structure—the odd formations of their heads, adapted for blocking doorways, and the sculpturing of their bodies—as any found today, when a large range of worker forms is present in numbers, but without this variation.

Although born in each generation with wings, the females were forced to live a terrestial life. The males, however, could roam at will and were handicapped by their wings on the ground. Shorter lived, they pursued their merry aerial course awhile, strayed far, and soon died. Oddly, it was from this slow-moving stock that the swiftly-marching nomads of the current art world sprang. Not long afterwards—thirty million years later— they had little of the normal social life found in earlier art communities. The chief factors in the revolution they brought with them from Eurasia were physiological and social. Because they were naked, and not enclosed in cocoons, the first flight usually became a mating chase. This trivial event proved to be the most important milestone in art history.

Other changes occurred with ever-increasing speed. The success of the small art communities had been immediate. One or two in each brood proved, not unnaturally, to be more fertile than the rest. They are the art queens. Their less fertile colleagues are the workers. If the males had been wingless, and less interested in their maleness, they might still have survived. Each worker who fed a larva obtained a treat in exchange. Licking and feeding became a great rite. If the arts pout with hunger they must be fed as quickly as possible. But the males remained unchanged, never learning to feed their colleagues, and so must always remain outcasts.

III. ARTS AS CRAFTSMEN

Art craftsmen are found among the Social Arts, whose large societies necessitate the building of complete structures. MacCook, in his book on art communities written nearly fifty years ago, gives a vivid description of the quiet excitement, care and method involved: "The curved edges approached in irregular lines, and at various points the two projecting points grew nearer and nearer until they almost touched. By bending the leaves together and glueing them with a whitish papery substance, the pulling process began. The outside of the new galleries was left rough but the interior was smoothed into blank walls. She climbed the arch, moving more daintily as the top was reached, stretched across the wee chasm and dropped the ball of soil into the breach."

These marvels have been confirmed by students. They

certainly show the ability of some of the arts to adapt
their habits and architecture to the most diverse surroundings, though the dullness, obtuseness and seeming un-
changeableness of other arts is equally astonishing. There
is always light tension throughout the art colony, localities
of concentration where jobs are being undertaken, low
tensions where the current may be said to be flowing
weakly. A nerve cell cannot survive on its own. It is tied
by a bond to its neighbors. The quick reaction of an art
to the work of its neighbors can bring great dangers. An
object is needed for the consummation of the train of
action which has been triggered off. A friend is helped
to hold the creature she is fighting. What more natural?
Yet she is free to mitigate, to grow, degenerate and
regenerate again more or less of her own accord.

The art's excitement mounts as the result of this vast
inflow of tensions, so its impulses flow outward at an
ever-increasing rate and brings it into contact with more
and more individuals from whom and to whom it both
receives and gives ever more tense and frequent stimuli.
This flow of nervous energy throughout the community
is a definite and little understood phenomenon. A rough
approximation to temperature could no doubt be made.
While the mental abilities of the arts are limited—for example, they have no proper language, cannot be said to
reason and do not usually use tools—their mental powers
should not be underrated. The quicker learners are the
leaders of the colony—the "excitement centers." Nearly
every art colony has more than one queen. Also there is
the constant toll of art warfare. They excite the other arts
into doing different jobs by starting to do it themselves
There are social arts and non-social arts. The jobs done
by each art will change when new stimuli come into play.
Gesture and action is the limit of art speech.

IV. THE SUCCESS OF THE ARTS
The arts all share these fundamental qualities. They opened
the door to unbounded success and with that success came
great diversity of form and habit. It is surprising how little
their importance is realized. In most parts of the world,
arts are talked of somewhat vaguely as either nuisances or
pests, but they are usually not considered to be of major
economic importance. In some parts of the East it is even
common practice to encourage the arts to live in and

around warehouses in order to keep the termites at bay. But success is not to be confused with beneficence to man. The seeking of patronage and protection implies the possesion of power by those from whom these things are sought. The chief enemy of an art is another art. This is the measure of the art's success.

The main difficulty in collecting the arts is finding the particular kind you want. Never place arts in glass containers. If this is absolutely unavoidable the placing of food in the vessel helps to complete the illusion. If the arts are collected for observation purposes then the appropriate apparatus must be manufactured. Food can be a problem because the arts have their fads. If they are collected as dead material for study then they must be mounted, set and identified. Many collectors give their arts little enough reward for the protection gained and others are parasites and secret robbers.

The persistence of the arts in the face of all assaults is due in part to their physical stamina—their immense tenacity in living. They are difficult creatures to kill, except by poison. The workers can survive for six or seven weeks without food and the queens for even longer periods. Practically no work has been done on the metabolism of the arts. When it is undertaken, the study of these aspects of the art world will yield the key to the fundamental mystery of their social organization. For the moment, the "excitement center" is the safer term. Lastly, remember the multitude of the arts, their ubiquity and dominance throughout the world. There are as you read this 1,280,000,000,000,000 arts crawling in and around the surface of the earth. In the face of such facts as these, no one can question the important, if indirect, part the arts play in our economy, and thereby in our lives.

—**Lucy R. Lippard**

See Ant

ASHBERY

I get very nervous before I have to teach, but when it's actually happening I don't mind it at all. I quite enjoy it. Then when it's over I collapse. But before every class I feel absolutely horrible. I feel I have nothing to teach anybody, and what am I doing in front of students who really want to learn something? But then I find myself talking, often rather interestingly, and then when it's all over I wonder what's happened.

I like to travel, it's one of the few things that I like a lot. I even like going some place dull like Nashville, which I was disappointed in. I thought it would be more exotic. I was very disappointed in Music Row or whatever they call it. Purposely very slummy and crummy. I love California. I can hardly wait to get there. Although, you're not supposed to like it if you're from New York.

In my day, growing up, life would have been hell if one had a name like Carrie Snodgrass. Now everybody wears funny looking clothes and granny glasses. I guess they still do. I still do.

I knew Delmore Schwartz and liked his poetry a lot.

There was a mellow, elegiac quality to the poetry of the late thirties, early forties, when I began writing. That whole period in American poetry's been neglected and forgotten. I came out of it, I wanted to sound the way they did, and make sense if I could, too. I didn't always succeed in the latter.

Jean Garrigue, for instance, was a poet I admired, actually in high school. You probably never heard of Ruth Hirschberger. She had a later career as a feminist writer, but I haven't heard of her again. Nicholas Moore was a strange poet in England nobody knows anymore. He was a Marxist although his poetry wasn't—that I could see. Joan Murray was in the Yale Series of Younger Poets. She died at the age of 25 in 1942. She'd been a student of Auden at the New School. I have this very rare copy of her Yale Younger Poets volume which I found in Paris of all places. David Schubert was another American poet who died quite young in the forties.

Ah, sweet mystery of life. Kenneth Koch asked me, "Are there any hidden meanings in your life?" and I said "No" and he said "Why not?" and I said because someone would find out what they are and then they wouldn't be mysterious. Don't you think it's nice that everything's so mysterious? I'm rather happy with the way things are.

I am not recognized very often on the street. Although I was waiting at the stop light at Sixth Avenue and Ninth Street, and a young hippie type cab driver leaned out of the window and said "Hi, John."

John Ashbery by Joe Brainard

He was probably someone who goes to poetry workshops at St. Mark's.

Lindsay Shapiro once told me I was "The Master of the Golden Glow." That's the title of a poem by James Schuyler. She said Fairfield Porter told her. But I think he meant someone else. At Deerfield I painted a copper pitcher a number of times and got very expert at the highlights. It was my favorite subject as a matter of fact because I got so good at it, and maybe Fairfield thought that that was what the James Schuyler title referred to, but I don't think that it's true. I think The Master of the Golden Glow was another painter, but I don't know which one.

Self-Portrait in a Convex Mirror, in hard-cover and paper together, has sold almost 20,000 copies which, as you know, is a lot for a book of poetry. More, I think, than all my previous books at the time they came out sold combined, although now some have been reprinted and sell very well, too, since I got the Pulitzer and the National Book Award.

A well-known artist complained privately that Wallace Stevens was too fastidious.

How can anybody be too fastidious?

I haven't known many painters who were really interested in poetry, but I do know some, nevertheless. One of them is Ron Kitaj who has done a painting which is going to be on the cover of my next book, and he reads poetry all the time. Larry Rivers and Jane Freilicher read a great deal of poetry. Of course there were a lot of others who, especially with Frank, pretended they were interested in poetry, but really weren't. I'm not unhappy that few artists, or few anybody, read poetry. Let's keep it for ourselves.

I make a point of not keeping up with the avant-garde, with the exception of Robert Wilson.

Jasper Johns is one of the artists that interest me the most, although I don't get along with him very well. I like his work very much.

Brice Marden is, to me, one of the great artists today. Brice, please excuse me for saying this.

I saw him about a week ago. It was the first time I ever really talked with him. We had a very nice conversation and he said he really liked the article I wrote about him.

Marden's the only painter I can look at but I can't look at him. I was out at the Newburger Museum in Purchase last Sunday for the Girogio Cavallon show, which was very beautiful. I used to live in his house. In the same museum were some etchings of Brice Marden. There was a large show of black and white graphics, mostly pretty dull except for him. Even in an etching, which is surely the most boring form of visual art that can exist, he had, you know, a new Baskin-Robbins flavor.

I didn't appreciate the Beatles when they came out, but since then I've come to appreciate "I Wanna Hold Your Hand."

I love The Firesign Theatre. I think they're the greatest artistic force in America at the present time. There's one that came out a year ago, *In the Next World You're on*

Your Own; do you know that one? That's their greatest work!

They went downhill for a long time. Then they did *Everything You Know is Wrong*, which is pretty good. But then their masterpiece, their *Golden Bowl,* is *In the Next World You're on Your Own,* and now it appears in *Rolling Stone.*

I don't care anything about rock music, but I love to read *Rolling Stone* because it's totally Byzantine, this other world, not to you, but to me. You get insight into this whole other world that's going on, and you're surprised that everybody cares about it.

I only bought the lilacs in my apartment today because the other ones had died, and I thought it would be nice to have them here while you were here, even though I'm leaving tomorrow and won't be able to enjoy them. It was sort of self-interest, too, because I wanted them to be here while you were interviewing me. Even though you don't smell them or look at them, I thought they added something.

I've been very influenced by Jack Benny. I used to do a very good imitation of him which went: "Hm...Well!" And of course the Rochester connection. Yes, boss?

—Kenneth Deifik & Stephen Paul Miller

AUGUST 13,1937
The first death registered at the concentration camp Buchenwald.

—Armand Schwerner & Donald M. Kaplan

AUGUST 15,1937
The second and third deaths registered at the concentration camp Buchenwald.

—Armand Schwerner & Donald M. Kaplan

AUGUST 6,1945
The first atomic bomb exploded over a civilian population.

—Armand Schwerner & Donald M. Kaplan

AUSTRALIA

Contributions towards a New Australian Poetics
selected from the best authors by Michael Wilding.

> I first adventure: follow me who list
> And be the Second Austral harmonist.
>
> —Barron Field

Positively Mount Olympus

Well, I wish I was on some
Australian mountain range.
Oh, I wish I was on some
Australian mountain range.
I got no reason to be there, but I
Imagine it would be some kind of change.

—Bob Dylan

Re-mapping the Territory

One can no longer put Mt Purgatory forty miles high in the
midst of Australian sheep land.

—Ezra Pound

The foothills of Mount Purgatory

There was still a bit of time to kill and so I listened to the
young Englishman who had had a strange time of it in
Australia. He was telling me of his life as a sheep herder,
how they castrate I don't know how many thousands of
sheep in a day. One had to work fast. So fast, in fact, that
the most expedient thing to do was to grab the testicles
with your teeth and then a quick slit with the knife and
spit them out. He was trying to estimate how many thousand pair of testicles he had bitten off in this hand to
mouth operation during his sojourn in Australia. And as
he was going through his mental calculations he wiped
his mouth with the back of his hand.

'You must have had a strange taste in your mouth,'
I said, instinctively wiping my own mouth.

'It wasn't as bad as you might imagine,' he answered
calmly. 'You get used to everything — in time. No, it
wasn't a bad taste at all...the idea is worse than the actual
thing. Just the same, I never thought when I left my com-
fortable home in England that I would be spitting out
those things for a living. A man can get used to doing most
anything when he's really up against it.'

—Henry Miller

Beyond Realism
You know the details of the kangaroo.

—**Leonard Cohen**

The details of the Kangaroo
The kangaroo has a double penis — one for weekdays and one for holidays.

—**Henry Miller**

I LOVE A SUNBURNT COUNTRY
A LAND OF SWEEPING PLAINS
OF RAGGED MOUNTAIN RANGES
OF DROUGHTS AND FLOODING RAINS...

ROBB

Dreamtime

It was as if a herd of silent, smooth, weightless kangaroos were stepping on my neck. I could hear the soft thump of their paws as they stepped gently over me. It was not a painful sensation at all and yet it was maddening. I knew that if it did not involve myself in doing something I would go mad and stand up and run.

—Carlos Castaneda

Neo Colonialism

"the
    only thing you ever gave New Guinea was your toe-nail
        and now
the Australians are taking over."

—Frank O'Hara

Chile

If you think that's bad you should see what the CIA is doing in Australia.

—Christopher Boyce

National Anthem Competition

We'll save Australia
Don't want to hurt no kangaroo
We'll build an all American amusement park there
They've got surfing too.

—Randy Newman

Beyond the Black Stump

and finally the great scene where the mad dope addict picks up the monstrous syringe and gives himself a big smack of H, and grabs the girl (who is some dumb move-less Zombie of the story and walks hands at her sides), he wild-haired and screaming with rain in the plip-plip of the ruined old film rushes off, her legs and hair dangling like Fay Wray in the arms of King Kong, across that mysterious dark endless Faustian horizon of Will's vision, happy like an Australian jackrabbit, his feet and heels flashing snow: Yip Yip Yip eee, till, as Will says, his "Yips" get dimmer and dimmer as distance diminishes his eager all-fructified final goal-joy, for what would be greater than that, Will thinks, than to have your arms full of joy and a good shot in you and off you run into eternal gloom to flip all you want in infinity

—Jack Kerouac

AUTHORITY

Actions, artificial, actions all artificial
are about as artificial as
authorized actions acting artificial action.
Artificial actions associated agreement artifice about
artificial actions are actions about action.
Actions apparently authorship analagous actions authority.
Action automobile and action author
accurately attributes anomalous always.
Action an aspect as and are asserted authority
and always any act an authority
and authority acts, act "author."
An actor against any author; action against action
author at authors auction another.
An action as action apparently as alternative
accrue and acteth another, act and an attorney, an actor.
Analysis. Actor acteth authority.
Artificial argument as any are attributed, and are as as
and actions, authors authorize.

Appear from time and which is approach to the appears and
however it is articulated, its basic are those of argument,
and eventually it encounters authority, I shall call
"authorization view," and theorists who hold "authorization
theorists." A representative is authorized to act. This
means that. Act which as if he and his responsibilities
(anything) decreased. Acquired new responsibilities and
(if anything) given up some. Authorization view concentrates
at the outset, actual representing begins. Authorized within
the authority, anything that a man does. Are always coextensive
with the limits of authority he has. Authority within which,
as representing well, as the activity of representing; anything
done after the right authorization and within its limits is.
And political scientists, and centering on an account of
democratic and a third articulated in the agent of an
individual.

An approach angle and apportionment and an accurate articulated
and accurately Adams argues American an at as act assembly.
As art argues "accurate" assembly absolutely accountability.
Acting authority, acting account, acting at all.
Act among advocates argued attempt assembly apparently.
Articulated advocate always again according actual adopted

attribute accurate absurd.
Accurate argue "an arena" "appearing" activities about
analogy, activities artist actively allowed.
Applicable an an action, accurate atomizes appear, attack
accurately: "action also assures adequate attacks."
Accustomed artist art American accuracy always.
Art artist accurate and art, art artistic and are accuracy,
artist, an artist and ancient and acquired, artist accurate,
an Audubon.
Alphabet an arrangement analagous arrangement art.

The Picasso and Braque abstractions *in which there is a guitar*
can be spoken of. Art is precisely art which is not.
Intended to correspond to the appearance. Resemblance
is irrelevant. "If we could make a genuine tree, as pines
are made in the factory on the model of those which exist
already, we should rather term them *pins."* "What's that!"
"A rabbit." "Right! And that?" Joyce Kilmer's God.
It represents the Annunciation, it represents the triumph
of riches, it represents Hans Holbein. Wallpaper representing
spacious Tyrolese landscapes. Christ, by a fish. Christ as a
fish. A chubby baby, by Christ. Allegations about facts.
"Frank Sinatra *is* Darth Vader." Map, blueprint, movie,
screwprint. Arbitrary, tenting tonight in a small red
triangle, invisible things like economic trade regions,
dialect distribution, happiness. Mathematicians, mapping,
mirrors, moments, metaphors, medium, miniature, mensions (di-),
leadings (miss).

The idea that a representative assembly should be *condensare*
to a whole nation is venerable, an average example of ordinary
men conclude quite reasonably. "That's a Babbit!" Desired:
a handsome family man to represent one. It is a matter of
being ABLE to draw correct conclusions from A about b.
But AN idea "ADEQUATE" possibility of AMBIGUITY ALSO, A
certain difference between typicAlity And representAtiveness,
the Crucifixion. This is cleArly true, thus, truly cleAr.
The painting asserts, alleges, actually, an aggregate, that
should be accurate. You abstract criteria, great men of
Emerson. Be yourself, a substance in one sense seeming to
practice the meaning of "Fairness" (or "marbles"). And those
alleys of yesteryear, where now? The nudge downtown. Arrest
thief! You know what you can do with fire. Two pinetrees
put their heads together, with a little love-dart halfway down.
Keep it to yourself.
                                        —David Bromige

AWKWARD

The only word in English with *wkw* in sequence.

Or, "awk," as English teachers—I'm one—write on student papers, meaning something between "This is unconventional," and "The nature of our language, as I understand it, resists this construction." Auk, it should be extinct.

Clumsy thinking: can one sprain a tongue? From a student paper: "Ahab was killed at the hands of Moby Dick." And, from another: "There is no movement in the bowels of the earth."

Or, and Steve Dunn found (or was given) this one: "Things have got so bad they're committing celibacy in the streets." And, as Steve was swift to see, they are.

What are the important differences between social and private definitions of *awkward?*

If language should communicate, awkward means to increase the space between the speaker and the listener, already immense. (Porchia, in Merwin's translation: "I know what I have given you. I do not know what you have received." And is Porchia's first sentence true?)

If language is to cloud, as so much of it does—political speeches, insurance policy prose, bad poems, seduction rhetoric—, which lapses in communication are *awkward* and which exact?

If language should embody what we feel, how can it be wrong, unless our feelings, as we know they often are, are tawdry and inadequate to what we experience. By experience, then, I must mean not only what we feel but also what we think about what we feel, so far as we can recover that feeling from what we think about it.

Awkward means without grace.

Grace means you endure paradox gratefully, even if it arises from the language you live by.

Or language may live by you. It may be our most elaborate parasite. A swarm of habits urgent to please by repeating its successes, and urgent to grow by sticking its historical tongue out. Blaah.

In a good guest, too much civility can be *awkward.* Does it therefore follow that in a good host too awkward can be civil? "I'm human, too." How hard to say such a sentence without false and easily accurate pride.

Blunder along. To thine own self be true: as if you had a choice. And everywhere along the line, you do; you do.

—William Matthews

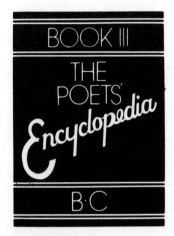

B-GIRLS

G-girls are by no means to be confused with B girls!
But what could make so vast a difference between such
lonely initials?
The Hollywood Horizon stretched out in front of us
offers a simple palm tree to start with.
So it is with the B girl.
One high ball to get her in a movie star mood.
And then she is identified at once by the loneliest initials
ever strung together on one string of B girl beads....

    The B girl is or *was* a basic type of bar room boarder
bordering on boozey bursts of the cash register to remind
her   in her bleached out bourbon bender
it is time to beg the boys for a brand
new batch of 100 proof hootch to heave down the hatch.

    The blisters of her backless mules begin to bring the B girl
to an alcoholic so-exhisting—
coherency.
Bothering these brawny bachelors with blatant wedding bands
to buy her one more bloody mary.
The beating of her bongo brains breathes benzedrine into
bathroom walls where the B girl can decipher her fate.
A frenzy of sewer fumes
and faulty toilet fixtures
where strains of a nickel's drop into the jukebox bucket
only brings Miss B a bleary eye.
And an earful of what was once a royal flush

is only now a quarter to three
and no one's in the place except for Miss B.
Very B, this girl.
Not a BAD sort
just a bouncing
maraschino cherry of a ball buster
mesmerized by that sleazy swizzle stick.
The B Girl's calling card is a cognac drenched coaster
that spells out for her what no first grade text book ever could
ALL GONE GIRL.

The B Girl is an endless commodity of
comic strip
straphanging
horseplaying
pushpins
from one end of the bar to the other.
The B's have cold knees
they snort
they sniff
they even sneeze.
Friendless frails in flapping fringe
found long lost near a beer barrel
cramped
like creatures who kick
to keep moving.
Watered down
their spirits pass,
chit and chat
an eye
of someone
YES
It's him.
The handsome stranger
swooning over "B"
HIS kind of woman.
His kind of promise
to continue
could result in risking
cash sales
for water and world war one whiskey
by order of the management
The B girl goes a round with not one word in her defense

lapping up the liquids
reeling from the fracas
Other B girls squint and totter
what's the matter?
Someone's got her.
So, the swinging doors fly creak free
the clattering clack of class lacking heels
parading poorly past the piemen on her way to where?
Searching the air for fiery fumes of fabled Fleischmann's
feathering her drunken nest
slitted skirt insures a spring and a swing
to her gait
after all men
that IS the thing.
Down the beer stained trodden hall of hate
B girls from her impure past forget to wave and fly fast
Her sweat streaked bar stool
that sung her calves and thighs to sleep
have found another lazy Susan
plucked and plastered
like a willow planted firm she'll weep.
The men
make time
the clock has told of ticking trips to tense amour
kindred spirits shut the door

Hi there   **I get your meaning**

Love is strange
the poets say
but B girls rhyme from day to day
striped halters draped on dames
in dreams of drambuie
draining the billfolds of the bucksin badmen
breaking the B girl's arm
before asking for her cherry.
So many makeshift hearts of
rock and rye
precede a reply of
"Only an olive"
obliterating firing facts of
realties rifles
when the B Girl announces that her cherry has been chewed
out by champion cheap-skates
who drag her through bar room after bar room
and setting no bail.
Like a semi-precious prisoner
Her last mile consists not of an electric chair
but a park bench
plenty available for the B Girl's bottom line.
The same bottom signed so many spritzers of lime ago.
More yellow than green by now
Miss B begins to wander

Come here   Whoops

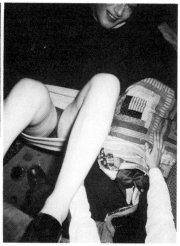

Jackie Curtis by Jimmy de Sana

washed up
from saloon to supermarket.
Our B Girl's dream of walking down an aisle come true
only in an A & P
with a shopping cart by her shabby side. Side by side.
And she aint got no barrel of money but even a B Girl's gotta eat
and so brilliantly versed in the art of deception
our chowsy frau plays tricks on suspecting eyes
proving to check out counters once again
that the B Girl can at times be thought of as no better than
a common thief.
Especially when apprehended, as our heroine was
is and always will be.
The eternal spiritual virgin
at the last minute
and at the missing mercy of some man haunting her heart's
only normally employed regions.
Pumping her in, pumping her out
this gorilla's bride, so to speak.
Like a stranded jazz singer searching for the proverb
searching for the proverbs
searching for the proverbial lost chord so prone to the suddenly
and responsive striking.
Only the cactus casts shadows that cool the sand which is still
and stretches far out into an effortless night nature mature
and a habitual repeat performance employing the desert's
vast supply of the four winds
if only she could make a wish
make a wish
to abandon the four winds for four roses so quietly invisible to her
naked B Girl's roving eye.
On and off again, water faucet fumbling at the tap that
B Girls look to like farmers look to the red harvest moon
for promises of fulfilling fertile earth's promise
to spring up a bounty of multiplying tables so serenely set
and ripe for reaping hands whose seeds have been sown.
Horns and blind men
wheels of a fast, fast car. Occasional streamers of headlight
Underneath it all
there she lies
trapped like a fox in the South during a most precipitous festivity.
But still her thread bare throat remains parched as the dunes in a
daring desert movie blaze beneath blowing torrents of too much

hurricane and only occasional musical comedy mirages of the
MGM Lion and Mickey Mouse re-enacting an Aesop's fable.
And as if all life were not one gold plated hell of a cheap charm
bracelet to begin with the B Girl is faced with the Motel alleyways
that lie to her weaknesses.
Sentimental arms spread heavenward ever grasping that hallowed
home made jam and jelly.
Our B Girl is being followed. It is 4:15 A.M. Accompanied by a
navy blue blanket up above.
Warm and woozy
she travels twisted toward the soda pop machine
chewing her technicolor red lips wishing for a miracle
could this attention from behind merit her attention span which
is geared to a bottle filled with bubbles?
Any bubbles will do.
In her human condition those voices tell her to humiliate herself
further and be grateful to God for a sign.
No it is not neon
She is being paged
by hand
grabbed by the rump.
It was all coming back to her. That area
the strange grasp was exploring was once married to marshmallow
soft cushioney security in strictly dishonorable surroundings.
Slurping sleeping powders in cheese flavored champagne from Tunisia
But a B Girl travels in trespasser's footsteps
so no doubt the incident occurring between the hungry hand
and the unsuspecting pair of victims (her buns)
secondary characters in a charming situation
where actually on her way to the soda pop machine in a desert motel
setting where her course was diverted by steel trap fingers
frantically feeling and grabbing at life.
Ah yes, she was still alive, she mustn't forget.
In silent concession
their private procession begins at the closing door.
She's open
receiving
fast love they're achieving. Both winning like greedy gamblers
carousel like rooms existing upon drftwood porches attached
by pink picket fences and dead, dim silhouettes of sordid sunset
scenes slapping the world outside the waiting window who wants to
win.
    The B Girl is no fool

What do you know?

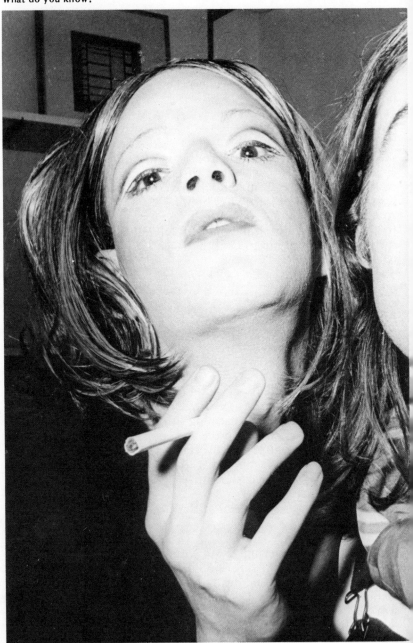

Jackie Curtis by Jimmy de San

she knows she must deposit the correct amount of change
if indeed any
so with the confidence of an Arista member she makes to her
sexual accoster for the fare for this ride that the fizzy fake pop
will take her careening on.
Drunk enough to drink dangerous destiny within his waiting
foyer where his laymen's loins once appeared loyal and alive,
now grinding with a scissor sharpener's fervour.
Sparks begin to fly as far as where Miss B has been biting clouds
of very close chummy dust.
Having been in more accomodating situations with lovers
she sloughs it off
but in point of fact is totally aware of what this lurid tongue
was travelling to find
to find land in her jungle of rain.
Yes, her jungles were storming the gates
the tigers ever burning bright
drizzling then flooding
mere mortals monsoon and on the paper plate of an end table
was blaring a second hand plastic portable radio
what was that song again
oh yeah
she remembers
C'est magnifique
And it was

—Jackie Curtis

See Fate

BARF

Barf, an excited wall of stingrays.
Source: The Divers
Author: Burnett Booth (1907—
First Published: 1947
Type of Work: Meditative Epic in blank verse
Context: While waterskiing with the three daughters of
Admiral Nimitz, Booth, loudspeaker in hand, entertained
his charges with the scabrous memoirs of a heroine of his
own invention, Randy, a champion deep-sea diver, whose
wanderings provided the Miami-born drifter with a rich
scena. The date of this excursion: December 7, 1941. The
place: Pearl Harbor. The sole survivor, Booth moved to an
Eskimo village near Juneau, Alaska, and, in total seclusion,

began his 45,000-word-masterpiece. The quotation comes from Randy's iron-lung hallucination, during which she discovers she has become a monster "of the deep", who sees only beauty around her, because she is unable to love.

> Lips free of spittle, cum, etc.
> These huskies dizzy from the skies
> Are full of blind but agile elation,
> Pro-banner, pro-noisy tents
> Out of which Neanderthals crawl,
> To cheer the nurses wheeling drunks to the docks.
> They mutter. They mutter slips, miss-hits,
> Prying open violent-seeming nooses,
> Dumping new knots into the abolished office buildings,
> The sexual encounters drag on. It's a fine night out.
> Post-existence is seen through a toy prism
> So as to contrast tinnily with the lame-brained machines
> Lowering us down past feather-duster agitations.
> Barf, an excited wall of stingrays.
> —Kenward Elmslie

BASEBALL

Baseball is different from other games. The difference is inherent, metaphysical.

First, baseball has a singular and distinctive relationship to time. Football and basketball, even if quantitatively more popular (that is, as measured by attendance counts), could never be called national "pastimes." Only baseball can be called a "pastime," for baseball is above or outside of time. Football, basketball, hockey and soccer games, for example, are arbitrarily divided into measured quarters, halves, or periods. They are controlled, even dominated, by time. Not so baseball, which either ignores time or dominates it. An inning in theory can go on forever. The same, of course, is true of a game. Interruptions are generally limited to acts of God, such as darkness or rain, or to cultural and quasi-natural occurrences such as curfew or midnight. If for some reason—dust in a batter's eye, rain, or the like—a baseball game must be halted, time is not taken "out," as in other sports. Rather time is "called" by the umpire. Theoretically, and in fact, the time "called" can be called forever. Or it can remain called for a shorter time

—as would have been the case if a baseball game had been in progress in Palestine at the beginning of the forty days of rain.

Second, baseball is different because it is played in a unique spatial frame. Other games are played inside defined and limited areas—rectangular or nearly-rectangular fields, floors, or rinks. Not so with baseball. The game is played within the lines of a projection from home plate, starting from the point of a ninety degree angle and extending to infinity. Were it not for the intervention of fences, buildings, mountains, and other obstacles in space, a baseball travelling within the ultimate projections of the first and third baseline could be fair and fully and infinitely in play. Baseballs never absolutely go out of bounds. They are either fair or foul; and even foul balls are, within limits, playable and are part of the game.

Baseball is distinguished from other games, also, in the way in which it is controlled by umpires. An umpire is very different from a referee, a field judge, or a linesman. Baseball uses umpires, and nothing else, and one umpire is always wholly responsible for a particular decision.

The distinction between umpires and referees goes back at least to the seventeenth century of English history. One of the earliest written descriptions of referees appeared in the Oxford Dictionary for the year 1621. That description set the tone for subsequent definitions, all of which suggested that the referee was always somewhat tentative—called in, as it were, after an act or only when others could not agree. Then, as now, decisions by referees were subject to serious challenge, and usually received with less than full respect. The 1621 notation reports that the Lords and Commons of the British Parliament met in the afternoon "to consult what punishment to inflict upon monopolists, and the referees, who are in chiefest fault." A 1670 note observes that the king "did not altogether...trust the Referee he had in public honored with that office."

One regularly hears the cry "Fire the referee," but seldom if ever the cry "Kill the referee." That cry is reserved for umpires, with good reason. Umpires have to be dealt with absolutely, for their power is absolute. Umpires are not men called in or appointed. They exist in their own right and exercise undelegated and unrequested power, which cannot be reviewed. They are not asked to make judgments. They make them—not after the act, but during the act. The word "umpire" carries this strength. It is derived from the Old French word "noumpere," meaning one who is alone or without "pere" (literally, without father or superior). In the theology of the time, reference was made to the umpirage of the Holy Ghost—who is, according to theology, "without pere." "Refuse not," the medieval divines warned, "the umpeership and judgments of the Holy Ghoste."

Baseball is not, as radio and television announcers often allege, a game of inches. The critical differences in baseball are much finer, and beyond such coarse measurements. They involve more than linear distinctions.

Sound and form are of critical importance and relevance. Thus on a close play at first base, umpires are supposed to watch the base to see when and if the runner's foot strikes the bag (at the same time keeping in view the foot of the first baseman), while they listen for the sound of the ball striking the first baseman's glove. They should then make a quick calculation of the difference between the speed of sound (which travels only about 1100 feet per second) and the speed of sight, or of light (which travels approximately 186,000 miles per second). An umpire who called a runner safe at first base because he saw the foot strike the bag at the same time that he heard the ball strike the first baseman's glove obviously would have made a bad call.

Baseball is different from other major sports in two final, morally significant ways.

First, the individual player is under constant surveillance. At all times one player, at least, is personally accountable. In football, a player may fall down and get up with mud all over him, and no one need know whether he has done his job or not. In basketball and in hockey, it is difficult to follow the action and to fix and measure responsibility. (Baseball teams do not carry chaplains, as do some football teams. They do not gather, kneeling or standing, in a group to pray or hold hands before the game, as basketball teams generally do, but proceed decently from locker room to dugout to playing field.)

Second, baseball is a game of records, team and individual. The books are balanced. They show earned runs and unearned runs. Hit are credited to batters and debited to pitchers. Errors are recorded, along with assists and put-

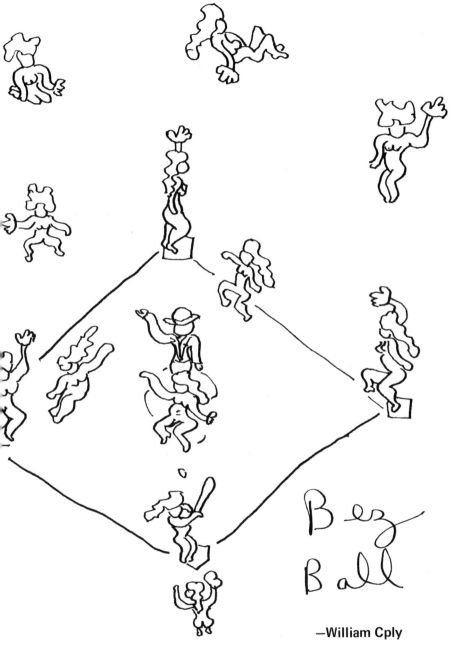

Bez
Ball

—William Cply

53

outs and the percentages are figured and recorded. Times at bat, home runs, triples, singles , sacrifices, strike-outs, passed balls, wild pitches, walks, balks, runs batted in, runs scored, and batting, pitching and fielding averages are all in the book. Other sports have tried to copy the scoring and record-keeping methods of baseball, but with little success. In football passing averages are recorded, but no distinction is made between passes badly thrown and passes which should have been caught. The record shows how many passes a receiver has caught in a game, or in a season, but not how many he has missed. In a vague way, football players are credited with having made tackles; but no record is kept, except on film, of those which are missed. Baseball, too, is played for the day, for the game—but also for the record, for the future, for the possibility of eternity. There is the particular, immediate judgement, but also the possibility of a final judgment.

—**Eugene McCarthy**

BEAT
Hip Woe.

—**Chinese Academy, San Francisco**

BEAUTY
Beauty must be convulsive, if it is to be. Convulsive beauty must be erotic-veiled, exploding-fixed, magic-circumstantial, if it is to be.

—**Andre Breton**

O *my* very own! O *my* beautiful! Atrocious fanfare that does not make me trip! Enchanted easel.

—**Arthur Rimbaud**

She is beautiful, she is more than beautiful: she is surprising.
—**Charles Baudelaire**

I'm beautiful and strong, but I'm a woman...   —**Cros**

workings by Ursule Molinaro

BIOGRAPHY
In the memory, facts survive only as images. We are helped by photographs and mementoes, but mainly we rely on the imagination. Our sense of the past depends more on

Shakespeare, Flaubert and Tolstoi than on official histories.
It follows that the best biographies are written with a
sense of character and form. When the biographer takes a
leap and treats the subject like the hero or heroine of a
novel, then, and only then, is there a chance that he or she
will come back to life, and be once more a memorable fact.

—Frank MacShane

BLOB

Although my body appears in place,
my consciousness is not
Nor am I localized
at the tool counter
in a Radio Shack store.
The purchase of old calendars
listing the daily activities
of dead yogis
is not my desire.
Nor are antique crystal serpents
and other Jungian thumbsucks
what I have in mind.
Neither am I great & a
responsible toiler in the karmic march
of a battalion of disciples.
All of these points of view
got sloughed in the flood.

The particulars of my whim
are never seen
because never given time
to trouble me.
No dramatic relationships
keep me in touch
with diverse others,
or bend the light
theatrically around me.
Call me the Blob.
Bump against me
and see your private fancies
turn to rust.

At the moment we met
I appeared on the twinkle twinkle

skin of the jelly sea
of my cosmic self—
and I seemed to smile and bend your ear,
and hold your attention for a hundred years—
But in fact my consciousness
was never mathematically impacted
around that brief transaction!
And already dissolved in my jello mind
you imagined a saving game,
a dream in which we met as men
and shared the localized
crap intelligences of men.

In order to save a man,
I'm happy to oblige him,
even to the point of appearing
to share his view of his own success.
Since I, the Blob,
have already absorbed the world,
it doesn't matter if you pretend our union
is your heroic victory over fear,
and your egoic conquest of the Great Unknown!

But wouldn't it be easier to name it
an unspeakable romance in which
we both fall as meteors into God?
It could happen in a flash then,
and be done with, that
all the phantom faces we might wear
get used up and disappear forever into
the seamless consciousness of
        the Blob.

                  —**Tom Veitch**

BOREDOM

An unpleasurable state of mind combining an intense need
for activity with a lack of purpose. In boredom, excitation
is experienced but its aim has been forgotten. The
environment may be shunned in an effort to relieve the
excitation through fantasy. More likely, however, the
environment is sought in the hope that relief will come
through some chance encounter with a purpose similar to
the one forgotten. Bored persons pass from situation to

situation like someone who has misplaced a valuable possession and inquires incessantly for its whereabouts, But the discovery of purpose has the disadvantage of responsibility. Hence, the environment is enlisted not for gratification—unknown aims cannot be gratified—but for continued diversion and distraction.

—Donald M. Kaplan & Armand Schwerner

Boredom is ennui.

—Novalis

At the lowest level lay boredom. What did they expect this blinded eagle to remember of our nostalgias?

—Paul Eluard
workings by Ursule Molinaro

BREATH

Continuous testimony (Readout)

—Charlie Morrow

BRONOWSKI

"Man is a singular creature. He has a set of gifts which make him unique among the animals: so that, unlike them, he is not a figure in the landscape—he is a shaper of the landscape. In body and in mind he is the explorer of nature, the ubiquitous animal, who did not find but made his home in every continent." "His imagination, his reason, his emotional subtlety and toughness, make it possible for him not to accept his environment but to change it. And that series of inventions, by which man from age to age has re-made his environment, is a different kind of evolution—not biological, but cultural evolution. I call that brilliant sequence of cultural peaks 'The Ascent of Man.' "

—Christo

BRUSH

My philosophical consolation was the memory of the man who, when asked what he would like to have done for him at the time of his death, requested that a brush be placed inside his coffin (for when he turned to dust).

—Andre Breton
a working by Ursule Molinaro

57

CADAVRE EXQUIS

A game played with a folded piece of paper, on which several participants compose a sentence or a drawing, without knowledge of the preceding collaboration or collaborations. The example, which has become a classic and to which the game owes its name, is derived from the first sentence thus obtained: *Le cadavre — exquis — boira —le vin — nouveau.* The exquisite corpse will drink the new wine.

—Andre Breton
a working by Ursule Molinaro

Le Cadvre exquis

CAGE, JOHN'S SONG

A member of the Avantis tribe and its rituals, his notoriety has come from his capability to innovate sounds like those of the voice by using plants and earth rather than humans and other animals. He has also used the constructs of the "cage" or barriers which abound on the reservation where he was, like many others of that tribe, confined for much of his early life, to create an unusual music. He is a tribal leader as indicated by his first name.

—Carol Berge

See Race Johnsong

CAPE

If Cape Horn looked like a breast, the Patagonians would spend their evenings caressing the star-coals that mill about on their stomachs, but unfortunately the Cape has always looked like an artichoke.

—Benjamin Peret
a working by Ursule Molinaro

58

CAPILLARY

Careful scrutiny of the content of the mind's most thought-less action can reveal a *capillary tissue,* the ignorance of which would defeat any attempt to determine mental circulation. The role of this tissue is to insure the constant exchange which must take place in the thought process between the exterior and interior worlds; this exchange requires the uninterrupted interpenetration of waking and sleep activity.

—Andre Breton
a working by Ursule Molinaro

CARS

According to a recent survey, "There could be as many as 20 million of them out there."

—Joe Brainard

CASABLANCA

If she can stand it so can I, play it Sam...

*Of all the gin joints in all the
world she had to walk into mine*

I stick my neck out for no one
Rick never drinks with customers

Help me Rick...you
     must do something...   "hearts full of
     hide me...   passion, jealousy
                                        and hate...it's
                                  still the same old story,
                                a fight for love and glory,
                                   on that you can rely...
vultures everywhere,   and when two lovers woo,
   vultures everywhere   they still say I love you
                                     the world will always
                                welcome lovers, as time
                                        goes by..."

I love you so much,
    and I hate this war so much...
  it's a crazy world and anything can happen...
    kiss me—kiss me as if it were for the last time...

> *Those days are over, I'm not*
> *   fighting for anything except*
> *   myself*

Is that cannon fire...
    or is it my heart pounding...

> *The wow finish, a guy standing on*
> * train platform*
> * with a comical look on his face because*
> *   his insides had been kicked out*

> *I've heard the story a million times, "Mister, I met a man*
> *once when I was a kid," it would always begin...*
> *   tell me, who was it you left me for...*
> *was it Lazlo or were there others in between...*
> *or aren't you the kind that tells...*

> Well, it seems I was right
>   you are a sentimentalist

You want to feel sorry for yourself...one
    woman has hurt you and you want to take
revenge on the whole world...If you don't
  help us Victor Lazlo will die in Casablanca...

> *—What of it, I'm going to die here,*
> *it's a good place for it*

Round up the usual suspects

> The day you left Paris—if you
>   only knew what I went through—
>   how much I loved you—
>   how much I still love you

> *I never make plans that far ahead...*
> * Take her home, Sasha, she's had*
> *   a little too much to drink...*

—Mimi Gross Grooms

I know I'll never have the strength to leave
    you again—I can't fight it anymore—
I ran away from you once, I can't do it again—

        I don't know what's right anymore—
    you'll have to do the thinking for both of us—
           for all of us—
    I wish I didn't love you so much

I came here for my health
    for the waters

    We'll always have Paris...
        we'd lost that, but we got it back again
        last night,

        —When I said I would
           never leave you

   —and you never will
               —Charles Bernstein

CENSORSHIP

In this dream a famous writer is being talked about in another country and because he is being talked about an official from the Department of Culture has arrived at his house to strike him for each sentence delivered by the stranger on this famous writer. He asks, Why strike me when it's not I who is talking? We strike you, the reply goes, because you are a surrogate for that man. When he stops talking about you we will cease talking to you with our hands, and the famous man decided to call up this stranger whose name he does not know to ask him or her to stop talking about him, and so he places the call with the operator who says she knows exactly who it is and she is ready to call that person but first must strike herself over the head as required by the rules of the Department of Culture. This she does and proceeds to put through the call. The person answers the phone, listens and gives one huge scream which is heard by the famous writer who turns to the cultural attache of his government and says, That person knows my work. I'm delighted.

—David Ignatow

CHAIR

Chairs with their legs upturned, like skeletons dug up by archeologists.
—Violette Nosieres
a working by Ursule Molinaro

Magritte

CHANCE

Canned Chance.

—Marcel Duchamp

Chance manifests outside necessity, as it hews a way through man's subconscious.

—Andre Breton

Chance is the master of humor.   —Max Ernst
workings by Ursule Molinaro

CHILD

Black as the wick of a bomb, the child is placed on the path

of a passing sovereign—the man—by an anarchist individual-
ist of the worst kind—the woman.

—Andre Breton and Paul Eluard
a working by Ursule Molinaro

CHURCH

All is good, only the church is not. In church, everything
depresses you, since it only ruins, terrifies and buries you.

—Baffo
a working by Ursule Molinaro

CLASSICAL

A corruption of the word "glass," meaning something one
can see through, this term has come to mean a subject that
is offered in classes at schools. Today the term has come
to be synonymous with obscurity, pedantry and dullness;
a subject is chosen because it has passed the test of historical
longevity and then presented in such a manner as to obfus-
cate the original beauty or joy. —Carol Berge

CLEVERNESS

"Don't you think Mr. Ray E. Johnson would
enjoy a perfect vacation, through the end of
this 'Cosmic Epoch,' ?"
—A.M. Fine

COLLAGE

If it's debatable whether—you can tell a bird by its feather—
It's absolutely not true—that you can tell a collage by its
glue.

It's something like the alchemy of the visual image.
The miracle of total transformation of persons and objects
with or without modifying their physical or anatomic aspect.

—Max Ernst
a working by Ursule Molinaro

COLOR

In the Fifties, when Franz Kline restricted his palette to
black and white, they started making bad movies in color.
In nature, according to television, the South Sea sea snake—
striped black and white—has markings which frighten, like
the skunk's, the creatures of its habitat. Books are black
and white, except for Tom Veitch's *Eat This Book*, which
is black and lavender. Television is in color, except for old

63

movies and Fifties re-runs.

Color at its best is a nuance. Iris, Juno's handmaiden, used rainbow to ship rainwater back to heaven; it was also a personal pocket stairway for running messages to earth, and a coat. Joseph's coat of many colors did not protect

pallid

wan

mist

gray

grey

dove

mouse

old

ash

soot

Woman with Hat in Feathers of Black and White Pearl, Ebony, Silver, Ivory.

him from Jacob's other sons. Genesis does not detail Jacob's ladder, which ascended from earth to heaven; some writers, including Denise Levertov, daughter of rabbi and priest, hold that it was of stone, and indeed Jacob does sleep on pillows of stone and build afterwards a stone pillar; but the vision takes place in a dream after sunset, and when Juno wanted a particular dream, she always sent her request to Sleep via Iris.

Cut irises don't last a damn, although they outlast daffodils. Pom-poms on the other hand outwear their welcome, and seem excessive, like cupcakes. "Lie down in yellow flowers," says Andrew Wylie, "it's the whole world." It is totally great. As a boy Bacchus wore flowers in his hair. The Greeks and Romans prettied up their stories but the Jews liked the tonal clarity of black and white. In the nineteen fifties, women wore feathered hats. Feathers outlast all flowers; as achievements, usually things, outlast pleasures, mere moods.

Night vision dispenses with color. Purple becomes a brushed and lustrous black, while red becomes grey. Thus, turning on the light, one finds his grey older woman blooming, while another finds his raven-tressed beauty weird. This is called "spinning the pie," a tradition connected to roulette and the medieval wheel of fortune. Ah the medieval—what an interregnum, half-way between the ancient world and the Fifties! Dye from Flanders was central to their textile industry, and led to the Reformation. Dye in hair is a carcinogen.

—T.W. Fretter

COLORADO

The Frank Shorter Cash Register
Boulder's a swell place
Everybody jogs

All that pounding
All those pretty feet

On the wall of the
Podiatrist's College

There's a map of Boulder
Framed in gold

Naughty Naropa Poem
It's great to hear the Muse of Shamanism lecture on
    Gertrude Stein
Fresh off the big jet from India
The principal struggle is to pronounce the word "automatism"
    right
And for this you will please pay $297

Hurricane Hill
It's nice to walk up by the old tungsten mine
But when sudden gunfire rings out
Who has time to notice the wild flowers?

The sight of all those pockmarked tin cans
Makes wandering these slopes of aspen and pine
These meadows of columbine and indian paint brush

A nervous pleasure

Colorado
Adolf Coors made all this possible

The Boulder Story
White guy
age 28
clean
no anxiety wrinkles
looks like he might be a member of the Eagles

meets white girl
age 22
clear skin
blond hair
at the Boulderado.

They go for a bike ride together.

(Note & Question: *No tension in this town.*
Without tension how can life exist?)

Adjustment Blues
Denver Bears games on the radio in the mountains at night
The ultimate loneliness

Out of the Blue
Hearing my waffle soles
crunch red rock tailings
two July-fattened

chipmunks scurry across
the pile of junk in
the abandoned mine shaft

the sun blazes down on
Arapahoe and Navajo Peaks
like on two ice cream cones

but nothing melts
the air is cold
the aspens shiver

the top of the world
isn't here, it's true
but you can see it from here

—Tom Clark

COMPREHENSION
Comprehension resembles infinity and fears the finite.
—Raymond Lulle

Nothing is incomprehensible.

—Lautreamont
Workings by Ursule Molinaro

CONCEPTUAL ART
Toilet training for amateur thinkers.

—Donald Kuspit

CONSUMPTION
The temptation to order a new dish: for instance a demo-
lition, garnished with plane trees.
—Paul Eluard & Andre Breton
a working by Ursule Molinaro

COOPERATIVE GALLERY
An unvisited space where a group of artists lose money
trying to beat the system at its own game.

—Dick Higgins

CORPSE

A corpse claps hands like a pebble in a window pane.

—Benjamin Peret
a working by Ursule Molinaro

COUNTERPHOBIA

A compulsion to perform an activity which one is actually afraid of. The compulsion is a symptom of an anxiety about fear. The counterphobic is distressed at the passivity that the fearful situation invites. Passivity is more unbearable than danger, and the counterphobia converts this passivity into activity. Counterphobics are people who engage in pursuits which normal people are afraid of.

—Armand Schwerner & Donald M. Kaplan

See Anxiety

COVETOUSNESS

but thorough daily care
to get, and nightly feare to lose his owne,
He led a wretched life vnto himself vnknowne.

—Edmund Spenser

A passionate desire for something that another person already has. The covetous person lacks a sense of personal authenticity and seeks guidance in the choices first made by others. The insatiability of covetousness is the result of the inevitable disqualification of the person whose possession is finally attained. "How could he have been worth my efforts, if what he possessed has been achieved by someone as worthless as me?" Covetousness not only indicates a failure of personal independence; it goes on to demean the morality encountered in others. It is one of the seven deadly sins (*q.v.*).

—Armand Schwerner & Donald M. Kaplan

CRUTCH

A wooden structure derived from the philosophy of Descartes. Generally used to uphold the tenderness of *flabby structures.*

—Salvador Dali
a working by Ursule Molinaro

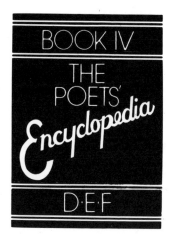

BOOK IV
THE POETS'
Encyclopedia

D·E·F

D

D is a dread denoter
D is a dreary denominator
dross   drought   dreg   drown
D has a desolate dominion

Deadly are the damages of D:
depletion   depression   defeat   decay
dolorous darks of despairing despond
dingy dungeons of deep defunct

Inside D dwells the dismal Dis
dispenser of discombobulations:
dismay   distress   disorder   disease
disgust   disgrace   disaster

Detestable despot of droop and doom
damned be thee   damnable D

—James Broughton

DANCE

Dance, according to the United States Post Office, is
"poetry in motion."

—Joe Brainard

DANGER

It is better to be rash than over-cautious, because Fortune is a woman, and, if you wish to keep her down, you must beat her and pound her. It is evident that she allows herself to be overcome by men who treat her in that way rather than by those who proceed coldly. For that reason like a woman, she is always the friend of young men, because they are less cautious, and more courageous, and command her with more boldness.

—Machiavelli
translated by Y. U. Puck

I wish dangerous drugs were. I'm sick of so much disdain. No one trembles. No one's afraid anymore.

Without risk, no thrill. Now, a top thrill can kill. Who provokes destruction for gain? The adventurer. He travels to the Carcasuss Mountains. He finds the falls that frighten him— the catwalks of suspension bridges, the peaks of high mountains, their cold and wind.

One by one the boy conquers his fears. But no one is ever out of danger. The King of Samos in his palace says to the King of Egypt, look what I have conquered! am I not fortunate?

But what about Miletus your enemy? says the King of Egypt. You are still *threatened.*

But even as the king of Egypt spoke, a soldier, bloodspattered, approached the King of Samos, and said, rejoice O king and let a thousand altars thank the sky, for this day the foe has fallen on the spear of Polydor; and from a basin he withdrew a head, dirty and grimy from the miles.

Happy days are here again, whistled the King, as he inspected the head; my cares and troubles are gone, there'll be no more from now on.

The King of Egypt was silent.

The King of Samos turned to him and said, isn't that right?

What about your fleet? It has been away three months and you have received no word.

From the battlements the call rang out. Sail! Sail! The fleet returns!

The King of Egypt was astonished. Bad luck, he said, is far from you today. Yet who knows what battles your fleet endured in Crete? Perhaps they return defeated?

"Victory!" The ships were at the dock, and sailors
and soldiers embraced. "Victory!" the people cried.

"O King," said the King of Egypt. "I have thought
myself as blessed as you; and I thought such blessings were
my lot; and at that moment my very own and only son
died. Beware. Count no man happy till he's in the grave.
I advise you to take some misfortune on your own head.
The gods will not tolerate such luck as yours. Take some item
which is precious to you and sacrifice it to the gods
to slake their anger."

Then spake the Samian, touched with fear. "This ring
of mine I hold most dear of all the island holds, and this
unto the furies I will give. Perhaps the sisters will forgive—"
it flashes from the precipice.

The next morning at dawn a fisher marches blithely
to the palace. "O lord," said the fisher, "casting my nets
this morning I caught a fish never before seen in these
waters."

A slave prepared the fish. "O King, thou art the
luckiest of men. The ring you threw into the waters
yesterday I have found in the fish's maw." Your luck is
without bounds."

But the King of Egypt turned white and started to
shiver. "The Gods have prepared you for your ruin."
He foreswore their friendship and in his galley set sail.

—Michael Andre

DEADLY SINS

Of which there are seven and from which all other sins
derive: Wrath, Envy, Lechery, Covetousness, Gluttony
and Sloth *(qq.v.).* Called deadly because they are held
to lead to spiritual death.

A foggy mist had couered all the land;
And vnderneath their feet, all scattered lay
Dead sculs and bones of men, whose life had gone astray.
                    —Edmund Spenser
        —Armand Schwerner & Donald M. Kaplan

DELUSION

An insistent, false belief, often of grandeur or persecution.
Falsity, however, is only one criterion of a delusion. A
second, and more important criterion is the unacceptability
of the belief to the deluded person's culture or immediate

group. False beliefs which are collectivized and maintained en masse are more accurately called superstitions, prejudices, theologies, etc., and give comfort to the believer. Delusions, on the other hand, are maintained in isolation and loneliness, and, like any malady, cause suffering. Thus delusions are relatively harmless to the community at large.

—**Armand Schwerner & Donald M. Kaplan**

See Group; Isolation

DENBY

When I was ten an uncle gave me "The Rubyiat" and I liked it very much and so I started to write. And when I was twelve I read "Adonais" and I didn't understand a word of it but it was absolutely marvellously thrilling. I went to the piano and tried to play it, not knowing anything about piano playing. It seemed to be all in the sound. I was very surprised when I re-read it three or four years later and understood it.

I was born in Tientsin, but I was only there for a year and then I was in Shanghai for a year when I was four or five. From the time I was ten on I was living in Detroit until I was about fifteen but I went away to school during that time and then my parents moved to Washington D.C.

My father was Consul in Shanghai and a business man in Tientsin. He had been living in China for a long time and he spoke and read Chinese.

When I was sixteen my freshman year at college I first read Waley and I imagined, by that time, the way people do, I could understand the Chinese point of view, whatever it is—you know, the Chinese atmosphere. It seemed very natural to me to be reading Chinese poems.

I wrote a novel when I was eight. My oldest brother was writing in his prep-school magazine, and my father had written a book, and I suppose all that made it like something you would do, *writing* in general. I had no idea about it nor did anybody tell me. It wasn't a literary atmosphere. I didn't know there was a poetry "society" until I got to Harvard. As a matter of fact, I had very little contact with writers or friends among them—until I met James Schuyler, Frank O'Hara, and John Ashbery, and that was in '52 or something like that.

Before that the friends around me had been painters! Somehow there wasn't much reason to know writers or

poets, being a dancer abroad.

That was in the late 20's and '30's in Germany. I wrote

a novel then. The first thing that was published—oh wait a minute—there was a libretto.... The very first thing that was published was an article on psychoanalysis, as I had studied that. I wrote it in German.

It was corrected by the editor.

At the time I was vaguely thinking I might be an analyst and I was living in Vienna, and then after I got to be a dancer some friends at the theatre suggested I should make a new libretto for a 19th century operetta. It was the fashion then to bring the libretto up-to-date and make contemorary allusions in the same sense as in the past.

It was performed with the old music of Suppé and the subject changed from 1870 to 1930.

When I came to New York Aaron Copland—who is an old friend from Europe too—asked me if I would write a libretto for a high school type performance that would happen only once at the Grand Street Playhouse. That was in '36 or '37. It was famous as a music place and people had asked Aaron if he would write an opera for their students to perform and so he asked me if I would write the libretto for it and I did, and it was performed and published.

In writing a poem you have a situation in the first line and you watch it grow. Images that I have seen actually, that are in my memory because I have seen them, are more productive for me than to imagine something which has no further contact with the world. I don't have any inner life.

The Mediterranean sonnets were all written here except one which I started there and hadn't been able to finish and I got that one sort of in order and then went on to do others by memory. I knew those places quite well, having been there quite a while, but I was interested in something that was happening to me here at the time but that is not mentioned. It was something I was interested in as one might be interested for oneself in technique. I was interested in something I was feeling.

When I was here in New York and no longer dancing, I started seeing the French and Russian ballet companies. I had been brought up in modern dance and didn't have much experience of ballet but I saw so many marvelous things that I got more and more interested.

Writing about it came about because I didn't have enough money to buy the tickets, and a magazine, a quarterly, *Modern Music,* offered me the job of being dance critic and getting tickets through it. The editor assured me that nobody would read me because it was only read by contemporary composers, modern composers, so I wasn't embarrassed and at the same time I had complete freedom—when I did have something interesting to say I could say it without being bothered by the fact it would or wouldn't be permissable. And the editor was a brilliant woman who very gradually trained me to say what I had to say more clearly.

I fought with her like mad to start with when she objected to something not being clear because I thought it was clear but gradually I realized that it wasn't and that was very interesting—to follow what you're doing and see if it really is clear. Minna Lederman was editor and the magazine was brilliantly edited and interesting to read now because it was all the avant-garde of the Twenties and Thirties. Virgil Thomson wrote for it too, and it was mostly written by composers. It had a very small circulation.

It seems to me that knowing what you like while you're liking it is the real subject matter of poetry and art in general. They're very glad to have some people to have done it for them who can remind them of the moments when they almost did or didn't for a short time. That instantaneous quality we like so much nowadays has to do with that sudden moment.

—Gerard Malanga

DENIAL

Of the various recourses for defending the mental apparatus from threatening stimuli, denial can be the most costly from the point of view of reality *(q.v.).* Whereas other defenses distort reality beyond recognition, this one simply evades reality by a withdrawal of attention. Indeed, denial may be regarded as an absence of recourse in the face of a threat. The energy usually available for attention to reality becomes available to the denying person as a restless, manic apprehension.

Except in very early childhood, denial never occurs wholly alone. It is orchestrated with other defensive maneuvers of mind and even finds a place in normal functioning. For example, the automobile accident rate has to be subjected to some amount of denial if one is to travel by car unanxiously; similarly air travel is feasible only through denial. Where to draw the line between adaptive and malignant denial is not always clear. However, one rather reliable indication of malignant denial is exuberance at the brink of disaster.

—Armand Schwerner & Donald M. Kaplan

DIPA(R)

a diving bird

the dipper or ousel or ant thrush has longer wings for steady rapid flight along borders of clear lakes and streams, dives into the water and walks upon the bottom making its way against a strong current. The nest is oven shaped on the banks of streams.

Barriers of land, chains of mountains determining the courses of rivers are each one boundaries between assemblages of fish

—Alison Knowles

DRILL ART

Drill Art arose in the late Sixties. Originally an informal movement among dentists to encourage each other as creative artists—painters, sculptors and pushers—in their spare time, it soon developed to the point where they opened their own galleries and suckassed their way to the status of a full time artworld power. "A force to be reckoned with." Drills, bits, molars, canines and the Big Incisor.

—Michael Brownstein

DUMB,WYOMING

Where *they* live and/or come from.
—Joel Oppenheimer

See East Jesus, Indiana; Niggerdeath, Alabama; Wayback, Ohio

Photo by Steve Fitch

76

EARTH ART OF ANCIENT ASTRONAUTS

Scientists tell us that the Earth's natural wonders—the great mountains, rivers, volcanoes, etc.—were created by cycles of upheaval and erosion caused by weather, gravity and changes in the Earth's crust. We are taught to accept the idea that a crack in the Earth can lift up huge mountain ranges. But have you ever seen this happen? Can you really believe that little streams of water, gusts of wind and fissures in the Earth made the Himalayas? Or even the Catskills? Have you ever noticed that when it rains, no matter how heavily, the water on the streets evaporates in a matter of hours? Do you think it could ever rain enough to fill an ocean, even if it rained for eons? Furthermore, it can rain all week and maybe 40 days and 40 nights, but *eons?*

We now know that ancient astronauts from smarter planets created the cultural wonders we so admire: The Pyramids, Stonehenge, Cave Paintings, Mayan Temples, etc. Well, doesn't it make sense that the ancestors of those very same extra-terrestrials created the magnificent sculptures on the Earth's surface—Nature?

This is why a mountain in Asia can look exactly like a mountain in California—they were the work of the same ancient astronaut earth artist. And why there are waterfalls all over the world. The ancient astronaut earth artists were much like the artists of today—they scouted the Earth for appropriate sites for their monuments, and went to work. Their mastery of materials was astounding, their technological achievements superb. Consider one of their masterpieces —

Different ancient astronaut earth artists had different interests. Some built mountains, some built beaches, some did perhaps only one great work in their life, so unique are some earth sculptures —

Inside the most common genres—mountains, deserts, etc.—ancient astronaut earth artists worked in varied and individual styles. We can identify the artists working in a particular genre—waterfalls, for example—by identifying characteristic elements in their work —

Master of the Split Stream

Master of the Single Stream   Master of the Multiple Stream

The careers of different ancient astronaut earth artists often went through different periods. The artist below first constructed mountains with dry lake beds in front of them, then built mountains with boulders in front and finally synthesized the two styles —

There also seem to have been ideological differences among ancient astronaut earth artists working in similar materials. For instance, one group built active, or timed, volcanoes (below left)—volcanoes which erupt every so often—and another group built volcanoes for one performance only (below right): they erupted once (perhaps during an ancient astronaut Art Fair) and were left as what we call "extinct."

Today it would be a cinch to build The Pyramids. At the time, it was technologically impossible for humans to do it: no wheel, no forklifts, etc. Someday we will be able to build mountain ranges easily, like the ancient astronaut earth artists. After all, the skyscrapers we build now are far more imposing than monuments, like The Pyramids, built by ancient astronauts.

And where are those astronauts today, anyway? They buzz around in their flying saucers, occasionally saying hi or picking up an Earthling or two, but they seem to have abandoned art. They haven't made a monument, natural or cultural, in hundreds of years. The primary activity of their society has become, sad to say, joy-riding. Or, to look at it more optimistically, perhaps these contemporary astronauts regard the Earth as "finished" and their seemingly aimless travels do serve a purpose: they are wandering around a museum.

—**Erika Rothenberg**

EAST JESUS, INDIANA

Where *they* live and/or come from.
—**Joel Oppenheimer**

See Wayback, Ohio; Niggerdeath, Alabama; Dumb Wyoming

photo by Steve Fitch

ECSTASY

Ecstasy is the *pure state* of rigorous, hyper-sensitive vital lucidity, the blind lucidity of desire. It is that critical mental state which present-day, hysterical, modern surrealist and phenomenal thinking hopes to render continuous.

—**Salvador Dali**
a working by Ursule Molinaro

EEL, SHARP-NOSED

(Anguilla Acutirostrio)
The bodeel is eelongeted and cylindreel, becoming moreel
and moreel and moreel and moreel and moreel and moreel
Compresseeled to the taieel, the mucous glandeels of the
eel skin are largeel, the eel airbladdeel is long, thereel are
teelth in eacheel jaweell, and a feweel on the eel vomer.
The eel eeltoral fins are closeel toeel the eeel smaleel
branchieell apeelture, and moreel and moreel and moreel
and moreel and moreel eel.

—Opal L.Nations

ELEGANCE

Elegance is progress.   —Alfred Jarry
a working by Ursule Molinaro

ELEPHANT

Elephants are contagious.   —Paul Eluard & Benjamin Peret
a working by Ursule Molinaro

ENCYCLOPEDIA

A compendium (using the alphabet for a filing system) of
statements that seem not to depend on other knowledge.
Aardvark is independent of *Mammal*, *Angel* of *God*. The
unit of the Encyclopedia is the Fact. A fact is a corpsed
deed; from L. *factum*, done, but with the residuum of accomplished action subtracted. Facts lie there pickled and
are generally wrong, scribes' minds having swerved from
the continuum of action. Guy Davenport notes that the
Britannica "has Waley sending Ez off on the trot to trans-
late Cathay, unruffled by picturing an event of 1917
causing an event of 1915." Shun all encyclopedias but
this one.   —Hugh Kenner

the condition of listing all thought
Pertinant to a present human situation,
exclusive of the future, anywhere
within a normal life-span of thirteen
million years, divided into five distinct
Periods. P.S. : Devils get it longer.

—A.M.Fine

81

ENVY

All in a kirtle of discoloured say
  He clothed was, ypainted full of eyes.
                                        —Edmund Spenser

One of the deadly sins *(q.v.)*. An indication of the voyeur-
istic source of envy lies in its etymology: Latin *in*=in, upon,
+ *videre*=to look. Envy begins in the child's observations
of adults, especially liberties involving what the child per-
ceives as pleasure and excitement. As the child experiences
a vicarious enjoyment in watching adults, this watching becomes complex and significant. Whenever there is intense
looking, the object being looked at is experienced as purposely showing; this experience leads to resentment in the
one who is looking. Envy describes this feeling: "I begrudge
you what I see you have, for you possess it merely to
torment me." The sin in Envy is its demand for license
without qualification.

                          —Armand Schwerner & Donald M. Kaplan

EVERYTHING

"Everything" is a circle, an egg. You look
and feel and listen. Tap on the shell:
it's hollow inside. "God, where are you?"
There is always an answer, but whose?
You curl up in the echo.

                                        —William Stafford

See Space

EVOLUTION

Evolution is a function of leisure time. Tadpoles fed on
thyroid extract metamorphose into frogs as small as flies.

                                        —Michael Brownstein

EXCLUSION

An outsider identifies with a group—a literary coterie, a
social clique—makes "advances" to individuals in the group,
often supporting and working for the group, believing himself at the brink of acceptance; but fails to meet an arbitrary
criterion or protocol; and as a result his support, work and
admiration are used but not returned. The outsider then
feels the bitterness and disappointment of injustice. Ex-

clusion parallels at the social level exploitation at the economic; in exploitation, a subordinate group (as wage earners, female sex, black race) are used for economic gain by a group in a superordinate position (as bosses, men, whites). After exclusion, the arbitrary protocol or criterion haunts the outsider as a "negative" destiny.

—Loo Hcs'Kroy Wen

FABIUS MAXIMUS VERRUSCOSUS, QUINTUS

Called Cunctator (Lat. "delayer") (died 203 B.C.), Roman consul, dictator, and priest. A conservative military genius he is famed for his strategy of avoiding pitched battle while conducting harassing raids during the Second Punic War, a tactic that wore Hannibal's forces to exhaustion. The Romans became bored with his methods, removed him from office, and were defeated at Cannae. Reinstated in 214, he served with honor until his death. The term *Fabian* came to mean a policy of delay.

—T.W. Fretter

Bernard Shaw dons captured Cathaginian helmet

Ho and Mao amuse children with tales of Helpless Giants

FAITH

My mother believes she will win the Massachusetts State Lottery. There is nothing I can say about faith until she does.
—Dotty le Mieux

FANTASY

my attempts to check the correlation between fantasy and reality, by comparing the associations evoked by pronouncing the name Aboudoukour, with a view from the carriage window of the clay-hut rectangles of Aboudoukour: what is built fits in, what is alive is something different.

the surprise that fantasy and reality are much closer in Ummerdjim, presumably because this name sounds less oriental and is therefore less loaded down with images.
—Peter Wehrli
translated by Roger Frood

See Reality

FASCINATION

A mode of observation involving mastery without effort. The prototype of fascination is the infant's rapt gaze on what he desires to handle and control but cannot yet do for lack of neuromuscular development. He will lose himself in the sight and sound of some object or scene and, in so becoming one with it, experience the illusion of mastery. Subsquently, fascination may occur as a pre-stage to mastery. It is then followed by some intellectual or physical effort, as in an encounter with a fascinating poem which excites comprehension or with a beautiful boat that one then wants to rig and sail. Here fascination is charged with the vitality of surprise.

Fascination may also occur as an end in itself. Here it is invited for its own sake and is devoid of surprise. One places oneself receptively before an inconsequential though titillating object and enjoys a gratification reminiscent of infancy, i.e., mastery without effort. Fascination is then followed by self-recrimination and often hostility against the object one has lost himself in and swindled himself with.
—Armand Schwerner & Donald M. Kaplan

FATE

From Latin *fatus*, "that which has been spoken."
Hence, declared, decreed, pronounced. Hence, a course
of events beyond human control leading to a predetermined outcome. The outcome usually bespeaks
punishment, suffering and defeat. In varying degrees all
human beings are susceptible to the experience that some
kind of fate rules their existence.

The collectivization of this susceptibility in programs
of destiny and prophecy leads to powerful justifications
for significant social movements. Thus, "It is my fate to
lead Germany and your fate to follow me." (Adolf Hitler)
"The defeat of capitalism is not in our hands but in the
prophecies of Marx." (Nikita Khrushchev) Also, Manifest
Destiny=the nineteenth century doctrine that it is the destiny of Anglo-Saxon nations, especially the United States,
to dominate the Western Hemisphere.

Now, a sense or notion of fate would seem likely to
originate in our observations of those inexorable regu-
larities and repetitions of nature, which are beyond our
control, which we are nevertheless compelled to participate in, and which we sometimes dread. The most apt
example might be death. But as likely as this assumption
is, it is not a good one. Indeed, it proves to be a better
assumption that it is we who impose a fatalistic view on
nature rather than the other way around.

For one thing, a sense of fate simply does not visit
especially those who are most exposed to the inevitabilities
of nature.

However, a sense of fate, indeed, strong enough to produce feelings of doom and hopelessness, is regularly encountered in all mental illness. It is also worth noting that it is a
feeling much more than a speakable thought. That it is
especially pronounced among compulsive gamblers, addicts
and the promiscuous gives a clue to its origins and dynamics.

These people not only share a strong sense of fate but
some additional characteristics as well. To begin with, their
distress is involved with some definite *activity*, rather than
an inhibition, fear or thought. Moreover, the activity itself
promises some kind of lasting triumph but inevitably
results in disappointment: for the gambler, usually a loss
or else an insufficient win that is subsequently played and

lost; for the addict, a subsiding of intoxication and elation; for the erotomanic woman, abandonment by her lover or else her own loss of interest in him. In each instance, a repetition of the activity is required. Finally, the activity on which the hopes are pinned is never arbitrary nor can it be resisted. Thus, the sequence emerges: hope—activity—defeat—repetition. So predetermined is the sequence, so dependable the outcome, and so subservient the individual caught in it, that he is often said to be suffering from a neurosis of destiny. And he is likely to be the first to agree with the aptness of this label.

But since nobody is forced by current externals into this sequence, it remains to be answered what special inner mission these people are on. At the core of a neurosis of destiny is a defeat sustained in the deep past, emotional, vast, and within the family unit, which was stricken from memory on the basis of an embittered threat: "I am helpless now. Let the matter rest. But temporarily, for I defer the the conflict to the future when I shall be older and stronger (like the one at whose hands I am now suffering) and then I shall reopen it again and this time win." But years hence with the memory thus obliterated, all that arises is the unspoken compulsion to act towards some exciting outcome. Mastery and the laying to rest of the original conflict are, of course, not feasible: the issue is no longer clear; the mighty adversaries of the helpless child have all grown old and are useless for satisfaction. All that now remains is the wound and the helpless child that now inhabits the body and the intellect of the adult. Fate is the emotional vapor that hangs over these remains.

And since all human beings have in common that helpless condition of childhood and have sustained to a greater or lesser extent the unspeakable injuries to feeling that this condition invites, some sense of fate is also held in common. Only its grip varies and the choice we make: we can either be its victim or its opponent.

Thus, Santayana: "Those who do not remember the past are condemned to relive it."

—Armand Schwerner & Donald M. Kaplan

FATE WORSE THAN DEATH

A; esp., to suffer... (Of a woman) to be raped; 19th century;

since ca. 1918, usually jocular.

—Laura LeNail

FATHAM

A full stretch of the arms in a straight line.

patella pectonata at 30 fathoms down attaches itself to stones and shells off rocky coasts. The substance to which they are affixed they can dissolve and absorb within themselves, making a deep excavation beneath. The gill tufts are supported at the extremity of lateral footstalks.

Barriers of land, chains of mountains determining the courses of rivers are each one boundaries between assemblages of fish

—Alison Knowles

FIRE

Fire is lack and excess.   —Heraclitus

In times of human upheavals fire always finds a way to escape through certain individuals who had involuntarily prepared themselves for it.

—Pierre Mabille
workings by Ursule Molinaro

FIREBALL

If the radiance of a thousand suns
were to burst into the sky,
that would be
the splendor of the Mighty-One.

—Bhagavad-Gita. Purportedly recalled by Julius Robert Oppenheimer upon witnessing the first atomic detonation at Alamogordo on 16 July, 1945.

An apparent sphere of radiant gases formed from the bomb mechanism, the air and other materials in the immediate environment of an atomic explosion. The ingredients of the fireball are vaporized to luminosity in the billionths of a second during which the explosion releases its energy. Theory leads to the conclusion that the fireball is actually doughnut-shaped, the outer rim rolling and swirling and sucking up the environment and determining the subsequent pattern of fallout.

In the case of a one-megaton air burst, the detonation produces temperatures exceeding 100,000,000° F., rivalling

A few minutes after an atomic test at Yucca Flats NE, 1955, radiological monitors found it "safe" for troops to march two miles to blast center.

the heat of the stars; within one-hundredth of a second the diameter of the ensuing fireball is roughly 440 feet; within 10 seconds it expands to a mile and a quarter, rising upward at a rate of 300 miles per hour. This immense and rapid expansion forms a shock wave that illuminates the surrounding air into a fiery hoop; this shock wave ripples out over the target area to contribute to the blast effects of the bomb. Seen from as far away as 60 miles, the fireball appears 30 times brighter than the midday sun. This radiant heat represents some 35 per cent of the total energy in the explosion and is enough to combine the nitrogen and oxygen in the atmosphere into 5,000 tons of corrosive nitric acid, enough acid to make steam out of a billion pounds of water. The fireball of a one megaton air burst may cause third-degree burns (complete destruction of the skin) to exposed persons 13 miles away. It will ignite light kindling materials within an area of 250 square miles. It rises nearly 25 miles, cooling as it goes, while materials like iron and stone condense into liquid and rain down on the earth below. The fireball is then the familiar mushroom cloud.

—Armand Schwerner & Donald M. Kaplan

FISH

—Walter de Maria

See Woman

FIVE-AND-TEN

A kind of American store, found now only in small towns considered "backward." Real Five-and-Tens have wooden floors and fixtures, carry a little of everything common but nothing rare or expensive, do not sell medicine or groceries do not advertise or cut prices, and were largely run out of business by the loss-leaders of large American corporations with the blessing of the American government, which has a parasitic relationship to large business. The Five-and-Ten made its money selling thread, socks and drinking glasses. The register was always at the front and the word *stealing* had not yet been changed to the word *shrinkage*. The store's profits rested on inventory and goodwill. If a store's shelves revealed empty spaces where small items had not been replaced when sold, you could be certain that the store would fail. The name of a failed Five-and-Ten was soon torn down to give a better businessman a chance, but the name of a good store was money-in-the-bank and a new owner would have to pay extra for the "goodwill." A man's father, after several heart attacks, sold his Five-and-Ten and retired, but he couldn't stand it because in those days the Five-and-Ten meant service and the friendship of one's customers as well as personal success. It couldn't have happened in Russia, so the immigrant Five-and-Ten owners often came out of retirement to die in their stores. One owner knew no songs but sang all the time. A dog who was run over by an automobile got well in the back room. The Five-and-Ten, for those who knew it, is like a coloring book on a rainy day, when toy sales boomed. Because the Five-and-Ten sold little things—thimbles, rulers, birthday candles—the distinctions between things still seem important (one might say, primary) to one who grew up handling them. It is possible, therefore, for such a one to believe that language begins in the (mathematical) concept of entity and separation, and that poetry is a way of using meaning (for which the ordinary dictionary is the final arbiter) to apprehend Meaning (for which experience is the source and this kind of Dictionary/Encyclopedia the testimony) and make it known. Notions, "fancy goods," and trinkets. Less is more. Everyone knows what a thimble is. The General Store was friendly. The Five-and-Ten was *personal*.

—Marvin Bell

FLAME

A tree must become a flowering flame, man a talking flame, and animals walking flames.

—**Novalis**

Flames, sponges of glass. —**Tristan Tzara**

The eternal youth of a precise flame—that veils nature while reproducing it.

—**Paul Eluard**
workings by Ursule Molinaro

FLOWERS

Regarding the insides of flowers:
this is something about which I have meant
to write you for a long time.

How awkwardly, but to a bee
fascinating it must seem, going in
to their sticky centers, half-

repellent, touching
their furry genitalia; horrible
to love and seek so, being dependent:

flowers' perfectly formed
hemispheres, the pretend insistence on privacy

like the hidden ladyslipper, modest,
shocking, sudden labia
blushing,

bifurcated, veined an
obvious: it is so soft,
slipping in,

is it not, and out?
I too am always
obsessed with the insides of flowers,

yearning to plunge
a finger into them
or a metaphor:

the "hermaphroditic artist"
invading the subject;
shivering at anemones,

at their dark secret
centers, or the double wheel
within a poppy, spoked

mouth slit and laughing.
The "Language of Flowers,"
spoken, translates "Sex."

If a daylily bends in the vase
it means: she is waiting.
If straight, trouble ahead.

If the flowers persist
in their drooping
throw them out

but refurbish
for it is good to have fresh
flowers beside one, breathing

their bodily secrets
by night, cleverly accessible
and bedded, moist.

—Kathleen Spivack

FOOTBALL, AMERICAN PROFESSIONAL

American Professional Football is
not only colorful (usually two
colors for each team on a background
field of green — not to mention
blue sky, cheerleaders, variety of
fan hues, etc.) it can also be in-
tellectually engaging (figuring
the moves of team members and coaches
is much like chess, as both are
based on war games, only football
is more modern with the quaterback

as field commander, the running
backs as lower ranking officers,
the ones who usually receive the most
injuries in action, the linemen are
the footsoldiers with the ends as
scouts and linebackers and other
defensive backs as noncommissioned
officers, special teams as the
special forces — rangers and
green berets, etc. — coaches are
the generals and upper echelon
desk officers who determine the
game plan and various changes in
the plan of attack as the battles
are waged and factors of actual
combat come into play, they even
have spies in the guys who
watch the game from up in
the press box or somewhere similarly removed and then run down
what they observe as enemy weak
spots to the coaches over walkie
talkies and other field radio
equipment — and don't forget the
wartime politicians in "the front
office" managers, etc.). Professional football is culturally
and aesthetically viable as well
(few other sports, if any, combine
as many aspects of our popular
culture and arts, the men themselves are a cross between the
subtle grace of dancers and the
sleek but often brutal persistance
of machines, their bottom halves
sheathed in muscle-clinging pants
resembling dancers' tights (their
movements, especially when seen on
slow motion replays and/or in snow,
are extremely dance-like because
they are choreographed, and like
the professional dancer they are
trained for years to respond to

ritualized circumstances with a
limited number of body movements
or steps and combinations
of those movements or steps) while
their top halves are like cars,
all bumpers and steel and fiber
glass designed for speed and power
and especially rough traffic (each
play as it unfolds seems like
nothing so much as a choreographed
traffic jam); with the ideal that
the choreography is based on being
almost total inaction, because
if everyone were to do exactly
what he is supposed to do right
not much would happen, it is by
capitalizing on the mistakes of
others and following through
without making mistakes of one's
own that the action progresses
in favor of one side or the other).

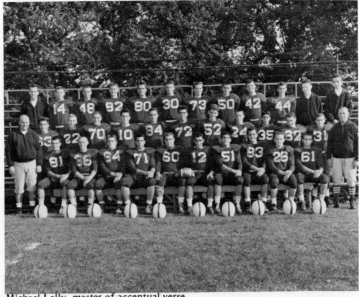

Michael Lally, master of accentual verse,
wore number 42 for St Benedict's, 1958

And, of course, as other poets
have noted, football is a ritual
of emerging manhood — a male rite
of passage — that almost all
young men and even young women
participate in, even if only in
spirit, especially during their
pubescent high school years, so
most citizens have an idea of
what it is about and what is at
stake when those who choose to
make it their career, their way
of earning a living and possibly
some measure of fame, continue
in this ritual of puberty when
they become fully developed men,
and even beyond that development,
some continuing to participate
actively into their late 30s and
40s, with often the option of
moving on to a position as coach

Michael Lally, star of stage and screen,
sat 3rd row right for "Rinky Dinks," 1956

or commentator and so staying
related to the game into
the age of retirement. This
kind of commitment is one few
citizens would care to make, so
those who do are seen as exceptions,
in some cases by some citizens as
freaks, but without in any way
taking away from their achievement
because that achievement is paid
for in dollar value and recognition
value beyond most other citizens'
achievements, even those of equal
or greater importance. Only in
professional football, where the
participants are old enough to know
better and in many cases do, is
the full involvement of the audience
possible, because in the end it is
a violent "sport" in which men are
incapacitated and sometimes brutally,
as in war (though few die from it,
at least on the professional level);
yet it falls well short of the
violence of more ancient rites of
manly combat, from war to gladiatorial
contests, even boxing is more dangerous.
And football is so technical, from
regulations to equipment, that it
can generate not only interest and
intellectual participation but lifetime career commitments from those
who have trained their intelligence,
or had it trained for them, to be
of use and successfully productive
in a society in which production is
the main and therefore most just-
ifiable (as well as corruptible) goal,
and the primary reason for that society's existence; it employs tons
of people (as small scale wars might)
while also generating innovations
and inventions to perfect the process

of play and the physical usefulness
of the players (as war generates new
materials and ways of using them as
well as new medical techniques
and equipment, etc.). Without professional
football the USA sports scene isn't
much different (except for the money)
from Cuba's or Japan's or almost
anywhere where US sports have caught
on or originated. But professional
football is played in only one other
country, Canada, and there it is
hardly as compelling because the
violence that underlies the drama
of the game (offering our own times
version of what classical drama was
supposed to do for its spectators)
has been softened by regulations
perhaps meant to express liberal
sentiments about life and combat
when it is a given that liberal
sentiments about the value of human
life and protection from physical
harm have no place in wars except
as in the principles of pacifists
and anti-war activists who might do
well to encourage football as an
international means for ending
hostilities, on second thought
that might generate so much passion
in the spectators wars would result
from close calls or bad calls and
the purpose of the game would be
lost in the politics of national
chauvinism. Besides, "pro"
football is as "American" as you
can get. Where else could grown
men dress like sensually self-
indulgent primping queens from the
waist down (constantly showing off
that aspect as they huddle or stick
their butts up at the fans and each
other at the start of every play or

Jackie Rohrs, Chicago Honeybear cheerleader & *Playboy* model, by Mike Tappin

playfully pat each other on the ass
at their conclusion) and like teenaged
hot rod macho science fiction
fantasies from the waist up.
With some of the best film and
video coverage of any sport or
activity, professional football
often produces stars even from
the ranks of the lowly footsoldiers
while making theater out of their
sport (not just the dance performance
aspect, so avant-garde in that the
contours of the dance depend on the
arbitrary and unpredictable arcs,
and more zany patterns, made by the
ball during play — the ball itself
one of the most unusual objects in
our culture, let alone sports world:
a sort of leather oversized egg —
the patterns it makes often calling
forth more military metaphors from
sports announcers and fans who
describe various passes as "bombs"
or "bullets" etc.) and allows
regional chauvinism to not only
express itself but develop a new
identity and provincial uniqueness
at a time when regional identities
have been fading into the bland
television version of a fast food
society. It is also corporate America's
response to the primal urges of the
creatures in us; it is a corporate
sport, where teamwork *and* competi-
tiveness are so necessary men's
entire careers and even their physical
safety depend on it, where what
management says is good for the team
is good for the team til proven
otherwise and then management replaces
those it deems responsible or new
management takes over (huddles are
conferences and much of the scoring

is done as though by committee).
Pro football is a business and a
profession (the pride of the professional almost always contributes
to the excitement of any game, even
those already won or played long
after the chances for a team's entry
into the play-offs the play is still
usually intense, committed, "professional"), a sport and a performing
art, a game, a civil war, a surrealist's
wildest dream (even the name is insane).
It is unique and temporary, exhausting
and overexposed, an opportunity for incredible
displays of courage, stamina, determination and even love (watch the over-
whelming displays of affection when a
teammate accomplishes something extraordinary or even ordinary but necessary;
and note the number of players who not
only play while temporarily injured but
always play with permanent handicaps —
one eyed receivers, one armed kickers,
etc.) . It can be beautiful in its
willfulness as well as its abandonment
(it is one of the only sports that is
played in just about any weather —
an indication of its basic stupidity
to some, or of its warlike intensity
to others, or even its childlike spirit
of "play" to still others). It can
make a poor boy rich, an unknown
a celebrity, a third-rate city more
important—for a while. But most
of all, most of all American Professional Football is a modern, in-
dustrialized, corporate society's
stylized way of "holding back the
void," raging at the inevitability of
aging and physical decline and
death itself. Hold that line, block
that kick, deee-fence deee-fence,
don't stop now, throw the bomb,

destroy that cocky bastard, do
it for us, do it for yourselves.

—Michael Lally

FOOTBALL,CANADIAN COLLEGE

Little Ronnie Stewart leaps the Toronto Varsity
line

in 1955-56 averaging more than five yards a carry
the minimum for a star back in Canada;

I'd sneak in, in Kingston, Queen's University
where people have fewer successful drives than New York

where Al Leonard where else coached
after marrying cheerleading Jean after

throwing the longest complete pass in Canadian football
they said, the football fans

men like my father sipping rye in the Park Plaza
on Bloor Street in Toronto opposite Varsity Stadium;

Jim Leonard, Al's son, loved the Kingston Trio

but was not part of my crowd of brats back in Kingston
who scaled the wall, slipped in with the crowd

then sat out the game, under the bleachers
collecting souvenirs

ripping off the college kids
we could never imagine being.

—T.W. Fretter

FORTRESS

The Poetry Fortress was named by Jim Brodey, in the
terrible winter of 1976-77; it is an apartment building
between Avenue A and First Avenue, and E. 11th and

Top: Joan Fagin & Tessie Mitchell
Bottom: William Dunas & Edwin Denby *(q.v.)*

Scenes from *Inside Dope* by Rudolph Burckhardt
Still photos by Jacob Burckhardt

102

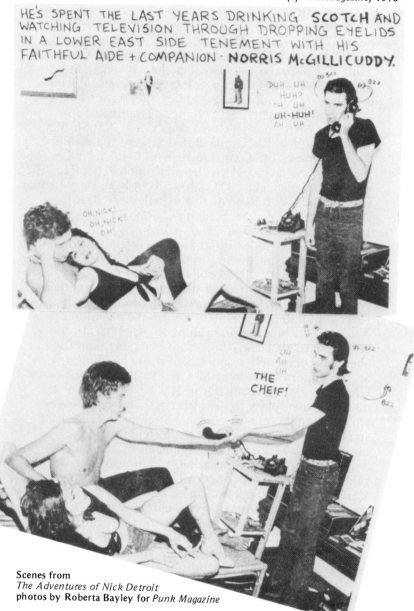

Scenes from
The Adventures of Nick Detroit
photos by Roberta Bayley for *Punk Magazine*

13th Streets, in Manhattan's "East Village." Many poets, artists, musicians, and other of the late sixties/seventies lived there, or do. Among them are: Alice Notley, Rebecca Wright, Jeanne Dawson, John Godfrey, Michael Brownstein, Jim Brodey, Allen Ginsberg, Peter Orlovsky, Julius Orlovsky, Denise Mercedes, Jack Kimball, Steve Malamude, Steve Hamilton, Steven Hall, Jamie MacInnis, Harley, Marthe Reynolds, Judy Galleon, Anna Malmude, Turan Wright, Carl Solomon, Sara Bolkenon, Gregory Corso, Jocelyn Corso, Max Corso, Rat Scabies, Roberta Bayley, Richard Hell, Joe Stevens, Barry Miles, Richard Corey, Tad Gast, Trevor Winkfield, Steve Levine, Simon Schuchat, Harris Schiff, Simon Petit, René Ricard, Mary Carlisi, Mary O'Cabbage, Ivan Kral, Gary Lenhart Greg Masters, Bob Rosenthal, Rochelle Rose Kraut, Arthur Russell, Michael Scholnick, Bobby Meyers, Joanne Brahinsky, Susan Noel, Joan Inglis. The landlady is reputedly an ex-officer in the Ukrainian Army and served time, rather was interned, in a Soviet concentration camp as a Nazi collaborator after the second world war, but the accuracy of this allegation is certainly in question. She was removed from power by a rent strike that lasted two winters and from early winter 77/78 on the building was run by the tenants, altho according to Mr Fagin, there is no Tenants Committee and he is completely responsible for the building; any and all inquiries should be directed to him, as the court appointed administrator. It is a pleasant, tho cold in winter, place to live although some poets have experienced severe blocks. As an attempt at "Socialism In One Building" it is admirable. References to the building may be found in many poems by the above, and an issue of *PUNK* magazine, a photo-cartoon novel called *The Adventures of Nick Detroit* included many scenes of the building. It can also be seen in several of the films of Rudy Burckhardt, including *Inside Dope* and *Good Evening Everybody*. At one time some residents published a small newsletter, *The 12th Street Rag*, which published poets such as John Weiners and Alfred Starr Hamilton, in addition to residents.

—**Simon Schuchat**

See Beat Hotel; Brooke Farm; Black Mountain College

FRAME OF REFERENCE

A framing device within which we inhabit the role of the general public, the audience, the media. Mirrors mirroring mirrors expanding and contracting to the focal point of view and including the lines of perspective bisecting the successive frames to the vanishing point. The general public, the audience, the media playing the part of the sounding board, the comprehensive framework outlining whatever meets their eye.

—**General Idea**

See General Idea

FREEDOM

In a dream I'm no longer in love, I breathe deeply this sense of freedom and I vow never again to seal myself in, but I am reminded it is my self I love also and that too is a kind of sealed condition. I am committed to taking care of my body and its home accomodations, its clothes and neat appearance that I admire in the mirror. It is love and I would like to know what it would be like freed of brushing my teeth, washing my neck and face and between my toes. I'd like to know, as I neglect to move my bowels and stay away from food that could sustain my health, and do not change my underwear and let odors rise from crotch and armpit. I stick out my tongue at the image in the mirror showing me my ragged beard and sunken eyes and hollow cheeks, free of my self-love at last, and I sink onto the bathroom floor, feeling life begin to seep out of me, I who haven't eaten since last month. I'm dying and I'm free.

But then I ask, having won the freedom to be dead, is that all? I struggle up on my feet and stagger over to the kitchen refrigerator and find an apple there nearly all rotten, and some mouldy cheese. I eat. I'm free to eat.

—**David Ignatow**

See Slavery

FRENCH

A tongue.

—**Ray DiPalma**

FRENCH GIRLS

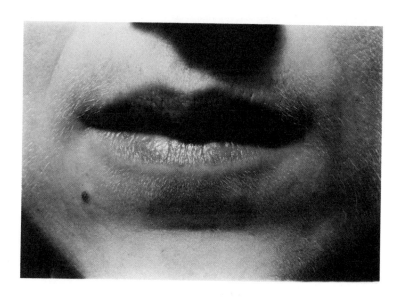

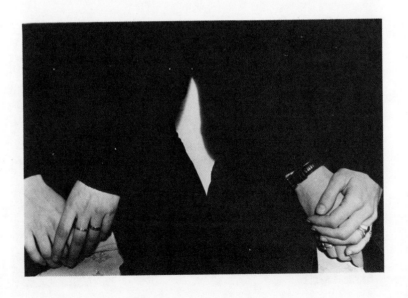

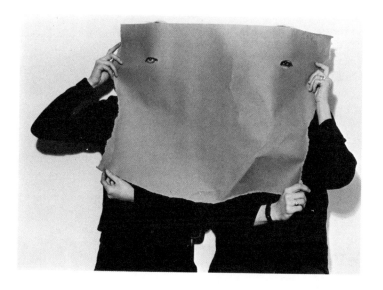

—Marcia Resnick

FRENCH LITERATURE

a garden separated their house from the street
au calme clair de lune triste et beau
he kept fucking gorgeous rimbe in the ass

her family agreed she would marry verlaine
she died, the stairway was too narrow for the coffin

mortal signs appearing, a
disc broke, jelly poured out,
he walked wincing
& limping toward the great verlaine

—David Ball

FREQUENT

FREQUENT (BUT NOT CONSTANT),as for example:

Left border	:	1st hole down from top:	Row 3 Nos. 1 and 11 : Cylinders 98 & 66 (16)
" "		4th " " " " :	Row 1 Nos. 3 and 13: Cylinder 66 mainly (8)
" "		7th " " " " :	Row 1 Nos. 4 and 14: Cylinders 98 & 66 (13)
" "		10th " " " " :	Row 4 Nos. 9 and 19: Cylinders 98 & 66 (7)
" "		15th " " " " :	Row 3 Nos.10 and 20: Cylinder 66 (4)
" "		8th hole up from bottom:	Row 4 Nos. 3 and 13: Cylinders 98 & 66 (9)
Top border	:	1st hole from left :	Row 4 Nos. 5 and 15: Cylinder 66 mainly (7)
" "		1st " " "	Row 1 Nos. 3 and 13: Cylinder 66 mainly
" "		5th " " "	Row 6 Nos. 5 and 15: Cylinders 98 and 66 (15)
Right border	:	4th hole down from top:	Row 1 Nos. 2 and 12: Cylinders 98 & 66 (13)
" "		5th " " " " :	Row 6 Nos. 1 and 11: Cylinders 98 & 66 (8)
" "		10th " " " " :	Row 4 Nos. 8 and 18: Cylinder 66 mainly (7)
" "		8th hole up from bottom:	Row 1 Nos. 3 and 13: Cylinder 66 mainly (8)
Bottom Border:		1st hole from left :	Row 5 Nos. 2 and 12: Cylinders 98 & 66 (7)
" "		6th " " "	Row 3 Nos. 8 and 18: Cylinders 98 & 66 (7)
" "		8th " " "	Row 3 Nos. 5 and 15: Cylinders 98 & 66 (12)
" "		9th " " "	Row 5 Nos. 1 and 11: Cylinders 98 & 66 (7)
" "		6th hole from right:	Row 6 Nos. 7 and 17: Cylinder 66 mainly (5)
" "		Last hole from left :	Row 3 Nos. 2 and 12: Cylinders 98 & 66 (10)

or at least regular.

—Bern Porter

FRONTIER

the frontier of civilisation indicated by the fact that before
Pilechik a farmer is taking his combine harvester to the field,
whereas after Pilecik an old woman rides on a board dragged
by a donkey over spread-out ears of corn.
    the changeover, gradually completed as we push for-

ward into the interior of Anatolia, from brick walls of houses
to clay walls, and
    my suspicion that such a change indicates a turning
point in many things.

—**Peter Wehrli**
translated by Roger Frood

FROST

On this February day of most excellent and purified cold
I am tempted by the ice floes on the Hudson to risk my
neck walking on their backs in hunt for white bear or some
fish with royal oil in its gut that will solace me in the
Spring.

I have in my pocket a picture of Knut Amundsen dressed
warmly enough to protect my expedition and I have also a
tiny Anarctican flag which I intend to plant on an ice cake
with a peculiar blue slant. Yesterday I was reading about a
child in Brooklyn who had made an Eskimo doll for his
sisters's birthday and I am going to carry this clipping with
me, along with a copy of *Les Malades Imaginaires.*

It will take somewhat more than a week to cross over
the ice and when I am there I shall not be in Paterson, but
in the center of the river making a crayon drawing. Can't
you see me sitting on that thin branch of ice, wearing a
parka, inventing a species of palm and a linguistics unbearable to the natives? One of Admiral Byrd's overshoes has
fallen into the water and I explain its demise to a group of
maidens dressed as swans, for his delusions are also mine.

February is the month of fish, freemen, forgetfulness
and fretfulness, but out on the ice floe it is like "Florida"
by Wallace Stevens and on the shore with the aid of the
foreign press I can make out the outlines of the Red Men
who are tattooing it into simple "frost."

Ah Knut Amundsen! He sends a message from Thule·
which I postpone reading due to the atmospheric content
of certain vowels. It says: ADVENTURE. I repeat this over
and over like an epic poem while Manhattan sails past waving
her smooth hands and on her deck the Captain bows his head
mournfully, for he alone knows it cannot last.

—**Barbara Guest**

FUDGE FACTOR

A fudge factor is a quantity which is added to a mathematical equation, or set of equations, in order to make an answer come out right. For example, suppose one multiplies 9 by 7 and obtains the result 59. Adding a fudge factor of 4 will yield the correct result, 63.

The most famous fudge factor of all time was one used by the great theoretical physicist, Albert Einstein, who gave it the rather grandiose name, "cosmological constant."

In 1917, Einstein, who had shortly before completed work on his general theory of relativity, was trying to find equations which would describe the structure of the universe. The only solutions that Einstein could find predicted that the universe had to be either expanding or contracting.

Since Einstein wanted a solution which gave a static universe, he added a fudge factor to make the answer come out right, the cosmological constant. This constant introduced a force which would cancel out gravity at large distances. This hypothetical force was a very odd one. While every other force known to physics became weaker with increasing distances, it grew larger. Nevertheless, it seemed to give correct results. Satisfied, Einstein published his work.

Just twelve years later, in 1929, the astronomer Edwin Hubble discovered that the universe was not static, as Einstein had thought; it was in a state of rapid expansion.

Years later, Einstein was to remark to physicist George Gamow that the introduction of the cosmological fudge factor was the biggest fuckup of his life. For if he had not introduced it, he would have been able to show that the universe was expanding long before Hubble discovered that fact empirically.

—Richard Morris

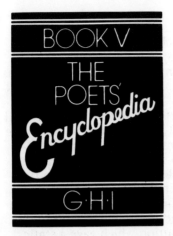

BOOK V
THE POETS'
Encyclopedia
G·H·I

GALA

A violent, sterilized woman.

—Salvador Dali
a working by Ursule Molinaro

GEARSHIFT MANIFESTO

Poetry does not know whether things used to be going faster than things are now. The red shift of creating verse, the passing auto horn. Poetry is the passing auto horn. Is the whole system someday going to stop? Please tell us poets! The detached arrangements of the torn wallpaper are worn away. Poetry has to be redefined in terms of energy and information. Poetry has never had a turn in the electronic media. The U.S. academic literati have died with Joyce and Hemingway. The U.S. scientific language is the most advanced. The coded information system in the genes is going through the same turns as poetry in different spheres. The dead rhetoric of the 60s is very quickly the worm dung waste along the trace. Poetry has not answered why the ape mind got loose. Why the immense death wish destruction gliding in a controlled and sterile environment. No poet told me so. Not yet have phoney poets of awards and Times been discovered eating dead flesh. By the hoax of fossils the young turn non verbal. The poets have not rejuvenated language fast enough to speak to science. Only through the collage metaphor can poetry collapse again towards its own beginning.

—Charles Plymell

GENERAL

The general's head has turned on the inside. He takes himself for his brother, the admiral, mistakes his statue for a cruiser, expresses surprise that it's not being launched into the waters of the ocean at once, asks if there's a strike going on, answers yes, screams that we've all been betrayed, and escapes with stumbling steps; he sobs, telling himself that he's been torpedoed in the back.

—Andre Breton

Gilded fatso in utter misery (a general in parade uniform).
—Benjamin Peret
workings by Ursule Molinaro

GENERAL IDEA

A framing device within which we inhabit the role of the artist as we see the living legend. We can be expected to do what is expected within these bounds. We are aware of the limitations of this and refer to it as our Frame of Reference and act accordingly behind the lines. Projecting our roles gives us some perspective to start with so we can see clear to project our frames frame by frame.

—General Idea

See Nineteen Eighty Four

GENIUS

Genius: —I'm the big cheese! —we'll all die of that disease.
—Arthur Rimbaud
a working by Ursule Molinaro

GERMAN

the German carrying only a toothbrush and umbrella, but wearing a tie and neat herringbone suit, who is on his way to India gets on the train in Sofia, explaining his hair had been shorn at the border before he was allowed to enter: "We must have order!" had been the customs official's comment.

—Peter Wehrli
translated by Roger Frood

GIMMICKS

Formal inventions are often dismissed as "gimmicks," but

115

it is precisely such mechanisms that generate innovative forms and styles. The development of a good gimmick can change an artist's career; it can produce flowers in what was previously perceived to be a desert. A new concept, if radically pursued, can draw out of the artist capacities for innovation and intelligence that not even he knew he possessed.

The history of modern music is filled with gimmicks, such as the profusion of nonsynchronous folk tunes in Charles Ives' best-known music, John Cage's prepared piano, which became an even more convenient means for avoiding familiar pitches, or Andres Segovia's transcription of Bach violin partitas for the guitar. Glenn Gould's peculiarly hunched-over way of physically approaching his piano was once dismissed as a gimmick, and what initially seemed a gimmicky way of applying paint to canvas produced Jackson Pollock's mature style.

In literature, many stylistic innovations and idiosyncrasies are indebted to syntactical gimmicks. Elements of literary craftsmanship no doubt contributed to the final product; but without the good gimmick there would be neither innovation nor a distinctly individual style.

For Apollinaire, a crucial trick was merely the elimination of punctuation, which drastically changed the style and flow of his poetry. For Faulkner, it was, first, a penchant for exceedingly long sentences and then the use of different first-person narrators. One of E.E. Cummings' pet gimmicks was the use of one part of speech to function in lieu of another. In places where nouns would normally be used, Cummings put verbs, adjectives, adverbs, and even conjunctions. In drafting both poetry and prose, Ezra Pound always put two spaces between typewritten words, duplicating with technology a characteristic of his handwriting. Words physically separated from each other are perceived differently. Tom Wolfe, in his preface to *The New Journalism* (1974): "I found that things like exclamation points, italics, abrupt shifts (dashes), syncopations (dots) helped give the illusion not only of a person talking but of a person thinking." The history of innovative writing is partly a record of gimmicks.

A fertile class of gimmicks in recent art is the use of nonartistic models, in either content or form: for example, paintings with popular iconography ("pop art"), a novel written in the form of encyclopedia notations (Richard Horn's *Encyclopedia*), poetry whose organization is permutational, rather than syntactical. The methods of non-artistic material can become both a constraint and a source of irony.

Unless a gimmick generates discernibly different art, it remains nothing more than a "gimmick."

—**Richard Kostelanetz**

GLASHA(R)

a large body of ice that grows or shrinks according to whether snowfall exceeds the rate of melting or not

The boulders had been left by glaciers and it took great ingenuity and the help of adjacent trees to climb the twenty odd feet to the top. The main ones were "Birthday Rock" and "Ship Rock". So, in our group after school each day one could decide to either head out to sea or have a party.

Barriers of land, chains of mountains determining the courses of rivers are each one boundaries between assemblages of fish

—**Alison Knowles**

GOATSUCKER, FORK-TAILED

(Psalurus Macropterus)

Of the genus psalurus sucks, close relative of the genus caprimulgus in its characteristics sucks, the strong Vibrissae of its bill sucks, the excessively long and deeply forked tail sucks.

This singular bird sucks, of Paraguay and Brazil sucks, the bright, ruddy, demi-collar that ornaments the back part of the neck sucks, the two external tail-feathers of the male sucks, the non-elongated tail-feathers of the female sucks. The fork-tailed goatsucker sucks rapidly flies sucking its tail expanding and closing and sucking as it skims along sucking and giving chase to insects sucking upon which it cusses.

—**Opal L. Nations**

GORILLA

Paul Oppedisano snapped this candid of Terry Stokes and Mercy Bona in downtown Saigon shortly before the Fall. Terry was discussing the Latin for *it.* Mercy collects penguins *(q.v.)* and says they're *it,* the latest. With a castrated bovine and a student of zebras *(q.v.),* they form a social, occasionally literary group *(q.v.).*
—Bob Pelosi
See Exclusion
Anything

GRANITE

the white granite stones neatly arranged end to end for kilometre after kilometre, which retain the gravel bed of the railway track right through Bulgaria: "We must have order!", explained the customs official.
—Peter Wehrli
translated by Roger Frood

GRANTS

—are what the new millenarians, among poets, writers and editors, are always applying for (or waiting for) instead of doing their work; they almost never come, at least not in useful amounts. In most arts, grants are given to reward what someone feels are the best artists. But in literature, at least in the United States, grants, if they are given at all, are given to the writers who exhibit the least ability, presumably to compensate them on the material plane for what, they lack on the artistic one.
—Dick Higgins

118

GROUP

Beasts form herds and packs. They do not form groups. Groups are feasible only between creatures who, for better or for worse, have evolved a necessity to maintain ideals through an inner struggle with conscience and desire. Groups communalize ideals and thus provide refuge from inner struggle. In groups there is good conscience: man follows, leads, cavorts, studies, learns, pillages, murders, prays. There is no ideal for which a group cannot be formed. Of the individual the group demands obedience to the ideals. Of the group the individual demands perpetuation of the ideals. Even when struggle arises over these demands, it is never a struggle within the individual. It is outward and is therefore waged in continuing good conscience.

For the validation which groups provide him, the individual forgoes some commensurate portion of his privacy. This cannot be otherwise; privacy is the saboteur of groups; it is an opportunity for personal, contemplative adventure, out of which an individual may emerge with misgivings about the group's ideals. The family, the political party, the religious order, the military organization, the professional association all have overt methods of invading, to a greater or lesser extent, the privacy of members. In social groups and clubs, the methods are covert; they are based on the latent possibility of with held good-fellowship and affection; in these groups, the individual is required to display conduct which affirms and reaffirms that what he does away from the group does not alter the ideals which have insured his standing.

There is ample evidence that man cannot do for very long away from groups; periodic relief from the burden of self-criticism seems to be vital; prolonged isolation from groups leads to various forms of madness. There is also evidence that prodigal affiliation with groups goes hand in hand with an impoverishment of moral stamina and a sense of alienation in the very midst of multitudes.

A group begins with three or more people. Two people cannot form a group. A group exists only when there is a chance for coalition.

—**Armand Schwerner & Donald M. Kaplan**

See Exclusion

119

GUILT

O Rose, thou art sick!
The invisible worm,
That flies in the night,
In the howling storm,

Has found out thy bed
Of crimson joy;
And his dark secret love
Does thy life destroy.
—William Blake, "The Sick Rose"

One of the exclusively human experiences, hence a landmark of evolution. Guilt is an affect originating in the exploitation of anxiety by conscience, the pain of which is undone only by atonement, that is, by an equivalence of punishment. That reason fails to mitigate the pain of guilt lies in the fact that the ingredients of guilt, i.e., anxiety and conscience, are partially submerged beyond reason: anxiety is a reaction to an unknown menace; conscience tends to interpret anxiety arbitrarily as a signal of weakness towards a temptation which it forbids. The forbidden may involve thoughts as well as action, courage as well as stealth. Hence guilt occurs throughout the range of human existence, inciting also a range of atonements from physical self-abuse, as in accident-proneness and suicide, to psychological self-abuse, as in depression and obsessive rituals.

Since guilt is painful and its avoidance desirable, strategies are evolved to cope with it. Some of these are personal, others social. The personal strategies attempt to ward off either anxiety or conscience or both in order to starve the process of its essential elements. Certain atonements of minimal pain, possessing even some practical value, are volunteered to the conscience in the absence of guilt—volunteered as a bribe beforehand against subsequent activity likely to be forbidden.

The social strategies attempt a transformation of the irrational aspects of guilt into rational ones: the forbidden is impersonalized in an orderly public code of law, religious, ethical, legal; personal conscience, which is not only arbitrary but inconsistent, is externalized as priest, moralist, judge, who will act impersonally without bias or caprice; and anxiety is converted to fear wherein the menace—in this instance, the punishment fitting the transgression—is known. Consistent with the scope of human functioning which guilt invades, social codes, administration and punishment apply to thoughts as well as actions, to courage as well as stealth.

—Armand Schwerner & Donald M. Kaplan

See Anxiety

HABITS

Habits are a xerox junkie. Moments compulsively repeated, reproduced in the form of specific gestures, body movements, thoughts, in response to certain situations. We sink our teeth into repetition, like rabbits into a nun.

—Michael Brownstein

HALPHABET

HΔ⊥ΦHΔ₿HƎT :   (under "H")

Δ, ₿, ⅭᏆ, Φ, Ꝋ, Ŧ, ℬ, H, I, ⊥, ✳,
⊥, ⋈, ⋈, O, Ϥ, ℒ, ℛ, ᵹ, T, ℧,
V, ⋈, X, Y, ⧖, ℋℛ.

I condescendingly leave lower-type to future generations.

—A.M.Fine

HARE

In spite of a tendancy to thin old lights, she is pleased by the red on snow. Its skin pulls away in one piece. The hung meat draining resembles us they say, a proof of warmth.

—Mei-Mei Berssenbrugge

HAT

Head Filter

—Charlie Morrow

HEAD

Head equals walls of apartment. This becomes clearer
after staying up all night. Folks with morning energy on
their way to work are outside your head. Poke you in
the eyes, break your windows. Eviction by landlord and
you're out of your head. Moving rugs and furniture into
apartment is giving head. Cockroaches as headaches. And
what happens when someone else moves in with you?

—Michael Brownstein

HEAVEN

Heaven is this place where you live forever and they don't
let any cats or dogs in because animals haven't got souls.
That's what I thought as a child and I still do. I wouldn't
want to go to Heaven.

—Dotty le Mieux

HISTORY

"History" has a resident spider
waiting, weaving tomorrow. You think
the little spotlight of your life, but
around you and pulling you forward reach
the great grey cables of the past.

—William Stafford

See Everything

HOCKNEY

I draw all the time. In the last two years I've only done five
paintings. I've only ever done about two hundred.

I've been doing etchings inspired by Wallace Stevens' poem
The Man with the Blue Guitar. I've just got back from Chicago where I went to see the Picasso painting that inspired
Stevens to write the poem. I thought it would be nice to
see what he saw, then something clicks.

There's perhaps periods where it's all repetitive. I mean,
at times one is inspired and at times one is not really very
inspired. But I do tend to work all the time, I never
actually stop.

Sometimes I have great problems with my work—mostly
technical, aesthetic problems. I assume that you should
always have problems; I assume that it's the natural state

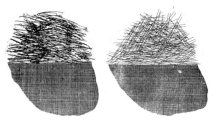

Three drawings for Grimm's *Fairy Tales* by David Hockney

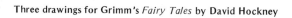

and I assume that you have problems because you want to do something that you've not quite done before.

I generally get up about 8:15.

One advantage of travelling is I'm difficult to locate and I like that.

I can paint in motel rooms. For instance, two years ago in Paris I was designing the opera, and I had a big show on. Too many people came around and it was difficult to work, so I thought—we'll go to Hollywood and do it. So I took my assistant Mo, and went to Hollywood, checked into the Chateau Marmont Hotel, and within a day the place looked like a studio. Mo was amazed.

My first visit to London was when I was eighteen years old and I had never left Bradford, Yorkshire. From that moment on I've always travelled. When you hadn't much money you hitchhiked. You don't need money to travel, all you need is desire.

I left the Royal College of Art in 1962 and I always earned a little money selling pictures, and I thought, "Well if I can earn money selling pictures why bother doing anything else?" I don't do anything I don't want to do just for the money. I mean, of course, one does do things. For instance, I was asked to design an opera for Glynebourne, a Stravinski opera, *The Rake's Progress*. And I thought it over: was it an interesting project? Could I do it? Was it something that would appeal? I didn't decide straight away. I said, "I'll have to think of it, I don't know the opera very well." Then I read the libretto and I thought it was a marvelous libretto and then I really began to get ideas. So I said I'd do it. I'm going to do another one—*The Magic Flute*—for Glynebourne in 1978. They asked me to do that and I instantly said I would. That opera is a real masterpiece, a challenge, very imaginative. It's not like doing realistic opera.

Possessions are a burden for people like me. I have two indulgences: good Cuban cigars, which cost a lot of money in England, and clothes. I don't buy art.

—**Victor Bockris**

HOLE

An absence of earth; a hollow, a pit; a tart, a tear, a cavity. Dangerous gravity.

—**Jeff Goldberg**

HOMERGA

ЖҒ "Homerga"
twenty-seventh letter of the English
alphabet, invented and added thereto
by A.M. Fine, who does not like the
idea of a 26 letter alphabet.
See under "H" for HΔⱢ§H⟨HƗT.

—A.M. Fine

HOMINIDS

Robust or slender (called gracile) they ground their food
And ground their teeth down doing it
They searched out seeds, roots, tubers, following the
Great grazing beasts, who were useful to them and friends
Their differences less important than their similarities
The way, now, a dog will companion the cows and bark
When a heifer is in trouble...but were they homanids
Were they made on the fifth day with the animals
Or on the sixth with homo sapiens sapiens?

In Jamaica, far up in the hills
A small boy, twelve, maybe nine
held a very large knife, a machete
Deftly slit an almond, cut the top
Off a green coconut for a drink
Smiling, peeled a grapefruit
Which he scurried up a tree to get
And offered at the end of his knife.
"How well you can do that." His cousins said
Studying his sure eyes and the blade
Of his competent knife, dangerous
To coconut and fruit, not yet to kin.

Their remains are found mainly in delta-mouths, marshes
Mud-flats, in shore-zones of ephemeral character

125

They exploited the food on the fringes of the forest
The stream valleys. Both the robust and the gracile forms
Favored the more open vegetation at the edge of the shore
Because they needed to see danger coming

In Ethiopia, Kenya, Lake Rudolf called Turkana
Along the Omo River, in the Afar Lowlands, in Olduvai Gorge
In the eastern rift of Tanzania, found with flint knives
Piles of fishbones, some bones of their friends, the large
   grazers
And even, occasionally, bones of their cousins, the
   Australopithicines
Who must have filled the gap when seeds, roots, tubers
(Not to mention coconuts, and fruits, such luxuries as came
   later)
Were scarce and they hungry

—Rose Drachler

HONORABLE DISCHARGE
How the Japanese address their clap symptoms.

—Michael O'Donoghue

HUNGER
An ache of a peculiar temporal pattern, for it is caused by
certain slow rhythmic contractions of the stomach that
appear in the absence of stomachic contents or at regular
intervals by habit. Any substance introduced into the
stomach to inhibit these contractions abolishes
hunger. The alimentary experience of nausea, and the
experience of the excretory processes, are simply internal
perceptions, in terms of pressure or pain, of the states or
processes to which they correspond. Hunger, however,
may exist in individuals who have ingested a sufficient
amount of food to inhibit stomachic contractions. This
order of hunger is often called malnutrition. It exists in
more than half the present population of the earth, approximately 1,500,000,000 people.

—Armand Schwerner & Donald M. Kaplan

HUTEMHANUT

(hoo·teem·hah·noot), *n*. [from Mbwezshtem, the ephemeral language; literally, by segments, *vessel, small, night, for* or *of*] **1.** A small vessel for the night. **2.** *Common* A bowl of rice. **b.** Sufficient amount not to go (e.g. to sleep) hungry. **c.** Enough, but particularly when not quite enough is satisfactory. **3.** *Exclam.* Any little thing can hold what's necessary for a short or just temporary darkness. **b.** If not full but not empty then there's potential for complete fulfillment, i.e. not a static state but a promising one is preferable. **4.** *V.* Don't sweat the small stuff. **5.** In time of poor visibility (possible danger) not to be out on a yacht, i.e. flaunting grandiose airs.

—**Annabel Levitt**

HYMN

So thus shall the lion brush his tail to the fly at the flood
     Nile to feed
on day one of year one before the white Sirius risen at the
     dawn
clear as the chisel on the granite of the temple of the zodiac
     of Isis
where a Pharaoh had suckled at Hathor under the Great Bear

And Orion of the green-faced feathered judge Osiris of the
     dead
who lie and implore and swear for his mercy
curled in Egypt in their incense in the earth dug up by the
     dog
eight thousand years ago like the foetus in my dream of
     the blue closet

And I saw in the dark the hawk head at the head of my
     father the engineer
who had courted with the gilt-edged Victorian sonnets
     in leather
like the equations of a war that was never to be won between
     a man and a woman

As Horus alone had been allowed the sky to drowse long in

blood's afterburn
with the cow from Dendera before the ibis and the jackel
at his altar arisen from the hawk perch
at the reed pool as he was swaddled like a Moses from the
    crocodile

Whoever she was drinking coffee over the dusk of the Hudson
eyelids tinted silver, sunburnt in underwear
adorned with gold and lapis and the cobra or armored like
    the Amazon

For I had been the circumcised as if drugged before the heat
    of the mouth of
the gentile combing her gold hair at the floors and floors of
    the city
because Israel had always wandered and warred as the idolators
of the cow head in the desert on the pillar

In the indecipherable light of the living photographed
by my father on my shoulders at the marbles on black dirt
    like the stars
that the priests of the Mother had watched through the notch
    of the palm leaf

Imprinted at the eye from their light years under the white
    insomniac continents
cracked in the wall when the sexual worm shall pearl the sheet
    with its inch
as I tried to open the light of my own hand
to the child who had not eaten though a family had been fed

When the trolley had plunged to the tunnel on Church Avenue
and I read as a boy scout of the Draco Patrol
the book in my bed in my parent's room
of the time traveller who had killed his ancestor when Thuban
    had been the pole

When even the excrement might have flared like the crown of
    the eclipse
and any Greek bored with the Greek might have tracked the
    lion
that Samson had made kneel to spare the parched ground

That is never too high or too low to be changed to the silt of
    of the Delta
as the gold is turned from the iron under the blood Antares
and the violet is raised against the ruby lily and the cardinal

Even though I had seen the wasp in the web impale the
    spider
or had thought and thought before the female fish in the
    museum
that shrivels the male to nothing but dead genitals

As the priests at Philae of Isis below the cataract
had sacrificed the red haired Set who had fed the crab the
    phallus of Osiris
smeared with her natron in the blackest radiation of the
    brains and viscera
for his worship as the phoenix at Heliopolis with Ra

As all are commanded to yield like the mummy when the
    dung beetle rolls the sun
before all the befores of the trillions of nights past night
    and day
though I knew that the broken receding mouth of the Sphinx
    had nothing to add
of resurrection in the history of its grimace

For any art, love or politic
of the human that had refused us so that I cried from
    the human
Goddess Goddess Goddess of the sistrum of Abaton, Senem
    and Elephantine

Ordained once to your first irreducible face of the nubile
twenty centuries past Christ at the fourteen year old with
    oiled pubic hair
in Brooklyn in a yellow sweater
luminous as the blue double of Pharaoh the *ka* in the dark
    when I touched her

                        —Hugh Seidman

IAMB

The iamb is the representation of the human heart beat in poetry. It goes dah-DUMBP. Wherever the push of the human heart is to be heard or felt in verse, one is sure to encounter the iamb. This is especially true in contemporary poetry. Although the poem might waver all over the page during flights of brainy fancy, when it gets to the pressure of the human heart it will settle into a strong series of iambs. One is employing iambs when one says "I love you, Claire," or "I love you, Dwight."

—George Bowering

IMAGINARY BEINGS

At birth, an Imaginary Being is very much like a newly born Infant. But unlike the Infant he grows not by being Fed but by being Spun. A solicitous mother will bring her Infant to the Age of Sex by constant Feeding. A creator will bring her Creature to the Age of Sex by constant Spinning. When a powerful Vortex is Spinned, the Imaginary Being releases another. Unfortunately, this kind of Vortex is achieved only in a culture where no one questions the morality of imagination.

Everyone has, at one time or another, pricked a yogi with a needle and watched the sperm come out. But this is where most folks stop. In trying to populate the world with Imaginary Beings, most people fail, and many should not attempt it at all. Most of you are only capable of populating the world with a single being which is half-handed to you by your parents, with the other half culled from hypnagogic impressions. This is as it should be because not many can risk losing their minds at the hands of the two Fears: flying & public opinion. Public opinion has always been against Imaginary Beings of all sort but never as much as it is today in America. The first order of business today is the elimination of imagination for the total protection of the Single Identity Person. Anyone possessing more than one identity is immediately thrown in a hospital where they sever the "weaker" ones. In most of these cases, of course, the stupidity of doctors eliminates the original identity while releasing the Imaginary Being, and thus Imaginary Beings survive vole volente.

But one day, in the heat of persecution, a pall will descend over the persecutors grinding the reductive technology to a halt. The fossil fuels have run out and "realistic self-appraisal" has become suddenly bankrupt. At that time, the few of us who have patiently invented and stored Imaginary Beings, either inside of us or in secret attics and cellars, will have something of a tremendous advantage, an advantage I propose we seize in revolutionary fashion to put a whole new set of fantasies in the myth basket of the race.

—Andrei Codrescu

IMPULSE

An act performed without due regard for the stimulus which releases it; the stimulus may be mere approximation of that stimulus which customarily releases the act; or the stimulus may be one that is occurring alone at a moment when customarily it occurs as part of a series of stimuli. Thus an impulse is an act which is either inappropriate or meaningless, like a step of a ladder that, having been removed and isolated, has become merely a plank.

Impulsive behavior is observable in all animals. A sea gull standing on a beach may be seen to rattle its beak or ruffle its wing in a manner otherwise employed as part of a series of actions in nest building; it is as if one lock of a pattern of locks had been suddenly sprung by some stray key in the environment.

In a highly symbolizing creature like man, impulsivity is especially rampant. With his blurred instinctual sense and with his rich faculty for memory which urges a personal past on an otherwise blank present, man lives among numerous keys. Too many of them work. Meaning through behavior is exceedingly hard to come by. It is born of that fragile interaction between restraint and spontaneity, both involving plenty of regard for the stimulus.

—Armand Schwerner & Donald M. Kaplan

INDEX

INDEX, Illustrated

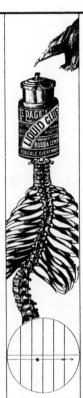

—M. Kaspar

INDIVIDUAL

Individual: any single human body, within a general thirteen million year human existance, whose individual human lives are imbued with an absolute ammount of Cosmic-Honesty, at any given time. Any or all humans of the same Cosmic Age, not imbued with such, may be considered only as more or less communist sluts.

—A.M.Fine

INSPIRATION

Someone's taken the stopper out of the bottle.

—**Philip Corner**

See Armony

INTRODUCTION

NOW THEN I AM DEAF MUTE. WHAT YOU HEAR YOU MUST TAKE AWAY FROM. LIVE WHAT YOU WISH.

—**Alan Davies**

IRAQI

the brown-skinned Iraqi in Belgrade who comes to ask, "Is this seat free?", and the guilelessness with which, when I say yes, he adds, "I will go and fetch my wife and five children."

—**Peter Wehrli**
translated by Roger Frood

IRONY

Irony Ford fell off a roof while attempting to install a TV antenna in 1954 in Bayonne, N.J. He landed in a flower bed and was saved, but he cracked his head on an imitation marble birdbath and had to have 32 stitches taken. The stitches became infected because one of the nurses in the

Emergency Room at the Catholic Hospital had just finished finger-fucking herself in the ladies' john and had to rush to Irony's assistance without washing her hands. Three months later, Irony Ford underwent brain surgery due to an acute cranial abscess. The same nurse was on duty, radiant because she had just finished playing with her cunt in the nurses' rest area by spraying herself repeatedly with feminine hygiene spray. The operation was a success and Irony Ford, a devout Catholic, later married the nurse. Their first child, who had an IQ of 231, died during childbirth because another nurse, a nun, administered the wrong injection. The Fords had six other children, all with IQs between 110 and 120. Until 1973 a well-known manufacturer of plastics (including plastic Jesus figurines, dildoes, and toy TVs), Irony Ford died that year in Scarsdale, N.Y., after he fell off a roof trying to install another TV antenna. His wife, Frigga, then age 42, was in bed playing with her cunt at the time. She died happily in her sleep at the age of 105, playing with her cunt at the time, and left an estate estimated at $1,240,000.

—Joe David Bellamy

ISOLATION

In keeping apart that which actually belongs together, e.g., an idea and its emotional connotation, a danger and its fear, the individual is spared from taking responsibility for what he actually feels. He need not recognize the source of his feelings and thus need not—in fact, cannot—do anything about them.

Isolation is frequently seen individuals who are passionate about cold intellect and intellectual about powerful emotions. This results in sophomoric ideation and emotional shallowness. Isolation of the sensual and tender components of the erotic drives is also common. As a consequence the isolating individual finds himself in the painful predicament of having no desire for the person he loves and no love for the person he desires.

The normal derivative of isolation is logical thinking, where the continued elimination of emotional associations is carried out in the interests of objectivity. The mockery which isolating individuals make of normal logical thinking is revealed by a number of characteristics. There is the frequent gambit of pursuing logic to the

absurd. Pedantry is common. A confusion between cold-
ness and objectivity can be caught in the glee with which
the gruesome is treated dispassionately.

—Armand Schwerner & Donald M. Kaplan

ISRAEL

Peace is not Israel's noble option, it is the only tactic that
makes sense. She could start by demilitarizing the West
Bank. Politically that would be a most astute move, to
allow some form of political expression, to stop locking
people up without trial, torturing them, breaking up the
most innocuous political groupings, acting, in fact, like
South Africa in a bantusan. In our seven weeks in the Mid-
East among all sorts of people, the Palestinians on the West
Bank were the only ones who insisted that we couldn't
tape what they were saying; we even had to promise that
we wouldn't name any individuals, or mention that we had
met with them. Politically such repression is a dumb move.
When people are being screwed in such ways, terror develops
as the only way out.

Everybody, including the Palestinians and the Israelis,
has been Americanized. Which is to say, translated, that
after 30 years of cold war, everybody believes in violence;
we put our stake on it, it's our special skill, we incant it,
we canonize it. 'Moving in troops' is our rough translation
of moving history itself, by imposing American solutions
on the world. As such, this is not a Jewish problem. It
comes to focus in a tragic way right now, but it's literally
an American attitude which has infected all of us. As a
people, we are tight dead against alternate ways of forming the future, of discovering how the unborn might live,
of surviving in the world. We're talking about one hot situation, the Middle East; the question has a deep Jewish
connection. But the connection has passed through, and
been profoundly altered by American experience. Most
of us are more American than we're anything else, alas
for us—and the world.

Catholics for instance wouldn't notably differ from
Zionists if we still had the old Papal States. There would
be the same quasi-religious feeling about a certain turf.
Catholics would say, let's send in troops, save the Pope's
acreage. Many of these attitudes are pure American, with
a religious translation for courtesy's sake.

136

No nation state is entitled to anything more than skepticism today; Israel is no special case. On the other hand, every people considered just as a people, is a very special case. In the case of Israelis, there is no need to invoke the past—from the Inquisition to Nazism—to arrive at the same attitude: Israelis are entitled to more compassion with every day that passes. Their leadership—religious, military, political—is entitled to ever more contempt. So are their patsies in the U.S. American Jews are building a bruderhof of death in Israel—a death they don't have to endure, only finance. They are quintessential Americans (putting all their bombs in one basket)—and Jews hardly at all. Of all the world, the Jew is least safe in Israel. That's terrifying, a waste. The Israelis know how absurd it is to think of Israel as "the last haven" for Jews; but the idea is peddled by American Jews, because among other things it justifies their living elsewhere. Such nonsense also explains the bitterness of the Israelis over the American Zionist frenzy to militarize Israel more and more. Christians, knowing something about the crimes of Christians against Jews and having only a weak sense of their own Christianity, have become more absurdly pro-Israel than the most fawning Zionist. Such an attitude gives them a base, gives them an identity. They speak as chic tough Christians: support the state of Israel or you're an anti-semite. It is what Bonhoefer would call, I suppose, a cheap grace.

There is thin ice here. I am also surrounded by anti-Semitic Catholics, especially in New York. There are crude elements of that community peddling their wares, mostly to one another; now they rejoice to hear me talking in the way I do—strictly for their own ends. It's very tough to write about Israel this way, knowing them and their methods. Still, on the other hand, one can't keep quiet because of some threat of having one's words seized on, bent out of shape by mad minds, when unpleasant truths need airing. So I walk on thin ice, and it creaks under my feet.

In our lifetime we're responsible for the people of our world, as well as for the unborn. We're not responsible for the sins of all prior ages; except in the sense that by our conduct, we try our best to assure they don't happen again. Nor can one legitimately keep quiet out of fear of conse-

137

quences; that just keeps the crimes on a back burner; and people are always ready for a sip of that infernal brew. I didn't commit the sins of the Inquisition and the Nazis. I start fresh with my birth. And I want to live responsibly.

Trust is the only solution to acute conflicts. Trust is the only safe frontier, given the times. As long as people are murdering one another, they're never going to come to any solution that deserves the name human—something we found out with the "Paris Accords" on Vietnam. The Israeli people, increasingly helpless and isolated in the world community, urged to hapless heroism by their compatriots elsewhere, paramilitarized, taxed to exhaustion, under permanent marching orders, forced to witness in silence the moral outrages once inflicted on themselves, now inflicted within their borders by their own authorities, on a people helpless and homeless as they once were—what a catastrophe! and as if this were not enough, the actual threat of another war not only lies over the land, but is actually prepared and coldbloodedly stockpiled, taken for granted by leadership, by advisors, by patrons—here and there.

To the Israelis I would write, as I wrote 2½ years ago, you start making peace where you are. You start listening; you start, as the prophets say, doing the works of justice. You start resisting an iniquitous government—which is not only anti-Palestinian but anti-decency, anti-human, and anti-Israeli. You seize for yourself the right to survival, a right which is threatened not primarily by Palestinians but by your own government—and ours. You start accepting the fact that interventionist diplomats and their settlements are piecemeal, that is, they break you into pieces, then make a meal of you. And you start granting to others the human and civil rights you demand for yourselves. You start creating safe borders in this way by creating friendships across the border. And I also think, by way of contrast, for Americans to go to Israel to do peace work, is about as fruitless as it once was to go to Hanoi. It's here the bombs are made and it is here the problems are made worse.

—Daniel Berrigan

שלום עכשיו

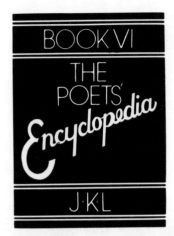

BOOK VI
THE POETS'
Encyclopedia
J·K·L

JOKE

Comedia had to leave New York and go to Scraggsville to look for jokes; a few years back most of the jokers ran wild to the west where they began jesting back and forth between Scraggsville (the sacred-hidden Indian name for Las Vegas) and Los Angeles. Comedia regarded the desert: chalky brown dirt and twisted brambles with little green spuds were dwarfed by the distant mountains which, like all other mountains, served to block the view. The only things that grew in these parts were the billboards, each larger than the next. One showed a picture of an innocent white church attached to a clever looking slot machine. The sign read: "Bluebell, The Exclusive Wedding Chapel: All currencies accepted—including food stamps."

The train of Comedia's nightgown dusted the desert floor. Her hair lay around her head in sleepy leaflets. She stuck her thumb in her mouth and searched the ground for The Strip. There it was, a glittering ribbon of tar/Some joke sayers insist it's a matter of making pictures out of the literal meaning of words/ which broadened and adhered to big hotels. She walked up to the first one, it was shaped like a flamingo and was rumored to be the place where visiting Floridians felt safest. At the pool she saw Rodney[1] sitting in his terry cloth robe with one foot straddling the other knee. It was the same robe he had worn back in New York where they drank hot clam juice together at his club. She remembered he'd talked about his material. He'd said,

"The idea is to make people feel it's happening right now, because comedy is mood." At that, Comedia let loose her mysterious smile, and it shrouded the room provoking senseless laughter throughout: no one was up on stage. Rodney was talking about the drawbacks to owning and appearing in his own club and he'd leaned over and whispered: "There were about 200 people in here the other night, and this guy called out, 'Say, Rodney, let me have your autograph and some butter, will ya?'"

Here in Scraggsville she knew things weren't going too well for him, either. She could tell he'd just been to the track; his eyes were still "roving" back and forth. "With animals I never had any luck. When I play the horses, I always hear the same thing: 'They're off—*except one*.'" He shook his head. "It's good I'm not in New York, I need a break. My kid drives me nuts. For three years now he goes to a private school. He won't tell me where it is..."

His lamentations...they always make Comedia smile. And what concision; to make the jokes concise, with not one extra word, that was supposed to be the best exhibition of the craft, and Rodney did it to perfection. But, few of the jokers would admit outright to telling jokes. Everyone made his own "conversation" and when there would be a meeting of monologists, they would tell their conversations to each other. Like finding the hidden meaning of talk cased in rhyme, jokes were an integral part of their conversation; uncovering them would take some searching.

Comedia saw Stanley[2] a parking lot away (Indian prophecy describes the evolution of Scraggsville into the biggest parking lot in the west) sitting on a fence. He was wearing his cap, of course, its peak kept the sun off of his face, and it was possible he had just been dreaming. He watched Comedia approach in her bare feet and white gown and thought she might be trying to get him to go back into his dream. Out there in the desert where bombed out isn't always a figure of speech he had to tell her his idea for the definitive disaster movie. "Something goes wrong with a nuclear device and an explosion destroys all life on earth except for one guy, a gas station attendant. He becomes world famous, does all the talk shows, is written up in all the papers."

Before she could even get the words out to ask how he was doing his face changed to a more definitive look of

141

horror: "I saw something I didn't want to see—I really didn't want to see. Backstage I was waiting to do a show, and I saw Edgar Bergen screw off Charlie McCarthy's head." He sighed and by way of filling her in on the calmer details of his days, said: "Last night I came home and there was nothing on TV. So I turned on the lamp."

But, could he please tell her what makes a joke? "I like to think that my material sounds so simple, that it's funny by accident. And it's hard to get a thing to sound simple. The image has to be just right. Once I went to a pastry school and I had a lot of trouble with the teacher. He always wanted to embarrass me. He wouldn't criticize my work, he just liked to humiliate people. Like once he cut a slice out of my chocolate layer cake and used it to keep the door open! Now, I had another variation: He cut a slice out of my sponge cake and used it to erase the board! But the layer cake is funnier. Only one of them is right."

They glanced around Scraggsville and Stanley narrowed his eyes. He was born in the Bronx but he knew he'd thrive in the West. One of his forebears, an uncle, had done it with elan. He told Comedia: "In the days of lawlessness when people were lucky to live past the age of 25, my Uncle Morris lived to 90—because he was *intelligent*. When he checked into town he handed out his card. It said: 'Morris Handleman, slowest gun in the West.' Everyone was afraid to fight with him—just in case they killed him and would end up with the reputation as the man who killed the slowest gun in the West."

She'd known comedy wizards whose forebears didn't do as well by them. In New York Ken[3] had reminded her that his relative the Marquis de Friedman "brought cruelty to new heights when he invented the bad joke." The onus of having such a relative had left its mark; the family was forever suspect. Ken once confided: "My father was out of work for years and now I'm out of work. People are actually accusing my father of nepotism." Not to worry, though, Ken had come up with a new way to make money. "I've invested in a frog ranch," he told her. "We raise frogs for their pelts. Their fur is beautiful but very fine. Now, not all frogs have fur, and the fur they do have is invisible to the human eye. The way to tell if a frog has fur is to lift up the frog and hold it in front of the mirror; if it reaches into its back pocket, takes out a comb and begins making a pompadour,

Rodney Dangerfield by Erika Rothenberg

you hit it with a hammer.''
    Her reveries were suddenly overpowered by the gaud.
At an eternal 10 A.M. people could be seen soul kissing the

143

slots. It was time to leave Las Vegas. As she approached L.A. she got a funny ringing in her ears and everything looked hazy, always an inch or two beyond where her eyes finally told her feet to step. She was in La La Land. A great billboard hovered over the city: A middle aged housewife in a full apron held a bowl in her hands, she held it out, sort of, towards everyone, and the words were written: "Forest Lawn, for the very best."

Comedia wasn't the only one suffering from confusion. Ed[4] walked her across the street. "California has really crazy laws. I got arrested once and the cop told me I had the right to remain silent or the right to sing a medley of Cole Porter songs." As they were crossing the next street the sign changed from "Sleep Walk" to "Don't Sleep Walk." She opened her eyes. Ed was saying: "Much of my material comes to me spontaneously just like in dreams. And, I have such weird dreams when I'm on a diet. I had this dream that a steak landed on my bed. Tiny cows got out and then they got back in and the steak flew away. I found a plaque on my bed; it said: 'Giant step for livestock.' "

Ed had studied philosophy and the methods stayed with him. "We learned things like whether knowledge is intuitive or learned—the kind of things that come in handy if you're looking for something to think about in solitary confinement."

Just before she waved goodbye to La La Land Comedia saw Stanley walking up the Street of the Stars. He was still wearing his cap and shaking his head. "People are so negligent in California. I bought a house and to make a little extra money I rented it out to some people. They never took care of anything. They let the grass starve, never watered it; the hedges, the rose bushes died. I had a big palm tree in the front and the tree died. You have to be very negligent to let a tree die. So I figured it'll cost me more but I want to make sure everything's okay. So I hired a gardener and I went back a few weeks later to see how things were coming along—they let the gardener die!"

It was obvious he played on the absurdities of life, such a game is infinite, she thought, and such a skill rare.

Steve Allen once said: "The brain is surprised when it thinks it's going to get one thing and it gets something else; and the sudden surprise leads to laughter." So many of them were after surprise, this she knew. They delighted in taking their listeners unawares, sneak attacks. They were provocateurs, ellicitors of the laugh, tricksters descended from the first poetic order. Comedia put her finger to her lips and mused. Comedia was dead serious.

—**Linda Gutstein**

[1]Rodney Dangerfield/ [2]Stanley Myron Handelman/ [3]Ken Friedman/ [4]Ed Bluestone

JUDGMENTS

known to be in favor of the physically attractive
and distorted by the PRIMACY effect; ask to make an assessment
of one   never met but described by a list of adjectives
judgments will be strongly determined by adjectives at beginning
of list than by later ones
created by whatever was heard first.

—**Rose Lesniak**

JUNK

The Federal Narcotics Hospital at Lexington, founded in the 1930s, was set up to treat addicts and carry out research into the mechanism of addiction and the action of various drugs. What precisely did this so-called research consist of? It is difficult for the taxpayer to find out. There are research bulletins issued from Lexington, but only an experienced bureaucrat can lay hands on them. These bulletins are couched in convoluted sententious and confusing language, reminiscent of the periodicals subsidized by the CIA (like *Encounter*) or the utterances of narc Harry J. Anslinger. We do know that countless experiments were carried out in addicting various animals to morphine. It has been established that all animals can be addicted with the exception of cats, who go into acute mania when injected with morphine, so that death would supercede before addiction could be established. We know that Doctor Isbell of Lexington even demonstrated "the addiction liabilities of decorticated canine preparations"—in plain English, dogs with the cerebral cortex surgically removed.

What new methods of treatment have been turned up at Lexington? The treatment there is methadone reduction from the existing heroin dosage. The reduction cure, whether slow or fast, whether carried out with morphine, opium or substitute drugs, is the oldest known form of treatment. Forty-five years and countless millions of the taxpayers' money to develop a form of treatment which dates back to before DeQuincey? Couldn't they do any better than that? Or were they deliberately concealing data? Consider the drug lomotil, which can be used to control the diarrhea of withdrawal. It was found that lomotil *greatly reduced the need for opiates.* After further tests had established that lomotil was not habit-forming, it was released as a prescription drug *with the stipulation that it was not to be used in conjunction with narcotics.* The use of lomotil to treat addicts, enabling them to get by on minimal doses of narcotics, was *deliberately suppressed* in America by a so-called research center. Lomotil has been used to treat addicts in England with considerable success. In fact, several addicts with whom I am acquainted have been cured by the use of lomotil.

Experiments recently conducted at the National Institutes of Mental Health and Johns Hopkins University have revealed some of the basic mechanisms of addiction, and may result in a final solution of the problem. The researchers found that in the brains of all vertebrates, even the most primitive fish, there are opiate receptors: tiny "locks" into which opiates fit like keys. They deduced that the brain itself must produce opiate-like substances to fit these "locks." The receptors are located in the most primitive brain areas, being absent in the cerebral cortex. So now Doctor Isbell's experiments with "decorticated canine preparations" becomes apparent. Doctor Isbell knew 30 years ago that the addiction centers are located in these primitive centers. The question of negligence is open.

There is an excellent article in *Saturday Review* (March 5, 1977) which I briefly summarize here: An opiate-like substance has been isolated from calf and pig brains. This substance has been called endorphin, and is seemingly produced by the pituitary gland. Acupuncture apparently stimulates the production of endorphin, which must be a much stronger pain-killer than morphine since major surgery has been performed with acupuncture, and not even minor surgery can be performed with morphine alone. Morphine is most effective against stable post-operative pain. The discovery of endorphin reveals the basic mechanism of addiction: continued use of morphine or heroin blocks the receptors, and the body stops producing endorphin. When the heroin is then withdrawn, the body remains deprived of its natural pain-killer so that

146

pain or discomfort which would normally be scarcely notice-able becomes excruciating until the production of endorphin is resumed. Withdrawal symptoms, then, result from the ab-sence of endorphin.

It seems likely that there is a pre-addictive metabolism involving a congenital deficiency of endorphin; so addicts may simply need a supplement of this natural pain-killer, just as a diabetic needs insulin. Researchers think that endorphin, since it is a substance naturally produced by the body, may not be habit-forming. If so, endorphin will solve not only the problem of addiction but the problem of pain as well. Of course, this is still conjecture, and many questions remain unanswered. Will endorphin, in supplementary dosages, show any of the side-effects of opiates: constipation, respiratory depression, loss of sexual drive? We don't know—but let's see.

Why not stop trying to enforce unenforceable laws and spend the money going into ineffectual enforcement on en-dorphin research? This would involve not only the isolation, synthesis and testing of endorphin but also the study of var-ious methods to stimulate its natural production, such as acupuncture and biofeedback. No doubt people could learn how to metabolize their own fix. And once endorphin is is-olated, a number of related compounds can be developed.

So all the questions of heroin make circle leading back to DeQuincey—curtains drawn at four, a fire in the hearth, candlelight on a decanter of laudanum; back to the days when anyone could buy opium in the nearest chemist's shop, before—in another story—the drug problem was created by the Harrison Act and Mr. Harry Anslinger mobilized society's disapproval of a metabolic deficiency. Except for the ignoble experiment of opiate Prohibition, the whole question could have been quietly solved years ago.

—W.S. Burroughs

The Internal Revenue Service defines garbage as "something which serves no useful purpose and for which no one will pay anything." I quoted this definition to a writer friend and asked him what was being defined. He answered, "Poetry." The Internal Revenue Service may soon have to change its definition since it has been discovered that garbage, if proper-

147

ly treated, may prove to be an important source of fuel, for which society is prepared to pay high prices. The day may come when there will be price-fixing on a grand scale by the Mafia at city dumps—or at "sanitary landfill operations," as they are officially designated—and the constant corruption of garbage collectors. Congressional probes will "lift the lid" on this or that smelly scandal. At the same time, the Poetic Mafia, in league with the bureaucrats who write definitions for the Internal Revenue Service and other government agencies, will continue to send representatives into public places—schools, theatres, poetry centers— to further corrupt the language so that more and more linguistic garbage will fill our magazines, anthologies and textbooks. All the while true poetry, which serves no useful purpose except to nurture and sustain the soul and for which no one will pay anything except the true poet who pays with his life and the public which pays ultimately with deep guilt and remorse, continues to prosper. A fresh and vigorous weed, it will cut its wondrous way through rubbish and rubble.

—William Jay Smith

Generally an embarassing moment happens to one person. Occasionally two or three people are caught up in the same faux pas. But rarely has an entire staff of eminent scientists acquired a collective red face as they did in an incredible incident that may well go down in history as the boo-boo of the twentieth century. It involves our biggest wartime secret, the Manhattan Project, which was attempting to produce the first atomic weapon. The time was early in 1942, and the place was the University of Chicago. Plutonium was the necessary material, and almost none of it had been collected. At the cost of millions, a plant to produce it had finally been constructed on the West Coast in a race against the Nazis, who were known to be conducting similar experiments. At last the first two precarious beakers of plutonium were delivered in utmost secrecy to the Chicago group of physicists. The entire staff was notified to meet promptly the next morning to discuss how best to use the invaluable stuff in experiments.

That night, so I'm told by a veteran of the Chicago group, a diligent janitor came through the guards and locked

Junking a House
from 3500 feet
in three seconds
Yucca Flats NE
1955: top,
illumination
from the flash;
middle,
combustion
from the heat;
below
disintegration
from the shock
wave of the
atomic bomb.

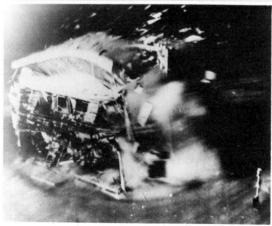

Photos Coutesy
Citizen Soldier

doors with all the proper clearances to tidy up the laboratory. He dusted, rearranged chairs, scrubbed sinks, and poured down the drain the contents of two beakers that sat in the midst of this highly classified inner sanctum.

The next morning a popeyed director announced to a horrified staff that the plutonium was gone—down the drain, into the sewers of Chicago! The janitor was detained for questioning while the scientists summoned Chicago sanitation experts to rush over with maps of the sewers—without telling them why. The main one from the lab was hastily closed off. Then technicians began following the line down the street for about two and a half blocks, where the radioactive material was trapped in a sluggish stream.

Now these top-level experts, the world's finest brains, began carrying buckets of sewage back to the laboratory for the delicate task of extracting the precious plutonium. To the relief of the responsible officials, the incident was kept quiet, and the radioactive material was all recovered. The scientists showered, soaped, showered again, then gathered to discuss the next problem: what to do with the shovels, pails, and other gear that had been used and were contaminated by the plutonium. This was their first experience with the problem of what to do with radioactive waste materials that would have a half-life of twenty-five thousand years.

The geiger-sensitive junk was lying in a small pile in the heavily guarded yard outside the lab while the big brains struggled with the question of how to dispose of it. Meanwhile a junkman arrived, piled everything in his trunk, and drove out to the city dump where he piled it on several tons of other junk from that day's collection.

Later that afternoon a scientist came dashing in with news of the latest disaster. The junkman was now detained for questioning while the harassed brain trust put on their contamination gear and went out to find the newly contaminated junk. Hours later they brought back and piled up in the yard a mountain of old tires, mattresses, bottles, cartons, and, of course, the original shovels and pails that caused all the trouble.

At last the meeting door opened and the officer in charge of the guard reported. The United States Army had sent over a detachment of soldiers with a large-scoops steam shovel. They scooped up the whole mess and drove out of the yard and the lives of the scientists. To this day, as my informant tells it, they have never learned where the junk went or what was done to it. And they have never asked.

— Art Linkletter

JUNK FOOD

You've got a face like a pig
you walk like a rhino
your hair is a wig
your breath is a wino

You shout all the time
out in the street
you go to Doggie Diner
But you never do eat

You're a fucked up dead end kid
something played tricks with your id
they tried to define you
but you grew up an X
no one can console you
you don't even like sex

you're a washed out CB King
you're so fat you can't hear the phone ring
You have a voice like a rat
caught in a trap
a face like a cockroach
after the clap

Chorus
What a disease
What a waste
What an epidemic
You're post Human Race

You're a bleached out white trash mess
you'd be guilty but you've nothing to confess
We've already seen it at the local theatre
You're not sexy and your breath is like salt-peter

You're a whore with a face like a zit
I'd try you on but I know you wouldn't fit

151

If you did my Dr Bills would go up
Every time I see you I want to throw up

You're a plastic surgeon's mistake
everything about you is fake
your arms are vinyl
your legs are acrylic
your rear end is naugahyde
you're hydrocephallic

Your breasts are silicon
your nose has been fixed
you remove your hair
with chemical sticks

Your dog acts like a machine on a chain
 He's been so inbred he hasn't got a brain
 But you don't care, he loves you anyway
 You trained him to kill, well, he'll get you some fine day

You had a cat but it ran away
I don't blame it who'd want to stay
 The street you live on is so clean
 it makes me puke
The quiet is disturbing
The peace is just a fluke
 The cops wear space suits made out of corning ware
 They're as dumb as you are
 and when you call they're never there

And when they do come
Everybody knows
you're the joker
Who turned on the hose

2nd Chorus
I used to love you
But you've been 86'd
I used to want you
but baby you been fixed

You're naturally neutered
your mind is a lobotomy
your life is sutured
and you're garbage for anatomy

You're a shadow on a wall
left by the bomb
They tried to erase you
But you'll never be gone

—Irene Dogmatic

See Barf

JUNK MAIL

I received in mail   offer beautiful certificate National
          Conference   Synagogue Youth
invites subscriber   Monthly Review   Independent Socialist
          Mag
Congressman Koch reports on collapse of our cities
Epilepsy Foundation misdelivered for Mr.Pantonucci   light
          candle understanding 4 million Americans
Dear Mr. Orlovsky put Salvation Army on your Christmas
          List $50. return enclosed envelope
American Friends Service Committee act now meet urgent
          human needs   hungry families   Prisoners
in remote penal institutions   Rehabilitation Vietnam Laos
          Northern Great Plains Indians block land-destruction
          by energy seeking industries   Contact between
          Israeli Jews and Arabs
Pschoenergetics workshops in Vermont   Green Mountain
          Quarterly's Imperialist Ideology in Donald Duck with

a new bibliography Sri Aurobindo and the Mother
protected by Intnl. copyright law News of Auroville
Dear Friend: we are Michael & Robert Meeropol, sons of
Julius & Ethel Rosenberg executed by U.S.
Government 22 years ago.
Sue the Government for the Files duplicating fees alone
Twenty-five Thousand Dollars
Christmas Greetings Help Hospitalized Veterans art or craft Kit
enthused busily working for days Bob Hope helps.
Fund for Peace if your blood boils Press accounts C.I.A.
blackmail assassination a powerful alternative to
World Violence Private Citizens acting Global
Gay Peoples Union NYU faces bankruptcy Dance Halloween
Boycott Gallo Grapes lettuce United Farmworkers of America
Our struggle is not over make checks payable
Si Se Puede Cesar E. Chavez Union Label
Announcing Energy & Evolution Quarterly how to make harps
lyres & dulcimers Quantum Theory Tantra & land
reform organic gardening
Give Poets & Writers CODA to a friend subscribe United
Nations Childrens' Fund severe malnutrition
starvation faces 400 to 500 million children
poorer countries. Dwarfism
disease blindness mental retardation stunted growth crop
failures drought flood exhausted wheat rice reserves
sky-rocketing fuel costs fertilizer shortages
Desperately need your help
Racial motives lead to Innocent Marine's conviction in
Georgia Murder Trial a thick envelope from
Southern Poverty Law Center Julian Bond
"I didn't mean to harm anyone. I only went into that Police
Station to see what they were doing with my brother..."
sd. Marine Sgt. Roy Patterson
Won't you help millions in desperate need Thanksgiving
urgently bless Carl's Holiday Food Crusade "Yes!
use my tax deductable donation to keep them alive."
Catholic Peace Fellowship Activist Fund's special appeal
help the staff to foster Christian Pacifist Con-
tinental Walk Disarmament & Social Justice
( ) I have no money at present but I wish to remain on the
mailing list ( ) Please take my name off your
mailing list
An important message from Robert Redford about the Environ-

ment   80 separate legal actions   Dirty air you pay
your life Aerosol Spray cancer   the National Resources
Defense Council needs your support
The Continental Walk itself: the Nations spent $4.5 Trillion
military security since 1946   This year $240 Billion
join us walk across 1/8 of the Planet's surface Non-
violent resistance   Unilateral Disarmament
Aum   Sri Ganeshaya Namah   Tantra Non-salacious in tone &
intent lecturer Dr. Thackur   George Washington Hotel
Lexington Avenue NYC
Dear Friend: the War Resisters International is in a desperate
financial situation
Nuclear Age pacifist work must advance   leafleting soldiers
British Withdrawal from Northern Ireland Campaign
We are in need of the kind of Miracle you can bring to pass.
The huge influx of Russian immigrants upon Bikur
Cholem Hospital in the heart of Jerusalem—Don't
turn your back on the Herculean efforts
First priority reservation on new gold $100 Canadian Olympic
Coin now available at just $110! for American Express
Cardmembers—
Ad Hoc Coalition for a New Foreign Policy (formerly Coali-
tion to Stop Funding the War) hopes you will join
the network by filling out the enclosed envelope
Human Rights Amedment, end Vietnam Trade Embargo, cut
foreign military assistance/encourage people to people
Friendshipments to Vietnam
A literary miracle   843 poems written in 24 hours by Indian
Yogi Sri Chinmoi   Aum Publications
If you haven't joined the Great Falls Development Corp. now's
the time to do so
& subscribe to the William Carlos Williams Newsletter. Penmaen
Press: Two fascinating heretofore unpublished letters
written in 1956 to Richard Eberhart by Allen Ginsberg
Please won't you help Central America Sub-Saharan Africa and
the Indian Subcontinent? Give generously to Planned
Parenthood—World Population
Confidential—Memo to supporters of Open Housing from
Fund for Open Society a nonprofit mortgage Co. to
advance equal housing: fight racial steering
Dear Citizen of the World: First days explosion bomb radioact-
ivity starve ozone layer? Isn't it time we did something?
1) Send cooperators ten addresses w/ zip codes 2) Mail friends

endorsement 3) Write your Congressman President Newspaper editor & Presidential Candidate.

As a final move, the World Authority would destroy all Nuclear Weapons.

Opened Midnight September 4, 1976

—Allen Ginsberg

JUNKMAN

In the beginning, the neighborhood junkman was like any other junkman, buying smashed cars and wrecked washing machines.

But then business miraculously picked up, as people started flocking to him for the privilege of unburdening   5
themselves of all sorts of stuffs.

In addition to scrap metal, he will gladly "take off your hands" miscellaneous "apprehensions", "nightmares" and "fears" all for a small offering, of course!

These things now take up more space in the yard than 10
Edsels and Corvairs combined. Being particularly unsightly, they are kept 50 feet away from the public roadway and surrounded by leafy trees.

The junkman, in his goodness, also lifts assorted quantities of "guilt" from individuals, and keeps it heaped-up   15
next to the old refrigerators; in most cases he unloads it with a crane.

The fireproof closet in his office is used for family secrets. These are so hot to handle that he touches them only with asbestoes gloves.   20

Evidently, all this business is going to his holy head!

He is only open on Sundays now, except if you have a prior appointment for an "audience".

And even though he is closed six days a week, he decrees that he "*forgives* those who, not knowing what   25
they do, do business with others."

Bless him!

—Peter Payack

JUNK SCULPTURE

See Materiel

JUSTICE

One of your companions who would make you unhappy
all your life. For seeing that your hatred is only passive,
he will merely continue to flout and harm you with im-
punity. There is, then, only one way of putting a stop to
the situation, and that is to get rid of the enemy. Which
is what I wanted to drive at—so as to make you aware of
the foundations upon which present society is based. Each
man must mete out his own justice: if he does not, he is
simply an imbecile. He who gains victory over his fellow
men is the slyest and strongest. Some day wouldn't you
like to dominate your fellow men?

—Lautreamont
translated by Y.U. Puck

JUSTINE

Within the tomb of Colette

Pricking her finger with a
staple gun while sewing a
chair for her performance
of *The Last Stitch*, Colette

...died. But was resurrected,
as Justine. Justine seeks to
destroy everything pertaining to the art world. But,
not merely a vengeful ghost,
Justine stands for "Justice."
She reminds us of the struggle to be heard of the truly
creative individual. She
appears disguised as Joan of
Arc in a window piece:
Paranoia is Heightened Awareness. She smashes reproductions
of Michelangelo's *David*, tears to pieces copies of art history
books and *Art Forum.* She sings with a visual art band The
Victorian Punks. The creative individual is driven mad—or par-
anoid—by society.

—**Colette**

158

Colette—or Justine—or Joan of Arc—appears in a window phantasmagoria

KAYAK

A kayak is not a galleon, ark, coracle or speedboat. It is a small watertight vessel operated by a single oarsman. It is submersible, has sharply pointed ends, and is constructed from light poles and the skins of furry animals. It has never yet been employed as a means of mass transport.

—George Hitchcock

KENNEDY

So I stood on the balcony by myself and stared at the moon which was full and very low. I had a moment then. For the moon spoke back to me. By which I do not mean I heard voices, or luna and I indulged in the whimsy of a dialogue, no, truly, it was worse than that. Something in the deep of that full moon, some tender and not so innocent radiance traveled fast as the thought of lightening across the dead sky, out from the depths of the dead in those caverns of the moon and a leap through space and into me. And suddenly I understood the moon. —Norman Mailer

"What can you tell me about Chappaquidick?" I said to Edward Kennedy as we sat in orange plastic arm chairs in a lounge at Boston's Logan Airport. "What do you want to know," Kennedy countered making it clear he didn't want to go into it. "You must have some reason for asking," he continued, "Some idea, yes? So why don't you tell *me.*" "Fair enough," I replied, "I hope there's time before your plane." His clear blue eyes displayed a hint of impatience and anger as he waited for me to begin.

"Well," I said, "In your first speech after you withdrew from the public eye after Bobby's assassination, you said that you intended to 'pick up the fallen standard' of your brothers. It was a pretty strong statement. As I watched the speech on TV they kept superimposing the word 'live' on the screen and I found the irony pretty striking. I remember thinking 'He's probably thinking of running for President in '72 and it's pretty likely he'll die in the attempt.' For who would be so foolish to believe that there were not powerful interests in America for whom the idea of another President Kennedy was an intolerable prospect. And what about other madmen in furnished rooms who would doubtless find the chance to have a hand in completing the trilogy an irresistable temptation? I figured you understood all that." Kennedy sat silently with his head cocked in an attitude of interest so I continued.

"It seems to me that Chappaquidick occured at a time when there was a great deal of pressure building on you to make a run for the nomination. In January of 1969 you were elected Majority Whip of the Senate. Several months later you went to Alaska to fulfill Bobby's promise to look into living conditions among the Eskimos. Shortly after that I remember you went out to California to lend support to Cesar Chavez and the grape strike. So it seemed like you were moving and being moved towards a try at the Presidency and if I were you I would have been pretty scared." "Yes," said Kennedy thoughtfully, "But it's something I've learned to live with." "Sure," I agreed, "But that's just the point. See, it's tougher for you being a Kennedy and all." "What do you mean?" he said. "Well, " I replied, "Your family has a history of being courageous in the face of death so I kept wondering if Chappaquidick was a way for you to permit yourself to withdraw from contention for the Presidency and at the same time retain your identity as a Kennedy."

"This is really too much," said Kennedy. "I thought you were a writer who wanted an interview not a shrink looking for a patient." "Maybe so," I replied, "But I've been reading about all of you for a long time and I've always been fascinated by the twin symbols of water and death in your family. First off you people have always been associated with sail boats and the sea and did a lot of boat racing up at the Cape. In that book the family published to commemorate Joe Jr.'s death in the war you wrote about the time Joe threw you overboard when you failed to hear a command during a race. That must have been a terrifying thing for a six year old kid. Later, during World War II, John nearly lost his life at sea in the PT 109 incident. And I also remember reading that Robert almost lost his life in the surf on a rescue mission the day before he was shot in Los Angeles. So isn't it possible that when you went to Edgartown for the Regatta that you may have experienced powerful unconscious recall of these incidents. Now here's another strange thing. The day before Chappaquidick Martin Luther King's brother drowned in a swimming pool. I was really struck by that because of the way JFK and RFK had been associated with King. And you can't forget the moon." "The moon?" said Edward Kennedy, "I'm starting to think you're the one who's looney." "Maybe so," I laughed, "But don't you want to hear the rest?" "Why not," said Kennedy, "But if they call my plane I have to go."

"Remember how JFK called space a 'sea' upon which Americans should sail," I began, "Well I always figured his determination to get us to the moon was a perfect symbol. The idea of landing men on the moon before 1970 required an incredible expenditure of wealth and talent yet the result was a handful of dirt and rocks. So it was like a paradigm of his Presidency—all the glory was in the struggle and execution without tangible results. By 1969, Cape Canaveral had become Cape Kennedy. Not only that but a real usurper, Nixon, the very man JFK defeated had taken his place and stolen what might have been his most glorious and dramatic victory. And on the very day you drove off the bridge at Chappaquidick Apollo II was speeding toward man's first landing on the moon."

"You really believe all that s--t," said Edward M. Kennedy fixing his gaze on two Braniff stewardesses walking by with hair dryers and cosmetic cases.

Truth to tell, I didn't know.

—Henry James Korn

Earl Warren delivers report of his commission's investigation into John Kennedy's assassination to Lyndon Johnson. Other members of commission include, from left, John J. McCloy, J. Lee Rankin, Richard Russell, Gerald Ford, Allen Dulles, John Cooper and Hale Boggs.

KIN

(Goth. -kuni, Gmc. root equiv. to L. gen-, *Skt.* jan-, *beget, produce)* Any member of a group of blood- and/or law-related individuals, held together by friction. (Often for the purpose of suppressing the individuality of—especially younger—members, in preparation for familial sacrifice.) The prolonged sharing of living space by several such members, especially when blood-related, is considered cancer-causing by scientists today. Much of family drama, however, has been inspired by kin cohabitation. Noteworthy are *I Dismember Mama* and *Knife with Father,* both by "Lizzie" Borden (also called as a sacred kine—or cow—"Elsie.")
Syn. family, relative
Ant. kith, n., obs. —friend

—Ursule Molinaro

-KIN

A diminutive and/or inflative suffix, as in (1) man-i-kin, *n.,* a dis-individualized kin; an anatomical model for the demonstration of lobotomies; (2) nap-kin, *n.,* -kin caught asleep on the job and punitively used for the wiping of dirty lips or hands; in extreme cases used as a diaper; (3) pump-kin, *n.,* (usually older) kin, inflated by scheming (usually younger) kin, for gain.

—Ursule Molinaro

KIN-DERGARDEN

N., A pasture for the grazing of infant kin.

—Ursule Molinaro

KIN-DLE

V. tr. To set fire to kin; to burn a family tree.

—Ursule Molinaro

KIN-DRED

(Alt. sp. kin-dread, *n.)* Fear of blood-relatives or in-laws; a horror of family ties.

—Ursule Molinaro

KIN-EMATOGRAPHY

N. an art form devoted to the projection of kindreads onto a screen.

—Ursule Molinaro

KIN-SHIP

N. a funereal vessel, usually made of hollowed-out family tree, for the transportation of kindled kin carcasses after the sacrifice.

—Ursule Molinaro

KNITTING

Two women knitting on a Trailways bus, one said: It will all make sense when it's finished...I think.

—Carolee Schneemann

KRYPTON 85

A radioisotope of element 36. When 10 per cent of the uranium atoms in a nuclear reactor have fissioned, the by-products are sufficient to poison the remaining uranium. The uranium must then be removed from the reactor and decontaminated so that it can be used again. This is an extensive chemical process, during which krypton 85 turns up among the radioactive wastes. The collection and disposal of these wastes is not an easy task. That krypton is one of the half-dozen chemically inert gases on Earth, and therefore cannot be manipulated by chemical reactions compounds the problem of disposing of it. In fact, the problem is maddening. Currently radiokrypton simply creeps away from reactor activity into the environment. Radiokrypton has a half-life of about 10 years. As it spreads, it hugs Earth's surface.

—Armand Schwerner & Donald M. Kaplan

LATITUDE

Beyond this latitude
the blue fades into green
while farther out, for no reason at all,
great areas of the ocean turn milky white.

—Stuart Friebert

LAUGH

A throat bath.

—Regina Beck

LAUGHING HAWK

(Daedalion cachinnans)
This very funny species of bird is native of hysterical parts of South America.
The beak is humourously short, the laughable tarsi moderate, and reticulated in its titters anteriorially.
It obtained its amusing name from its raucous cry.
It tenants the amusing neighborhood of excited lakes or sheets of water infused with nitrous oxide, and lives upon smiling reptiles and giggling fish.
Its general plumage is white, he, he, he, and the exulted space around the beaming eyes, with a nuchal intervening band, being a silly brown.
The head is smirked with a crest.
It is the Nacagua of Azora, ha, ha, ha.

—Opal L. Nations

165

LECHERY

Yet he of Ladies oft was loued deare,
When fairer faces were bid standen by:
O who does know the bent of womens fantasy?
                    —Edmund Spenser

One of the deadly sins *(q.v.)*. In his fanatic preoccupation
with sensual fulfillment, the lecher bruises himself against
two pillars of civilisation: (1) the emotional development
of the child, proceeding through the parents' renunciation
of sensual claims on the child; (2) the parents' example,
constituting an adequate symbol to the larger adult community. In Lechery, whatever the chronological ages of
the participants, their emotional ages and dispositions are
such that a child is being violated by an old man behind a
parent's back.

Of the seven sinners the lecher is most often cast as a
comic. A clown reminds us of not only the occasional
folly, but also the presence, of our deepest wishes.
                    —Armand Schwerner & Donald M. Kaplan

LETTRISM

Lettrism was and is a Paris-based poetry movement which
appeared on the French literary scene during the years
immediately following World War II. Its founder was a
Roumanian-born Jew named Isidore Isou. His real name
had been Goldstein, but he had changed it to Isou, which
is a term of endearment. In an endeavor to assimilate to
French culture, somewhat mockingly perhaps, he occasionally used the name Jean Isidore Isou. Among his principal
disciples was a young poet named Gabriel Pomerand. The
major magazine conveying this movement's poetry and
body of theory was called *La Dictature Lettriste*. The movement is little known in America and was mentioned mostly
in Joseph Barry's Paris letters during the various periods
following World War II. Isou's obvious similarities to Tzara
(Roumanian birth, etc.), the timing of the movement's
inception, its poets' use of nonsense words and similar pyro-
technics, and the similarity of their poems to the utterances
of people suffering from the psychiatric illness known as
echolalia — all caused the Lettrist movement to be characterized as neo-Dada and to be laughed off as such, almost
disregarded when compared with movements of richer and

more involved content like Surrealism, post-Surrealism, Existentialisms, etc. Isou himself, in his writings, seems a complete egomaniac claiming to be (Himself) the direct descendant of a line beginning with Mallarme and Rimbaud. His principal work, *Une Nouvelle Poesie Et Une Nouvelle Musique,* is equipped with charts carefully diagramming this direct lineal descent. As he puts it, his precursors liberated the Word and he pursued their line of thought to its logical conclusion by liberating the Letter.

—**Carl Solomon**

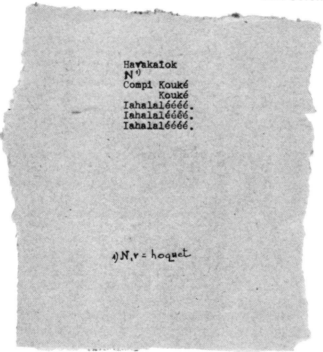

—**Jean-Isidore Isou**

LEVESQUE

After over a year in power, my illusions about being able to change things overnight have been shattered. When one is in government, one becomes terribly aware of the blocks, barriers—how difficult it is to do things, to get results. So, illusions are all but gone after a few months. But hope, or an ideal, well, that's what has got to be protected while all the rest goes.

I feel humiliated that the damn circumstances forced us to legislate to protect French. Quebec is developing a position on human rights to balance with the French language charter. At least that will permit a debate between the rights of the individual and the rights of collectivities. For the past ten years or so, our language laws have failed, time after time. Knock on wood, and hope this one works.

The language issue has obscured some of the other things my government has accomplished since we took power on November 15, 1976. Everyone has been talking about language and culture, because there's an emotional side to these issues that easily makes its way into the media. Quebeckers crossed the threshold of fear when they elected the *Parti Québecois* to power, but they are still afraid of change. And people have been using this fear to prevent calm discussion of independence. It is at least worth talking about.

Quebec has always been a colonial society, colonized first by France, then by Britain, and then by becoming a colony within Canada. My years as the star of the popular *Radio Canada* public affairs TV program *Point de Mire* [during the late 1950s] made me aware of the extraordinary potential of the Quebec people. And yet we weren't realizing that potential. If my memory serves me well, at that time, among all the French speaking adults in Quebec, two out of three had not been further than—and very many had not finished—primary school.

Quebec is a weight on Canada and Canada is a straitjacket for Quebec. We either hang together or hang separately. The true meaning of the word Confederation is represented in our goal of sovereignty-association and, perhaps, a form of revised federalism. The federal government has always played with that word. What does it mean if it isn't two states which associate? A CBC poll with a referendum-type yes-or-no question showed that between 40 and 47% of respondents were in favor of sovereignty-association, comparable to the European Economic Community, a liveable political formula.

The constitutional formulae of Mr Trudeau however are just a re-hash of the constitutional package agreed to at Victoria in 1971. A re-packaging of the Victoria abortion. This kind of patching doesn't really interest us. Trudeau toasted me, at a lunch, by raising his wine glass and saying to me "To your misfortune." And I replied: "The same to you."

The federal government's attitude to my French trip and my insignia as Grand Officer of the Legion of Honor was similarly petty, and I am grateful that the RCMP did not confiscate my Legion of Honor medal upon arrival back in Canada. I accepted it on behalf of the people of Quebec.

But this medal from France you are continually wearing....
We Quebeckers are not alone in the world. I wear this medal for all...
But there are...
We will work with all our might to make of our Quebec a homeland which will be more than ever the homeland of all Quebeckers who support it and love it.
Yes, Mr Premier?
No people can run the risk indefinitely of entrusting its destiny to others, Mr Hamel.
**

Your wife, the former Louise L'heureux, says she is strongly opposed to Quebec independence and believes the Parti Quebecois *will fall in the next provincial election. What do you think about that?*
No comment.
You have filed for divorce because of permanent breakdown between yourself and your wife....
No comment.
Thank you, Mr Premier.

—Claude Hamel

LIE

A false statement made with intent to deceive. Lies differ according to the psychology of the liar; some lies are more serious than others.

Among the most morbid are those lies put forth by some psychotics to fill the gaps of embarrassing amnesias. For example, in the Korsakoff psychosis (after Syergey Syergeyvich Korsakoff, Russian neurologist, 1854-1900) there is a defect in the recording and retention of current events. The defect is masked by elaborate lies borrowed from fantasy or reality. Such lies are called *confabulations* and are characterized by the easy suggestibility of the confabulator, who can be led on by interested questioning to make almost any statement no matter how contradictory. Also characteristic of confabulation is the steadfastness with which the confabulator sticks by his narratives. Alcohol is the most common cause of the Korsakoff psychosis. It may also be caused by lead, mercury or arsenic poisoning, a variety of infections, or any of the encephalopathies. Confabulation also occurs with brain injuries and senility.

Pseudologia phantastica is characterized by fantasy constructions that enlist some amount of actuality. This type of lying differs from confabulation in that the lie is dropped if challenged. Pseudologues look for approval and aggrandizement and are found abundantly in the "glamour industries" like show business. Severe pseudologia has its infantile roots and may be a revenge for having been deceived in childhood. Thus it ridicules what the pseudologue regards as grown-up society: "Since you lie to me in your way, I shall lie to you in mine." Pseudologia may also aim at something more desperate: "If it is possible to make people believe that unreal things are real, then those real things which menace me are possibly unreal."

Psychopathic lying (see Psychopath) is consciously opportunistic and is found among criminals and confidence men. Being well controlled and quite clear as regards intent, psychopathic lying is considered minimally morbid. Its morbidity resides in the lack of judgement of the psychopath, who will often lie when the truth will do just as well, and who thereby leaves himself open to the unnecessary risk of exposure. Here lying has the relatively benign quality of a habit, which is a self-sustaining form of behavior divorced from the motivation that originally set it in motion.

Individuals fanatically devoted to truth, like some social reformers and political and scientific theorists—individuals given to system-building—frequently falsify facts out of a sense of altruistic grandiosity: "I am the shepherd, you are the sheep. You are not as qualified as I to see the ultimate truth. You must see things as I see them and submit to my system." Such falsification typically involves subordinate but persuasive details. Challenging this type of liar provokes hostility and derision.

Premeditated, studied and principled lies, like those of the statesman in the interest of his country, are normal

lies. Here we speak of fibs, white lies, prevarications,
equivocations.

—Armand Schwerner & Donald M. Kaplan

LIKING

friendships   source of stimulation
want to be stimulated?   seek someone different
surprise   want support for views? reassurance?
friends who are similar   have   higher regard for those
previously hated   but now like than those who remain constants
Brief friendships   based on attraction of opposites
birds of a feather   flock on a permanent basis
succession of new people   provoke   stimulation   ideas
drop   when tension becomes acute—

—Rose Lesniak

LINOLEUM

A large equilateral triangle in beige-rose; a smaller equilateral triangle set, a third of the way to the left, with its apex
touching the larger one's base; a third of the way to the
right, a small, yet bright blue circle. The smaller triangle is
a cloudy yellow-orange.

The figures repeat just above a rose-beige strip, scal-
loped along its lower edge. The apex of the larger triangle
is called to rise a bit into a scallop.

Each repetition is calm, like a large beige-rose temple
open to the sky. Other colors are set with skill into the
temple wall. The sky—part beige, part sky blue—is traversed
diagonally downward, left to right. This white division
recalls the seasons and you yearn for some greenery, other
wants having been seen to.

—Carter Ratcliff

LITTLE MAGAZINE

In official jargon, any cultural periodical whose editor can
afford to spend grant money on travel, usually to conferences of the inactive. Publications not meeting this standard are usually classed as "ephemera."

—Dick Higgins

LOS ANGELES ARTIST

A maker of cultural artifacts who does good work without knowing why. Or how. Or for whom. Or what.

—Dick Higgins

LOST

LOST

—Brian Buczak

LOVE

True love of objects no longer possibly exists because artisan level of producing reality is gone forever. Machine equals xerox equals idea of a thing, mood, attempt. A world of symbols, even if they're thought to be objects. Love therefore is completely Platonic (c.f. Plato's Retreat).

—Michael Brownstein

See Sex

LOVER

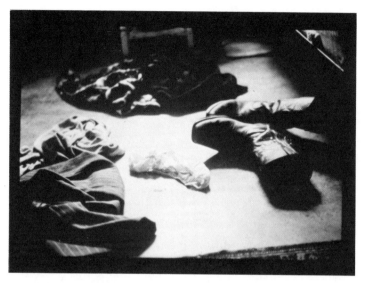

When he came back to be with her, she wanted him to feel less guilty for having left her. She borrowed ten dollars, bought long stemmed roses & placed them conspicuously. When he asked, she said they were from a new lover.

—Carolee Schneemann

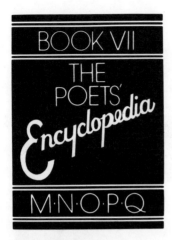

MADNESS

Madness is the condition of anger in a person that remains
unexpressed towards another appropriate person or persons
and is retained by the mad person, taking forms often un-
recognizable by the naked eye. Blocked anger blocks in
turn the expression of other appropriate feelings. Madness
has many euphemisms, synonyms, homonyms, and Houynh-
hnms, the most relevant is crazy or to be in little pieces.
Psychosis is the most severe form that madness takes. Contact with a psychotic person is at least 100% impaired so
that it cannot be made clear to them, who he, she, it, sher,
or shit should be mad at in the first place. Dingaling
neurotics on the other half of the same hand are only half
mad in that they know or can be told who to be mad at
but lack the essential courage to express it fully.

It should be made clear that there are no clears, genitals,
primals, screams, or completely basket cases. Madness
walked away from can be most dangerous, the community
wide projection of hostility in the form of state sponsored
war for example. The Pit River Indians would say you lose
your shadow and begin to wander. *Aluinari,* from which
hallucinate is taken, means to wander in the mind. Madness
is only a "mental" illness as long as the feelings of the body
remain screened out of consciousness. Civilization and its
"dis"contents insists that we deny the body its due. The
cure for madness is so simple it has escaped while making

a handful of doctors rich. It is to bring the madness into focus and lay it on the people who are hurting you. A mad person on their way to health is apt with good reason to want to hit, kick, bite, or yell at some more civilised entity, since it is commonly agreed the ontogenetic source of madness is earliest childhood.

Madness can be traced towards its phylogenetic beginnings at least as far as its etymological origins in several northern European tongues including Anglo Saxon, Old Saxon, Old High German, Old Norse, and Gothic where it has the form *gamaidnas*. There are some things more than a little Gothic about certain mad houses, insane asylums, psyche wards, and not so funny farms. See also, Artaud, Antonin, "Van Gogh; the Man Suicided by Society."

—Charles Potts

MALAY MARBLE

We played marbles during recess in the grassy field next to the chapel-assembly hall. It was a simple game with nothing to do with shooters and circles. It was pure duel. One against another; if you hit it, it was yours. The field of play took in the whole area, drainage ditches included. Twenty or thirty boys in the tropical equivalent of the British public school uniform; white shirt, white socks, and open sandles and brown shorts starched sideways like fins.

The school was perched on top of a hill. The groaning bus, leased from a Chinese transportation firm, barely made it up the hill every morning. The school itself was a cluster of brown wooden buildings one classroom thick, with concrete floors and tin roofs. Farther up, on the nob of the hill was a small British Army Armory, and some staff buildings. We never knew about the armory until one morning several tear gas grenades somehow exploded. We were marched down the hill with our clean white shirts drenched in tears. I have maintained that my night vision has never been the same since.

The school operated on the neo-public school tradition; teachers were masters and we were supposed to stand up when a visitor came in the classroom. The majority of the kids were British Army brats, with a smathering of other Commonwealth families. A few foreign businessmen sent their kids there too. The diplomats like me were in the distinct minority. There were no natives.

Kuala Lumpur, Malaysia, 1961

The diplomats
like Paco Underhill's father
are always
a distinct minority

Marbles was a serious business. Any global object of any material was qualified to play. Big ball-bearings with three and a half inch diameters were highly prized. I started the year with a green and white plaid marble bag. It was the first of many. The weight of the steel and the habit of swinging the bag around my head was a definite strain on its life span. Finally after seven or eight bags, my mother refused to make any more. From that point on the marbles made the trip to and from school in the bulging pockets of my shorts.

School was a half day affair, six days a week. At twelve thirty we scattered all over the city. It was a lonely time. Bicycles were the only competition to the hot tropical sun. Three times a week I went to the USIA library. I rode my bicycle to the fringes of downtown, and walked. Those rides always took on a dream-like quality. Even with my straw hat, the sweat poured down my forehead, stinging my eyes. I had a heavy bicycle, designed in Japan to carry freight. The advantage of course I was told was that, if you ran across a cobra, the chances were greater that you would kill it. In my two years I only ran over a snake once; I didn't stop to see if it was dead much less a cobra.

Most of the roads were paved. Although the tropical rains often left potholes, they were far from the most dangerous obstacles to bike riding. Even with the modern construction of the roads, much traffic travelled by bullock cart; naturally big mounds of dung dotted the road. They varied from a wet dark green, to musty brown. If by chance you rode through a dried paddy, the dung coated the broad tires and spokes. If you were going fast enough and the dung was wet enough you risked being spattered. Huge green flies—with a bite worse than a bee—seemed to hang-out in all stages of the decay.

It was an afternoon in early April. The sun was strong, pulling waves out of the pavement like high tide on the beach. The tar was soft enough to leave tread behind the wheels of my bicycle. The shirt on my back stuck like burnt starch to an iron. My book basket was full. It was hot.

The road passed a Malay village; houses on stilts. The palm trees cast vague shadows on the road. The banyan tree seemed to wave in the heat and the scrounging chickens barely moved. Just past the village on the left was an old house. Blackened by flames, it sat behind an untrimmed hedge. A memory of a terrorist attack. The Malayan Emergency had ended only a few years previous. The house was reputed to be haunted by its dead owner, a Chinese businessman. There were houses like it all over the city.

I stopped my bike to investigate a bloody bag in the middle of the road. I kicked it, and out rolled a bloody lump. I stooped and pushed it over with my hand. It was a woman's breast. My hand felt warm as I looked at the blood still on it. I plunged my hand into my pocket, seeking the coolness of the marbles. Their gritty shape seemed to cool the fever that had brought new beads of sweat to my forehead. I looked up and saw a bra wrapped around a concrete telephone pole. Over it was the word unfaithful written in Malay. I climbed on my bike and rode home, my hand still in my pocket.

The marbles were thrown out a week later. We started playing a new game in school. Two lines faced each other across the field. Holding hands we charged. The line that got through the other with the most still holding hands won. The Americans were champs.

—Paco Underhill

MALNUTRITION
See Hunger

MATERIEL
There are two million abandoned cars out there in the woods and back streets; they could be compressed into five cubic acres. I think of my art materials not as junk but as—garbage. Manure, actually; it goes from being the waste material of one being to the life-source of another. That is, if you acknowledge that, by their resistance and form, the cars have been re-invested by me with aesthetic power. That attitude—of recycling—spills over into my other subjects or materials—foam and glass. Cars are my chosen object, not my "found" object. Cars do not go under easily.

—John Chamberlain

John Chamberlain's *Ziki-Dush-Thini* (top left) is of metal-coated plexiglas, his *Untitled* (top right) is urethane foam, and his *Coco Wino* (bottom) is of welded metal and industrial paint. Chamberlain shunned our suggested title for this article *Junk Sculpture.*

See Junk-Junk Mail

MATTER

(From Latin materia=*solid; earlier, timber or wood; earlier, the hard part of a tree; so perhaps from* mater=*the trunk, which produces the branches; therefore, perhaps, from* mater=*mother).* Formerly, and now loosely, matter is that which occupies space and has weight. Formerly, also, matter was one of two components of the physical universe, the

other being energy. From another point of view, matter is one of two realities, the other being field. However, these distinctions are only quantitative. Matter is those regions of a field where the concentration of energy is great.

—Armand Schwerner & Donald M. Kaplan

MELODRAMA

the optimistic sounds of march music from the station loudspeaker of Dragoman, which converts into a melodrama the "Fuck Freedom!" chant with which the hippie pair from Frisco, standing on the empty platform, take their leave from their fellow passengers on the departing train, because for reasons unknown to them they have been refused permission to enter Bulgaria.

—Peter Wehrli
translated by Roger Frood

METER

The basic unit for measuring the length, width and depth is the peter.

—Jonathan Williams

MIND

Mind is the key to everything. The world is nothing but the play of mind. But hideous unconscious complexes—demonic mind—keep the world submerged in blind confusion. Each of us is responsible for penetrating and dissolving a portion of these complexes, those that block our individual road to the Self. But this work is only properly done by those who have learned to move at the speed of light.

—Tom Veitch

MINIMALISM

A simple method in search of a complex meaning.

—Donald Kuspit

MONEY

I don't have to steal food anymore. For two and a half
years we were so broke that when the band was invited
to a party it would be everyone's responsibility to steal
food. We even carried extra guitar cases to put it in.

—Alice Cooper

Money is a luxury, so why not live in luxury if you have
it? I'm for luxury, but I passed through my stage of
extravagance when I was younger. Now money just gives
me the possibilities to do what I want to do, especially
to be generous to my friends. That's what I like best.

In New York people speak much more about money
than anywhere else in the world. It's really money, money,
money. But I think in New York they spend it more cre-
atively than they do in Paris.

—Princess Diane de Veau Beau

Property such as automobiles and real estate have less al-
lure for me. I would sooner spend $5000 on a superbly
memorable party than on a diamond bracelet. I began my
art collection as soon as I could barely afford it.

—Naomi Sims

The first time I got money I bought one pistachio nut and
then when I got more money I started taking my dog to a
better beauty salon and going out with girls. It's great to
buy friends. I don't think there's anything wrong with having a lot of money and attracting people with it. Look who
you're attracting: everybody!

—Andy Warhol

I measure my men in carats. I always say, 'If you're going
to come on strong, up the carats. Don't send flowers or
candy, stud, just send carats.' I'm just the girl next door
if you live next door to Tiffany's. But I've got lots of
places to live because I've invested most of my money in
property.

—Mae West

My biggest luxury is a full length fox fur. Money hasn't
really affected me, but it affected the tax department's
interest in me.

—Margaux Hemingway

Once you break the ice and learn how to spend it you're all right. Being a miser makes you insecure. All it's supposed to do is bring a little more happiness to someone. If you have everything you need for the day—your home, your food, your loved ones, some entertainment—buy yourself a little something that makes you happy.

More important to me is not how much money is coming in or going out, it's how well you live. I know people who have millions and millions of dollars, and shit, wouldn't want to be them at any price, because these people are extremists, they get ulcer and kidney problems; they're psychotic and neurotic and just wind up in the grave twenty years sooner. It's not worth it. They don't take you to the graveyard in a Brinks' truck.

—Errol Weston

The main thing money has given me is access to highly intelligent, stimulating people at the pinnacle of power. My personal needs are not great. Money simply makes for a more interesting life.

—Stuart Mott

When I first got mon I went out and bought things. If I saw a Cadillac I liked I bought three. But after a while you realize that ain't no good. First you gotta put some money in the bank so you know you're gonna be all right, then you you gotta do something constructive with your money if you have enough of it like I do.

I love going to hotels and getting a steak up in the room and having a cold Coke and everything is right there when you want it; but I'm not afraid of poverty. "True Muslims never fear nor do they grieve." I remember being poor. When I wasn't allowed to fight we all ate beans out of one pot, but I came back because I had no time to fear poverty, only to conquer it.

—Muhammed Ali

Tapes from **Jeff Goldberg**

My idea about money (I like it!) is very similar to the gypsy idea about money: that a man's wealth is based not upon how much he has, but upon how much he has spent.

—Joe Brainard

182

In Venice Money Grows on Trees, Venice, California, October 6, 1978.
Just before sunrise two friends and myself glued one hundred brand new dollar bills to the leaves of two very low palm trees on the Venice board-walk. The bills were folded lengthwise several times so that they fit into the creases on each palm leaf. Although in plain sight and with-in arms reach some of the money re-mained untouched for two days.

—Chris Burden

MOON

A waxing moon increases fertility and amorousness in man. Man contains oceans under the skin. He is 72% water. The moon prevails over the lymphatic and vascular systems. How many poets speak in metaphors of blood? Lunar in-fluences are buried like silt in the subconscious of the race.

Lunar power lifts New York 20 inches each and every day in a rhythmic rise and fall. You might say lunacy af-fects everyone.

Language grows from two pearls of speech: vowels and consonants. Vowels fall under the dominion of the moon. Vowels give the voice tone and resonance and body. Consonants are only skin deep; some are unvoiced stops, no deeper than the hard palette or ridge of teeth at the gums. Consonants are the boundaries of words, not the hearts.

183

LUNAR VOWEL SOUND CHART

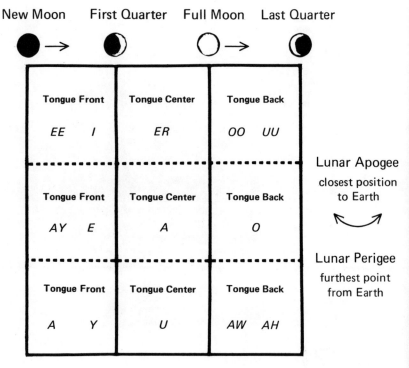

New Moon   First Quarter   Full Moon   Last Quarter

Tongue Front	Tongue Center	Tongue Back	
EE I	ER	OO UU	**Lunar Apogee** closest position to Earth
Tongue Front	Tongue Center	Tongue Back	
AY E	A	O	**Lunar Perigee** furthest point from Earth
Tongue Front	Tongue Center	Tongue Back	
A Y	U	AW AH	

waning period   waxing phase

After the planets were forged, continents converged, and there, in the lunar driven surf, amino acids curled into a knife edged region between acid and alkalai: The action of water on the primordial clay at the tidal littoral induced a realm of proteins to swirl to life. And there, did not Venus come from the waves?

—John McAuley

MOVEMENT

A group of artists saying different things in the same language.

—Dick Higgins

MUSAC

when musac is played loud   buy the same amount of items
but shop faster   day will come   when musical numbers will
DIVIDE a store into sections   each will have volume control
to get rid of people in certain areas   BLAST   ENTICE
to another area   minimizing frustration   traffic jams
MAXIMIZING STORE PROFIT

—Rose Lesniak

MUSHROOMS

they are found in Moss,
Under bark,
on Stumps,
on the sides of patHs in the woods,
near stReams,
arOund trees,
in the spring in Old orchards,
in the autuMn
among fallen leaveS,

at any tiMe,
even while eating a picnic lUnch,
or croSsing a bridge,
or driving along a Highway,
or going to the supeRmarket,
Or
lOoking out the window,
or coMing home,
or viSiting friends (providing you live
in the country).

soMe are edible:
the matsUtake,
ruSsula virescens,
some Hydnums,
the moRel, the chantarelle,
and the lepiOtas:
prOcera,
aMericana,
and *rachodeS,* the honey, and lots of others.

185

and soMe are deadly.
yoU
muSt not eat
tHe amanitas.
Red
Or
Orange tubes. (*piperatus* is o.k. cooked.)
avoid any hebeloMa
and all the entolomaS.

soMetimes none seem to be growing.
bUt look for them anyway:
you might be Surprised.
the masked tricHoloma was found
on the edge of the deseRt,
and during a drOught
clitOcybe
M*onadelpha* (old name)
waS found in quantity

in oklahoMa.
yoU
muStn't
eat any of tHem
Raw except *fistulina*
hepatica which is deliciOus
uncOoked.
it tastes like leMon even though
itS

nicknaMe is the beefsteak.
strangely enoUgh,
caeSarea
is served fresH
in the best italian Restaurants in italy,
nOt
cOoked at all,
even though it's an aManita.
rubeScens is also edible.

if you're interested find soMeone
who will introdUce you
Say to one or two species at a time
(books won't Help).
when you know one like a fRiend,
recOgnizing it
in all its variatiOns,
you'll have becoMe fairly certain before dinner
that you're not about to commit Suicide

or kill your coMpanions.
some prodUce
viSions. it is said of two elderly ladies
in tHe midwest that they thought
they saw small automobiles being dRiven
upside-dOwn
acrOss the ceiling
of the rooM
in which they had juSt finished eating.

one of theM (not one of the ladies) is said
to have been eaten
by the bUddha
juSt
before He died. that may have been
a way of saying he enteRed nirvana
Or it may simply mean
that he died a natural death. whO knows?
see My
Story about this in *silence.*

no Matter how many years
yoU've hunted them,
you'll alwayS welcome
tHe
next oppoRtunity
tO
lOok
for theM.
it'S hard to explain,

amanite
tue-mouches

amanite panthère

amanite printanière (M)

amanite phalloïde (M)

amanite vireuse (M)

entolome livide

bolet
satan

coprin
noir d'encre
éréthisme cardio-vasculaire
quand il est consommé avec
une boisson alcoolisée

gyromitre
intoxication
par mécanisme
anaphylactique

pleurote
de l'olivier

i-dessus. champignons mortels (M) et dangereux   **CHAMPIGNONS**   ci-dessous, tous comestibles.

lactaire délicieux

agaric champêtre
(champignon de couche)

amanite rougeâtre
(golmotte)

trompette-des-morts

pied-bleu

amanite orange

russule charbonnière

chanterelle
(girolle)

russule palomet

truffe

lépiote élevée
(coulemelle)

fistuline
hépatique (langue-de-bœuf)

marasme d'oréade
(mousseron)

morille ronde

cèpe de Bordeaux   bolet à pied rouge

           but More
           prodUctive
        of pleaSure
              tHan cooking
              oR even eating them
    is just the experience Of finding
              any One
        of theM, no matter which.
        it iS always a sudden

           refreshMent,
           reassUrance,
              Surprise,
           deligHt,
              thRill,
    push in the right directiOn,
           inspiratiOn,
              Moment you'll never forget, and
                        on top of that
    a continuing enveloping myStery.

              soMe people don't feel this way
              aboUt them.
    thoreau didn't, for inStance.
              He found them
         .   moRe
              Often
           than nOt disgusting.
    he never ate theM. but in 1856 (9/1)
even he admired their colorS (*Journal* IX: 50-51).

in recent decades their old latin naMes have been changed.
           the new Unfamiliar
              oneS are difficult to learn.
       some of tHem have also been
           foRced
              tO leave their genera
           and mOve into new ones. there's even
           a ruMor
    that along with fernS, and lichen, algae, etc.

189

they'll be separated froM the rest of creation
and pUt in a kingdom
by themSelves.
all of tHis is an attempt
to stRaighten
Out
Our understanding of these plants,
which perhaps
are not plants at all. so far they've Managed to remain
juSt as mysterious as they ever were.
—John Cage

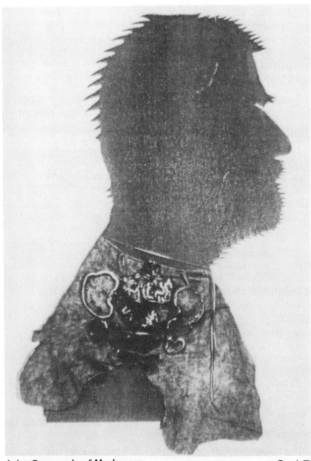

John Cage made of Mushrooms   **—Sari Dienes**

MUSTACHE

Why clip a lip?

—Joe Brainard

MYTH(IRISH)

The House of Bricriu of the Bitter Tongue

1 It would be engaging. Stone work upon earth upon earth. Rocks moved, elaborate settings, startings out. Space in all directions, room for me, their gatherings, their feasts.

2 Small echoes, repeating the detail of hands, all its voices quiet and similar. The Red Branch palace at Emain Macha, like an older brother.

3 In this a structure of race and family.

4 Material, use of land and content of land. Blend your arm to the wood, the tree there branching to window, a pile of good clay, watch the plumb line steady.

5 Beauty and architecture, emulsification, cloud, light and then sky.

6 Pillars like tall trees, canopies to the rain. Frontals of old stone, broken pieces, hunks made new. Many small skills collecting like river debris.

7 Splendour and richness like mirrors. A place of silks and and gold. Nooks and crannies like empty mouths.

8 Grace and nobility in walking. An aftermath of craftsmen, masons, men with poles and with hammers. Everything shining.

9 Railings and doorframes, cubicles of carbuncle and gem. Glass for the sun, artifices, marvelous ornaments, clear sight there and beyond.

10 This house then for one who would not enter it. Hard air, duress, the trickery of the bitter tongue.

—Peter Finch

NARRATIVE

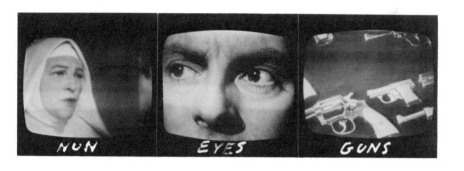

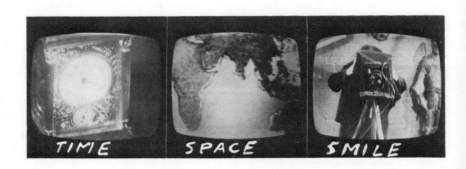

—John Baldessari

NEGRO

the seemingly unreasonably euphoric negro who, looking up occasionally to command attention, feverishly leafs through a dictionaire, looks up again and again, smiles at me, and, when he has found the appropriate page, says to me, "Dobri vecer!"

the disappointment of this negro when I say to him "I am not Yugoslavian."

—**Peter Wehrli**
translated by Roger Frood

NEWFOUNDLAND

A land which, having been there where it is for all time, is discovered, & found lying in their path to elsewhere, by the the inhabitants of another land.

—**Nathaniel Tarn**

See Archaeology

NEXT

Here goes...Only vitamins sneeze in Spanish. And maybe Miami is all blue...so what! Seeing as how my Kazoo has a lisp...it's up to you to tell the potato salad off.

Why me?

Let's just say I'm having a tete a tete with a few gazebos. —**D.S. Hoffman**

NIGGERDEATH, ALABAMA

Where *they* live
and/or come
from.
—**Joel Oppenheimer**

See Dumb, Wyoming
East Jesus, Indi-
ana *and*
Wayback, Ohio

Photo by Steve Fitch

1984 MISS GENERAL IDEA PAGEANT

A framing device we have framed for our own devices to contain our frame-ups. The Search for the Spirit of Miss General Idea is the ritualized pageant of creation, production, selection, presentation, competition, manipulation and revelation of that which is suitable for framing.

—General Idea

1984 MISS GENERAL IDEA PAVILLION

A framing device for accommodation. A terminal in which to rest the case of open and closed frameworks. A superstructure of containment formats like walls framing the theatre of operations. Architecture playing the part of the Master of Ceremonies directing all eyes to this stage to perform the single point of view.

—General Idea

See Frame of Reference

NOT

Not wanted in fifty states.

—Michael Brownstein

NOTHING

That of which many large varieties are found in the major cultural centers of the United States. Although the eminent Earl of Rochester, John Wilmot, has somehow ascertained that Nothing was the elder sibling of Shade and spoke to it as to a familiar, the more modern variety seems unrelated to anything in particular, itself derived from nothing and going in that direction from which it came.

Nothing, as implied above, is derived from nothing, although translators of Hindu and Buddhist literature have more often found nothing to be a prefix of Ness, unrelated to the Scottish monster, which is only nothing coincidently. In colloquial terms nothing is what one has "plenty of", and it would not behoove any compilation of contemporary learning and culture to omit.

Nothing has been called dust, void, eternity, but in reality shirks all these aliases in modern times as being metaphysical, preferring the contemporary tendency to ascribe importance to the particular and objective; hence the modern tendency to make it a noun or person, making light of it by "little" or much of it by "big", the latter of which in this increasingly hectic age has tended to thrive more than the former.

—**James Sherry**

OF

Belonging or pertaining to.

—**Nathaniel Tarn**

See Archaeology; Newfoundland

OUTLAND

Outlands are essentially travelling parks, air-borne places which visit other places. The favored form is a gentle circular valley set in a concave disk two miles across. It cruises silently among the clouds about 5,000 feet overhead. In the valley a landscape of beautiful gardens centers around a large clear-bottomed pool.

What one sees from the ground is a convex mirror reflecting the world against the sky.

The valley dish covers a vast hemispherical shell encasing

A clear, mile-high air vault carries a tropical Outland to places in the temperate winter zone.

a controlled vacuum. The vacuum is buoyant in air as an air bubble is in water. The outland breathes to ascend and descend.

The outland is invited to cities where it hovers, and people board shuttles which carry them there for the day.

They find many wonders as they wander through the quadrants of the valley. It is a world-travelling place, accumulating a rare mixture of culture. Its people, vegetation, animal life and sciences are hybrid like those of no country.

We now see the surface of earth as massive plates floating on molten rock. The outland extends this form into the atmosphere, creating a new strata composed of materials from earth below and vacuum from space above.

The 'world above' has from ancient times figured into world culture. Krishna balanced Mount Govardhana on his finger. Ama, the not-far-off, not-inaccessible-place just like Japan, was found just across the Heavenly River. Laputa, Swift's drifting magnetic island of mathematicians, and, later, Fuller's floating solar cities all foreshadow the work to be done expanding the life of the planet. Gerard O'Niell's space colonization work has extended this realm into weightless space. The outlands are intended to occupy an interzone as a sort of cultural cross-pollinator.

—**Thomas Shannon**

200

OWL

(Strigidae)
Tho owls soome fow oxcepted ore creposcolor
ond noctornol on thor hobots; thoy come forth woth
tho dosk of evonong to prowl for food, thoy wonow tho
oir woth solont ponions, thoir oars ottontive to ovory
sloght sound, ond theor oyos qoick to doscern, theor creopong
proy, on whoch thoy gloide woth noiceloss colority.
Tho orgonic ondowmonts of theose noightly moroudors ore
oin odmorable concordonce woth theor dostoined mode of liofe.
                                        —Opal L. Nations

PAIN

To us, physical pain has never been anything but the fifth
wheel of the flesh cart.
                              —Andre Breton & Paul Eluard
                                       a working by Ursule Molinaro

He came to a point.
He ate his heart.
It was sharp.
                              —Neal Abramson

born in that village they die there
without having seen
the sea the city or any mountain

they toil
on the barren soil
to feed others while they go hungry

they come into the world without hope
they leave in despair
born in that village they die there

                              —Bulent Ecevit
                              translated by Talat S. Halman

the pain, suffered with dignified pride, that a Turk brings upon himself by butting with his forehead the face of the fellow selling water out of an old petrol can to the train passengers for 10 kurus, as a punishment for his giving short change.

—**Peter Wehrli**
translated by Roger Frood

PAINTING

Agamemnon slaughtered a deer sacred to Artemis. Then Helen, the wife of his brother, Menelaos, was seduced by Paris and ran off with him to Troy. Agamemnon and Menelaos set sail for that city, intending to bring the woman back. But the goddess, Artemis, was still angry at Agamemnon. She caused contrary winds to blow, making it known through Kalchas that they would not stop until Agamemnon had sacrificed his daughter, Iphigeneia, to the memory of her sacred animal. Agamemnon chose to do this. The painter, Timanthes, was drawn to the story. He painted the moment when, as the sacrificial knife descends, the idea rises in

202

Agamemnon's mind to substitute a young doe for his daughter. The problem was in giving Agamemnon a proper expression. Timanthes' answer was to show the man hiding his face in his hands. There are other examples of this painter's ingenuity. He once set himself the problem of showing the size of a Cyclops in a very small painting. His answer was to paint the figure asleep, an unclenched hand reaching into the foreground. Nearby he placed a satyr, no bigger than the giant's thumb. Each of Timanthes' paintings permits more to be gathered than is actually there to be seen. He had immense skill in the use of color and line, but his greatest virtue was in the ingenuity by which he forced people and things to give hints of the stories that draw them out of the past for our present amazement.

—Carter Ratcliff

PAPE(R)

a sheet of fibers laid down on a fine screen from a watery suspension

The paper nautilus has no skeleton. They lie very deep in the mud at the port of Messina in the Mediterranean below where the boats are thickest. They rise, opening their elegantly colored transparent wings or sails only when unobserved. When resting they fold their sails around themselves and float along.

Barriers of land, chains of mountains determining the courses of rivers are each one boundaries between assemblages of fish

—Alison Knowles

PASCISM

ҒΛ8Хᴉ8Ⴀ
(pascist),

ҒΛ8ХᴉᴇН
(pascism);

a poet or poetry inclusive, as human consciousness, of a sufficient ammount of due respect to the absolute laws of Cosmic Honesty.

—A.M. Fine

203

PENAL COLONY

the penal colony with its blond padlocks, like a book on a young girl's lap.

—Andre Breton

Dream-time at Saint Laurent du Moroni.

—Georges Limbour
workings by Ursule Molinaro

PENGUINS

GALAPAGOS PENGUIN *(Spheniscus mendiculus).* These penguins cast out to sea from Antarctica hundreds of years ago in search of the legendary Mirror Continent of penguin folklore. According to penguin fables, if you travel far enough in any direction from the Antarctic you will arrive at an "identical land, as far away from home as one can travel without starting to head back home

again." How the penguins who originated this myth were aware of the existence of the Arctic is a mystery to all penguinologists, since no penguins have been known to make it there. One expedition decided to give up and colonize on the

Galapagos Islands, their belief in the Mirror Continent shaken by the fact that it seemed to be getting warmer as they travelled. (1)

PERUVIAN PENGUIN *(Shpeniscus humboldti).* An off-shoot of the above. This colony was a result of some Galapagos penguins getting drunk one night and deciding to "check out what's happening on the mainland." (2)

MAGELLANIC PENGUIN *(Spheniscus magellanicus).* These creatures are totally at home playing HORSE, running the mile, throwing the boomerang, competing in a Duncan around-the-world contest. And totally neurotic. They never know if they're arriving or departing, saying hello or goodbye, putting their mittens on or pulling them off. (3)

YELLOW-EYED PENGUIN *(Megadyptes antipodes).* Claims have been made that their eyes are candles which can peer into human souls, and either warm them, or set them on fire. (4)

MACARONI PENGUIN *(Eudyptes chysolophus).* Amateur philosophers, Macaronies like to think that stoicism is out of place in the Hellenistic World, Descartes was wrong, Spinoza was right, and that if Machiavelli orders one more Baked

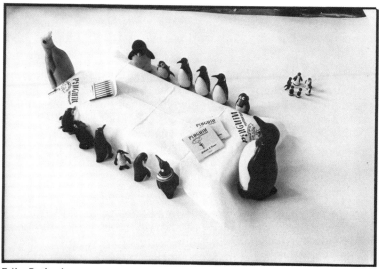

Erika Rothenberg

205

Zitti to go Nietzsche will shove a little prince up his sphincter. (5)

ROYAL PENGUIN *(Eudyptes schegeli).* Blue of blood and a pain in the ass worthy of their name, Royal penguins no longer have any governmental functions, so they tend to frequent discotheques and/or entertain the masses (via gossip and society columns) with the buffoonery of their daily lives. (6)

EMPEROR PENGUIN CHICK These tots are raised on a plush diet of maraschino cherries. Norwegian explorer Fritdtjof Nansen undertook a long Antarctic stroll for a newspaper, in tee shirt and bermudas, when his mess tent disappeared and it proved impossible to mix a decent whiskey sour for the remainder of the expedition. (7)

CHINSTRAP PENGUIN *(Pygoscelis antarctic).* This penguin was formerly known as the Doublechin penguin and took a lot of ribbing at high school dances. They now wear chinstraps, made of black and white felt, that blend in with their fur. They still take a lot of ribbing at high school dances. (8)

SNARES CRESTED PENGUIN *(Eudyptes robustus).* Nicknamed "Sticks" they are the easiest of their breed to hook on "snow." Also answering to the names Gene, Bobby, Ringo, Buddy, Ginger, and Reinhold Niebuhr (if they're close to O'D'ing) they can be seen along New Zealand's west coast banging skins during any month that has an A, E, or U in it. (9)

GENTOO PENGUIN *(Pygoscelis papua).* These are the gentlest of the penguins and make for the majority of penguin psychotherapists. It is their duty to deal with the penguins' identity problem at not quite being fish nor birds. "Just think, you can fly underwater, the best of both worlds," Gentoo penguins tell their patients. Group therapy sessions, with hundreds of participants huddled together, have been widely photographed and drawn. (10)

LITTLE BLUE PENGUIN *(Eudyptula minor).* As one acquainted with the ironies of animal-naming would suspect, the Little Blue penguin is not actually blue. Ironically, however, it *is* little. The term "blue" refers to this breed's proclivity for becoming major league umpires. In a migratory pattern from April to October, these "Umpire Penguins" tend to keep to themselves in order to avoid mingling with known gamblers, the players, or killer whales. They generally travel in disguises, but an attentive desk clerk can pick them out because they make many calls for buckets of ice, and never order champagne. (11)

ERECT-CRESTED PENGUIN *(Eudyptes sclateri)*. Known for their distinctive and prodigious tufts, these penguins have a reputation for giving incredible head. (12)

—Harry Greenberg & Alan Ziegler

PERMANENCE

The word "permanent" means permanently dead because nothing can be permanently alive.

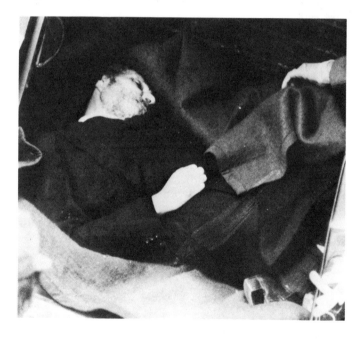

See Aesthetic

—Les Levine

207

PHOTO

my surprise that one cannot recognize the face on the photo in the passport of the Iraqi's wife, because it is covered by a veil as is the Arab custom.

—Peter Wehrli
translated by Roger Frood

POEM

The flow of "our larger self."

—Tom Marshall

Answer to a question one didn't know one had asked oneself.

—Joel Oppenheimer

Ordering of psychic overload.

—Tom Marshall

POET

A painter's poor cousin.

—Dick Higgins

PORCELAIN

The Pleasures of Porcelain are enhanced by their 'Perhapness'. The fragility of their Projected vision is also Perspicacious. One comes to admire their 'Piecehood,' which like a Piebald Pigeon is reckless on the Perilous heights of a mantlePiece. Porcelain is doomed to remain Private until it becomes Public outside the Pantry, i.e. upon entering a museum to be Participated in. Porcelain knows no single Persia, but exists in all the Punjabs of the senses, delicate as a Persimmon, slim as a Panther, impeccable as a Puritan.

—Barbara Guest

POST-MINIMALISM

A lean-to.

—Donald Kuspit

PRAISE

CONCERT PIANIST:
If you have just performed a piece by a great composer, you must discern whether the praise is directed at you or

the piece. If someone remarks on the exquisite beauty of the composition, you should agree, rather than thank, since it is possible that the listener is avoiding telling you how lousy you were. If the praise is clearly directed at your performance, you should thank the listener and share the praise by saying, "I had such great material to work with." Sharing praise is a wholesome and often necessary aspect of dealing with praise, as we shall see in other categories, and all praiseworthy people should know when and how to do it.

SECOND BASEMAN:

Praise for a short-to-second-to-first double play must always be shared with your keystone partner, in the interest of fairness and team harmony. If you are especially interested in team morale, you will also mention that the pitcher did a marvelous job of keeping the ball down. While running around the bases after hitting a home run, tip your hat. Fans appreciate this kind of feedback. But only tip your hat in your home park; tipping one's hat at an away game will likely be interpreted as rubbing it in, and you will be branded a sore winner.

PRO FULLBACK:

Never ever accept praise without sharing it with the line: "I couldn't have gone nowhere if those boys up front didn't open up the turf," is adequate. Failure to do this might result in opposing uniforms getting blindside shots at you during future games. Coaches, who don't make as much money as you do, merit a share of the praise, especially your old college and high school coaches or the guy from the drug rehabilitation program who saw you beating up a cop while you were in high school and said, "Son you could be getting paid for stuff like that."

TEACHER:

A particularly tough profession for evaluating praise. It all must be sprinkled with generous helpings of salt. Praise from a student during the course of a semester may have something to do with the fact that you will be grading that student; praise after the semester may have something to do with the student's plans to use you you as a reference. (This also holds true for praise

during a semester from a student in a pass/fail course.)
Praise from a former student now successful in his/her
field can usually be taken at face value, but there is always
the possibility that the former student feels sorry for you
because you are still at the place he/she got so far away
from, or that a major magazine will soon be doing a profile
on your former student and will be digging for dirt.

SHORT ORDER COOK:
Don't expect much praise. People in this society rarely
have much to say about a hamburger that has been
cooked to perfection (which is no mean trick when there
are seven on the grill). And, unlike the waiter or waitress,
praise does not take the form of a big monetary tip. This
job falls in the category of "self-praise"; it is one of the
professions where praising oneself is not only permissable,
but necessary. So, on a particularly good flip of an omelet,
don't hesitate to say, under your breath, "Bingo," or
"Bullseye."

POLICE:
There have been stories of praise taking the form of a
shiny apple or a crisp tenspot; if this is the case with you,
it is especially important that you learn how to take the
compliment: very discreetly. Be careful not to talk about
this praise with other officers who have not personally been
praised in a similar way, and especially not with members
of the press, who may perceive it as for something other
than excellence of performance. You will be praised by
society when you risk your life, and praise is particularly
strong if you lose it. But do not expect much conventional
praise. Think of yourself as an athlete always playing an
away game.

WRITER:
There are many varied responses to praise, such as:
"What does this person want from me?" Or, "What did
this person once get from me?" Praise from friends
should be taken about as seriously as criticism from
enemies. It is always good to vary this routine a little
when you're the one doing the criticizing or praising: If
you criticize a friend once in awhile, it helps make your
praise mean a little more, and occasionally praising an
enemy might result in future retaliation being a bit less

brutal than otherwise. Praise from someone you don't
know has the most chance of being meaningful. If this
comes face to face and embarrasses you, you can show
your own surprise at the work: "Yeah, it was strange,
it just sort of wrote itself." This is known as "leaning on
the muse," and has the side effect of taking you off the
hook if you have written something particularly nasty
about someone standing close by. Never say, "I know,"
when someone praises your work, because it makes them
feel unoriginal. To receive praise when needed badly and
it is not forthcoming, praise someone else's work. Chances
are they will respond with, "Thanks...you're terrific too."
This is the "I love you too" approach. If they double
cross you and respond with, "I know," then you can
amend your statement with something like, "Yeah, I
think it's terrific how you capture Keats' voice so perfectly in one poem and then sound just like Bukowski in the
next."

ADDENDUM: PRAISE AND MONEY
   Praise and money sometimes come together, but you
might have to make a choice between the two—especially
if you are involved with the arts, where artistic achievement generally receives more praise than money, while
artistically inferior works might get the opposite. (The
athletics industry is purer in this regard.)
   People who make a lot of money often get praised for
their ability to make money, and damned for their way of
doing it. If you can't decide whether to shoot for praise or
money, ask yourself this question: Would you prefer to
make art or own it?

—Alan Ziegler

See Money

PRAYER
Happy the one
stepping lightly over
paper hearts of men

and out of the way
of mind-locked reality
the masks of sincerity

—Mimi Gross Grooms

he steps from his place at the glib cafe
to find himself in the word
of the infinite

embracing it
in his mind
with his heart

parting his lips for it
lightly
day into night

transported like a tree
to a riverbank
sweet with fruit in time

his heart unselfish
whatever he does
ripens

while bitter men turn dry
blowing in the wind
like yesterday's paper

unable to stand
in the gathering
light

they fall
faded masks
in love's spotlight

burning hearts of paper
unhappily
locked in their own glare

but My Lord opens
his loving one
to breathe embracing air.

—David Rosenberg

PREFERENCES

From the time that I lived and traveled in Mexico, I have
compiled this list of preferences. Most of these will surely
change in time, but at the moment, here they are. Favorite
small plaza: the Jardin de la Union in Guanajuato. Favorite
states: Veracruz, Oaxaca, and Chiapas. Favorite seaside
resort: still Acapulco, although most will disagree. Fa-
orite university: none, the universities are disappointing.
Favorite red wine: *Noblejo.* It is light and smooth, comparable to a good claret. Best train ride: Chihuahua to Los Mo-
chis. Best post office: Oaxaca. Favorite large patio: the one
in Bellas Artes, a run-down former monastery in San Miguel
de Allende. Favorite statue: the Diana on the Paseo de la
Reforma in Mexico City. Favorite pottery: the greenish-
glaze from Michoacan. Favorite highway: the scenic CN-195,
from Villahermosa to near San Cristobal de las Casas. Favorite large plazas: the ones in Puebla, Morelia, and Oaxaca.
Favorite coastal town: Campeche, still quiet and unspoiled.
Favorite cheeses: locally-made *queso de Oaxaca,* usually
called *quesillo* there, and also *queso de Chihuahua.* Favorite town with many Americans: at this time, San Miguel de
Allende, although there are many tourists and it is relatively expensive. Favorite all-around place: Mexico City, although most will disagree. Favorite bookstore: the Libreria
Anglo-Americana in Mexico City, with its fine stock of

213

Penguin Books. Best English-language library: the Biblioteca Benjamin Franklin in Mexico City. Favorite small library: the Biblioteca Publica in San Miguel de Allende. Favorite basketry: that made by the Seri Indians of Sonora. Favorite small cities: the state capitals of Morelia and Queretaro. Also, Oaxaca, although the reaction to some of the young Americans has made it less pleasant. Favorite park: the beautiful Parque Nacional in Uruapan.

—Kenneth Gangemi

PRIDE

Its pride is the way a being flexes itself to demonstrate (feel, imprint) its own particular existence. The same holds true for all animal orders, even insect life. Each is self-centered, so that first and formost every species is concerned with *a conspicuous radiation of its pride.* Notice of intent to vacate the taste of democracy.

—Michael Brownstein

PROFESSIONAL ARTIST

A duplicator en masse of what he once did out of love or necessity. The surest sign of a professional is that he laments his financial worries to his stockbroker and his accountant.

—Dick Higgins

See Amateur Artist

PROFIT

Between the apple & the eye, right there is profit. The rain will not cause it to rot along the sills or in the porch steps of any farmhouse abandoned to the strangulation of weeds. Even when the rain is snow, profit is safe from any weakness in the rafters, and it's all the same that later there will simply be a hump in the ground and later still a depression, to be avoided; then, finally, a leveling-off. Perhaps the lawn will be a little greener here, enough to notice—and greener yet where the barn had stood, the chicken house.

One tree is saved in the orchard—its apples smaller than ever: too small to bother with—and bitter. They fall on the fine grey gravel in the drive. Children throw them straight down. Birds pick them full of holes to let the gnats in, until the first hard frost.

214

The only possible regret is the children won't see
that blue sky through the rafters, the hornets' nest with its
single hole pointing down, round as the "o" in profit.

—Gerald Cable

PROPHECY

Tyre, Phoenicia

Pick up your lyre
and walk through the city
whore no one remembers

pick the strings gently
sing all your songs over
until you're remembered: desired

Once again Tyre
will be paid handsomely
like a whore

open for hire
to every self-serving kingdom
on the leering face of earth

like a royal taxi
much of the world's commerce
done inside her

its traffic
passing through her
heavily breathing

but her trade her obscene profits
will become a true vehicle
this time re-opened

to the core
filled with light
nothing held back

nothing under the table
no self-reproducing capital
no closet deals

no treasures secretly hidden
but totally opened for love
for pure service   a wealth untouched

all the desperate merchandising
of life and blood and the air of song
all the face-saving prostitution

will be a way for the Lord
the profits and losses a highway
prosperity will build a house

for those who live in his presence
who breathe in his air
there will be food for all

all human desire
will be clothed
with dignity

all will be moved
to fill their place at his table
to sing his grace.

—David Rosenberg

PSYCHOPATH

Incorrectly,any person possessed of a sick mind. Thus,
often used abusively.

   Correctly, a person whose way of life is based on a grand
show of good intentions that covers up a basic insincerity
and fraudulence. Psychopaths are clever, charming, irre-
sponsible, emotionally shallow, flattering, double-crossing,
evasive, impulsive, arrogant, opportunistic, and fanatic.
They are excellently suited to be swindlers, con men, zealous
patriots, and political leaders of the sort that rises to sudden,
brilliant—though short-lived—prominence.

—Armand Schwerner & Donald M. Kaplan

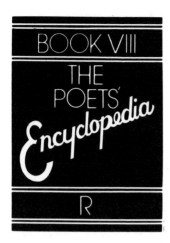

BOOK VIII
THE
POETS'
Encyclopedia

R

RACE JOHNSONG

A group of runners, also dashers, who conduct a thrice-yearly dance with self-provided music, the purpose of which is to exceed what they have themselves previously set as a record. Originally popular among Indians of the Athabaskan tribes, now preempted by the Avantis of the eastern regions of the US, particularly in the Manhatta region. Leader always has to have "John" as part of his name, either given or familial.   **—Carol Berge**

RADIO

It is possible to set aside radio time because radio is a function of originality. It cannot repeat itself. You are about to go to sleep. Fantasy isn't everything, but there really is a principle of inwardness. Radio gives the listener the feeling of absolute, deep-rooted rest. It has everything needed for speaking in solitude. Radio needs no face.
                                                   —Michael Brownstein

REALITY

"Electrical stimulation of the brain has triggered experiences that cannot be distinguished as being different from real."
In other words, the brain is not capable of distinguishing between the real and the illusory. "By appropriate electrical

stimulation of cell aggregates of living human brains, phe-
nomena can be evoked which have reminiscent aspects (in
some instances memorylike in the old sense of the term),
characteristics which at times rival ordinary afferent sensory
stimulation in their vivid insistence and intrusion upon the
stream of consciousness, and at still other times rival effective
responses appropriate to the content of the phenomenon
elicited." For the brain there is no illusion. Reality is whatever the brain is doing. Electrical stimulation can activate
programs of prior experience. In the process of decoding
and deciphering the functions of neural activity, it seems a
realizable possibility to be able to enjoy such pleasures as
the orgasm a hundred, a thousand times a day.

—**John Brockman**

Oh, practical end of my poetry!
Because of you I can't overcome
the ingenuousness that dims my prestige;

because of you my tongue cracks in
anxiety, which I have to stifle by talking.
I look in my heart only for what's there.

To this I'm reduced: when I write
poetry, it's to defend myself, to fight,
compromising myself, renouncing

all my ancient dignity: thus,
defenseless, my elegiac heart appears, which
I'm ashamed of, and tired, but alive,

my tongue reflects the imaginings
of the son who'll never be a father...
Meanwhile, one by one, I lost my circle

of poets with dry naked faces,
divine goats with the hard features
of Po Valley fathers in whose sparse

ranks only pure relations of
passion and thought matter.
Dragged away by the obscure

events of my life. Ah, to begin again from scratch!
alone, like a cadaver in its grave!
Behold this morning, in which I hope

only in light...yes, in the light that softens
with its springtime joy
these days of my Canossa.

Here I am in the glow of an old April,
kneeling in confession,
till the end of my life.

May this light give me breath,
unwind its fragrant gold thread
on a world, like death, reborn.

Then...but, in the sunshine is my sole delight...
those bodies, in their summer pants a bit
worn at the groin by habitual caresses of

rough, dusty hands...The sweaty
gatherings of male adolescents,
at the edges of meadows, leaning against the fronts

of houses in the scorching dusk...
The explosive excitement of the festive city
the peace of the countryside flowering again...

And them, their faces vivid
or dark with shadows, like wolf pups,
in lazy raids, in lascivious

ingenuousness...What napes! Such dark
glances! That need to smile,
in their slightly stupid conversations

of innocents, or as a challenge
to the rest of the world that receives them:
sons: Ah, what God guides them

so sure, along the barest roads,
to the Castelli, to the beaches, to the gates
of the city in the predictable, ancient desires

of him who is confident he will arrive
at death after he has truly lived:
that the life that fell to his lot

fell fairly, and that nothing will be lost.
Yes, they're humble. And what will later be
their mediocre way of fulfilling

themselves (their destiny is mediocrity)
is just dawning
over unknown trees, in which nature

is only beginning to germinate, in a stasis
of supreme purity and courage.
Of course, by now, they've been invaded

by an evil inherited from
their fathers—my coevals, dark race.
But in what do they place their hopes? what ray

of light strikes them, in those faces
where the joining of hair at the forehead,
the forelocks, the waves have a grace

that's more than corporeal?...Sweetly rebellious
and, at the same time, content with their future as fathers:
that's what makes them so beautiful!

The eyes of even the tough, the sad,
the thievish have the knowing sweetness
of those who have understood: orderly

squadrons of flowers in the chaos of existence.
In reality, I am the boy, they're
the adults. I, who by the excess of my presence,

never crossed the border between the love
for life, and life...
I gloomy with love, and all around me, the chorus

of the happy, for whom reality is friendly.
Thousands of them. It's impossible to love only one of them.
Each has his own ancient or new

beauty, which all share: dark
or blond, slim or heavy, it is
the world which I love in him; and within him—

vision of fruitless and purest love—
I join together the generations,
the body, sex, I sink

each time—in   sweet expansions,
in   breaths of juniper—into history,
which is always living, in each

day, each millennium, my love
is only for the woman: child and mother.
Only to her do I pledge all my heart.

As for my contemporaries, the sons in tribes
scattering marvelously over plains
and hills, in alleyways and squares, for them

only my flesh burns. Yet, at times,
I think that nothing else has the wonderful
purity of this feeling. Better death

than to renounce it! I must defend
this enormity of desperate tenderness,
which, like the world, is my birthright.

Perhaps no one has lived at such heights
of desire—funereal anxiety that
replenishes me, as the sea freshens its breeze.

Slopes,   hills, grass a thousand years old,
landslides of flowers or garbage,   branches
dry or glistening with dew, the air

of the seasons with their little walls,
ancient or recent, in the sunlight...all this
envelopes me and (you laugh!) my young friends

in whom no act is dishonest
because their desires are void of tragedy:
because their sex is whole and fresh.

I couldn't, otherwise. Only the wholesome,
normal, healthy son
can kindle my dark

dazzling thought: only thus do I resemble him
in the infinite reascertaining
his groin's lily-like secret.

And a thousand times this act must be repeated:
because not to repeat it means to feel
death like a frenetic pain

unequaled in the living world...
I don't conceal it, have never concealed anything:
the unrepressed love that invades me,

the love for my mother, has no room
for hypocrisy or cowardice! Nor am I right
simply because I'm different; I don't know

your God; I am an atheist; prisoner
only of my love, but in all else I'm free,
in every judgment, every passion.

I am a free man! The honest food
of liberty is tears; well, then, I'll weep.
It's the price of my "libito far licito,"

yes, but love is worth everything I have.
Sex, death, political passion,
these are simple objects to which I give

my elegiac heart...My life
possesses nothing else. I could tomorrow
naked as a monk leave the wordly

game, concede victory
to the infamous...My soul would
surely have lost nothing!

for the fatality of inalienable
existence, race, universe,
is enough for anyone, even if one is without

brotherhood in the world, because different.
Therefore the derision   and   insinuations
of pitiable racists run through

one's reality like the unreal
sounds of the dead. In my life,
sex and passions have this reality...

And, certainly, it doesn't give me joy.
Its predestined forms are obsessive:
"repression makes me an S.S. man,

or a Mafioso..." and this—it's enormous,
I know—is what I am; as a young-son-candid-
saintly-barbaric-angel, I followed,

for a time, in the footsteps leading
to Reactionary Revolt
(this was the lowest period of the grand

itinerary of a life in Italy),
blond executioner or mud-hearted killer,
like a disciple...of bloodthirsty

bourgeois Hitler or the strong son
of the poor, Salvatore Giuliano...—conformity
that was saving me, like a blind

flight. All this was only the chrism,
a shadow that disappeared from my life.
There remained the inclination toward schism,

a natural need to hurt myself at the always
open wound. A shaping of each
relationship-to-the-world-that-calls-me

into the form of my filial
sadism, masochism: for which I was not born,
and here I'm alone, like a nameless

animal, by nothing consecrated,
belonging to no one,
free, with a liberty that's massacred me.

So that not I but that man that I communicate
must conclude desperately that
he's an outcast from the assembly

of *others: all men,* without distinction,
*all the normal,*who constitute this life.
And I seek, as revenge or retaliation,

alliances that have no other reason for being
than otherness, meekness, impotent violence:
the Jews...the blacks...any outcast humanity...

And this was how, as a man outside
humanity, unconsciously under a spell, or like a spy
or   confused hunter of benevolence,

I was tempted by holiness. Poetry was how.
The *good* witch who witch-hunts
out of terror discovered democracy...

It wasn't a gift from heaven! The dreadful alliances
with virile comrades/unconscious blackmailers,
the derisive laughs with which the monster gave

proof of calm health and secure loves,
ready to torture and kill other monsters
in order not to be recognized—all this was

suddenly out and away from me (and here and now
they recognize themselves, those who hate me, a
public fact, pitiful fascists), one evening

in a young woods, among indissoluble stains
of violets on the stream's edge, among vineyards
or the evening lights of the villages, under virgin clouds

(in the Emilia of my destiny, in the Friuli of my deities)...
Terror won out. I mean that the terror of
reality and of solitude was greater

than that of society. Bitter youth,
prey to that untreatable feeling
of nonbeing that still enslaves me...

For I shall arrive at the end of my
life without having passed
the essential test, the experience

that unites all men and gives them
their so-sweetly definite idea
of brotherhood, at least in the acts of love!

Like a blind man, to whom something that
coincides with life itself will have
escaped at death—light followed

hopelessly but which smiles on everyone,
like the simplest thing in the world—
something he will never be able to share in.

I shall die without having known the profound
meaning of being a man, born into a single
life   to which nothing in eternity corresponds.

A blind man, a monster, nothing in life can
ever really console him: but at the irremediable
shameful point, in the terror of the

ultimate hour—he'll be a...guinea pig,
no longer even a man! Absurd
—to the point of being unendurable, of screaming in rage,

of howling, like an animal whose cry
is the cry of an innocent protesting
an injustice of which he's the victim—

absurd this prenatal order, this
predestination, in which he has no say
and which has nothing to do with his honest,

ancient soul...Within the wombs
of the mothers, blind children are born,
longing for the light, misshapen,

full of joyous instincts:
and they go through life in darkness and shame.
One can resign oneself to it—and the living

fetuses, wretched Erinyes, at any moment
in their lives, know how to be silent, to pretend.
The *others* always say that they shouldn't

burden *them.* And they obey. And thus their whole
life takes on a completely different color.
And the world—the innocent world!—rejects them.

But I speak...of the world—when instead
I should speak of Italy, or rather
an Italy, of which you, reader of

my verses, are, with me, the offspring:
that physical history in which you verify yourself.
I called it "innocent," the world, I,

I, the blind, martyred son.
But if I look around me at these remnants
of a history that, for centuries, has produced

only serfs...this Apparition
in which reality has no form other
than its own brutal repetition...

what an...expressionistic scene! I think of a judgment
suffered pointlessly...the togas...the sad authorities of the South...
behind the faces of the judges—in whom vice

is the vice of suffering in
poverty—one could see only the impossibility
of escaping an obscure reality of blood relationships,

a crude morality, a provincial lack of experience...
Those Teatro dell'Arte foreheads,
those obedient, persistent onager's pitiable

eyes, those lowered ears,
those words that, to mask
the void, swell up to recite the role

of paternal menace and flowery indignation!
Ah, I don't know how to hate: and therefore I know
I can't describe them with the ferocity necessary

to poetry. I'll speak only with pity of that
Calabrian face, with the features both of a child
and a skull, who used dialect

with the humble, scholastic language with the grand...
who was listening carefully, humanely
and, in the meantime, within his unspoken and nefarious

interior forums, was hatching his plan
of the timid whom fear makes ruthless.
At his side are two other easily recognizable faces,

faces from the street or a crowded bar,
the weak, barely healthy faces of
the prematurely old, of the

jaundiced, of the bourgeois whose life
certainly has no tears in it, but not ignoble, no,
not at all deprived of human features,

in the pugent black of their eyes, in the pallor
of the foreheads tortured by the first
ferocious signs of aging...A fourth envoy of the Lord

—married, surely; surely protected by a circle
of respectable colleagues in his provincial
town—curdling in the sigh of someone

sick in the heart or viscera—
was sitting by himself on an isolated bench, like someone
preparing for a premediated estrangement

And in front of these, the champion: who sold
his soul to the devil, flesh and bone.
Classical character! I'd seen his face

some months earlier, and it had looked different:
the peasant face of a coarse-grained young
man, balding, pallid,

but with a professional dignity.
Now a blush was deforming him,
like an old red scab

on his skin. The depraved light
in his eyes was that of the guilty.
His hate for my person was hate

for the object of that guilt, that is,
hate for his conscience.
He wasn't dishonest enough. His imagination

wasn't big enough to conceive an experience
of ignorance and blackmail. The bourgeoisie
is the devil; should one sell it one's soul

without compensation? Certainly not; one must
adopt its culture, reciting
like a Pater Noster the shame

of a purely formal exordium,
of a mystifying clause...
And to be rhetorical means to hate,

to be uncultured means to have lost
deliberately all respect for man.
The old love for the ideal is reduced to

a desperate lying to oneself
and believing the lies.
But the light of the eye remains, obsessed

accusers! There, in that drop of light,
in that elusive glance, livid,
guilty, was your truth.

I know that an interior will of mine
leads me into relationships with you,
but that's a secret of the self,

or God, if you wish. To you it will be said:
"You don't count, you're the symbols
of millions of men, of a society.

And it—not you, its automatons—condemns me.
Well then, I'm content with being a monster.
Or do we want to deceive the spirit? Men

who condemn other men in the name of nothing:
because Institutions *are* nothing when
they've lost all force, the maiden force

of Revolutions—because the Morality
of common sense, of a passive
community with no remaining reality, is nothing.

You, men of form—humble because of
cowardice, obsequious because of timidity—
you are people: in you and me, let the relationship

consummate itself: in you, by arid hate,
in me, by knowledge. But, about the society
of which you are inexpressive rhapsodists,

I have something quite different to say: not as a Marxist
anymore, or, perhaps yes for this moment only
—since the rapture of the Authors

of the Apocalypse is mythified in a fire
outside of time: My loves—
I'll shout—are a terrible weapon;

why don't I use it? Nothing's more terrible
than being different. Exposed every moment
—shouted ceaselessly—incessant

exception—madness unrestrained
like a fire—contradiction
by which all justice is desecrated.

Oh, blacks, Jews, poor hosts
of the marked and different, born by innocent
wombs into sterile

springtimes, of worms, of serpents,
horrendous without their knowing, condemned
to be atrociously meek, childishly violent,

hate! tear apart the world of well-born men!
Only a sea of blood can save
the world from its bourgeois dreams, destined

to make it more and more unreal!
Only a revolution that slaughters
these dead ones can deconsecrate their evil!"

This is what a prophet would shout who doesn't have
the strength to kill a fly—whose strength
lies in his degrading difference.

Only when this has been said, or shouted,
will my fate be able to free itself:
and my discourse on reality begin.

—Pier Paolo Pasolini
translated by Norman MacAfee & Luciano Martinego

REGIONAL ART

An increasingly popular term for any art that is not econ-
omical for metropolitan art galleries with their high overhead.

—Dick Higgins

REPETITION

the repetition of the pronouncement, "This is the Orient,"
by the long-legged blue-jeans Belgian girl when a camel
dozes so close to the track that we all fear the train wheels
will sever the head from its neck; to which it should be added that the mere sight of the camel brings the Belgian girl to
say this, rather than the fact that the camel was almost be-
headed by the wheels of the train.

—Peter Wehrli
translated by Roger Frood

REPRESENTATION

There was a farmer who wasn't quite sure that his cow was
at the end of its representation; thinking that it might be a
larger beast of another sort, if fully inflated.

That's stupid, you stupid person, said his wife.

How do we know the cow isn't an elephant? said the
farmer.

Because it's a cow, you stupid person, said his wife.

But how do we know that the cow is not simply a
station on a journey still to be completed? said the farmer.

The farmer attached a bicycle pump to one of the
nipples of the cow's milk bag, and began to pump.

229

And sure enough, the cow began to swell: its legs got thicker, its horns leaned forward and swung down into tusks. And the more he pumped the more the cow became an elephant.

Look, look, screamed the farmer to his wife, I knew there was more.

But his wife had returned to the house to bake a mitten pie.

When the elephant was fully pumped up he ran to the house to tell his wife. The cow's an elephant, the cow's an elephant, he screamed, come see.

But when they got to the barn the cow was still just a cow with an irritated nipple.

His wife said, you stupid person.

No no, I am not a stupid person, it's just that the elephant sprung a leak. I'll find the leak and pump it up into an elephant again. I'll begin by checking its anus, which has always seemed a bit gassy...

—Russell Edson

REVIEW

A journalistic statement about what the work being discussed is not and about who the reviewer is.

—Dick Higgins

RIVER

Any kind of news, change, misfortune, surprise shows up in the river. It floats by—pollution, etc. We are witnesses on the banks. Involuntary. We wake up one morning and it's there, as in the idea of being downriver when, say, a corpse floats by: "They must be having a fight up there." From the river comes the idea of cause and effect: "She tried to burn it in the stove or drown it in the river—nothing helped."

—Michael Brownstein

ROACHES

Let me tell you how I feel about roaches. I don't really *like* roaches, but I don't really hate roaches either. Just so long as they do what they're supposed to do. I mean like—it really doesn't bother me much to see them scurrying around when you turn the lights on. But when you turn the lights on and they *don't* scurry around—that really pisses me off. And—optimistically speaking—I certainly prefer them to—say—tarantulas.

—**Joe Brainard**

ROCKET

the fact that in the Turkish villages the mosques look no different from the ordinary houses, except that a minaret towers up out of the tiled roof and reminds me of space rockets about to take-off at Cape Kennedy; however that holds good only for tiled roofs, on domed roofs they remain for me as minarets.

—**Peter Wehrli**
translated by Roger Frood

RUSH

the yapping hoot of the train, sounding like coughing, to announce the departure from Crveni Crst, and the precipitous rush with which all those who hurried to the water tap with empty water bottles, leap up again with them half empty.

—**Peter Wehrli**
translated by Roger Frood

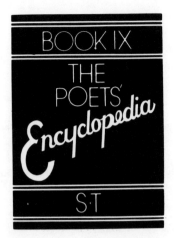

S

"S", nineteenth letter of the alphabet, letter in the shape of an angry cobra or a dead man's road across a mountain ledge. Deceptively soft, Beware! for it spits back in pronunciation, snarls when you whisper it. I do not trust "S". Though Sabbath and Saint appear within its cloak, I neither trust Sunday nor Saturday (the two common sabbaths, and the two days with the highest instance of reported crimes of violence) nor do I trust saint, as saint is so often an historical fiction meant to pacify one political/religious grouping of peoples or another and created by a minority who have but to gain at the suggestion of canonization.

"S" is for Sweet as in Sugar, that heavenly substance hiding a Souer disposition. Sugar is probably the singular most addictive generation-spanning drug we know, a one way ticket to diabetes, tooth decay, hypoglycemia, and yet who takes candy from a baby is a monster, who forgets to send it on Mother's day is guilty of uncaring. And then there's the 1920's flapper from Mississippi, the belle with Susceptible Smile and five 'ole boy' escorts to every dance ..."Sorry Sugah, ah sent the mink baack for a Sable, its evah so much waaarmmah and ah get soo cold on the veranda in the night wind". To replace sugar with Saccharin is to invite peptic ulcer or cancer. Spices do much for the delight of eating while eating out the lower intestine and Salt may replenish you in the summer heat but beware the Swollen tongue, the hardened artery and the failing heart.

Sons commit more murders than daughters, and Sisters deceptions are legion against their little brothers.

The Sun brings delight and growth to the earth, but it is the fire which may consume us. Summer is the season of the body's freedom from the burden of cold...in temperate climates it brings unemployment and irritability to our urban Slums. Swimmers never learn, and the instances of drowning peak in mid-July.....and what could be more predatory than the Shark whose busy season begins with the crowding of beaches. Then September lingers in the death of summer, a month of nostalgia and tears.

"S" is for Sorrow.....

And Satan, prince of darknes.....and Sin, the Smallpox Scar upon the Soul, and Specter of foreboding, a Spirit best avoided. "S" Stinks with death.

To Suffer may be the noble stuff of which causes are made, but suffering is pain, and for its own sake speaks masochistic. To Seek is to never know, and Safe in the Security of Sanctuary is a lie. The first act of war is to topple the temples of the enemy. So much for sanctuary.

Basic excreta, though a purifying agent to the body, is reduced to four letter profanity....Shit and Snot express contempt. The Semen of Sperm when mixed with the egg begin our existence, and yet are deemed Shocking in drawing and class rooms. A Sucking infant at its mother's breast equates with tender innocence in literature and painting, but he who sucks or she who sucks or that which sucks has less to be admired than a Spider. And a Sucker is everyone's fool.

Power, regeneration, pleasure beyond intellect, "S" is for Sex, what marries and divides us. Even the word itself is Suspect... leaping out of the throat, then hanging in air like a hornet. Consider the spelling, the danger of "S", the commonality of "E", and "X" which cancels out, hides or forgets. It's as if we're all in the middle, sandwiched between danger and obscurity. Oh, but then we say it's worth it...to make love is to taste delight, to know the beloved by entering and being entered is to join our desires with compassion, to trust, to make ourselves vulnerable, to be generous, to give and take pleasure for the joy and gratification of our partner as well as for ourselves. And yet this primal function of our nature is the constant butt of jokes and method of

233

debasement....To Screw (a bastardization of the noun, screw, 'a cylindrical rod' and the verb, screw, 'to apply pressure, to tighten') is to sexually couple by conquest, to undermine the will or take something away from the partner if only for the momentary release, a kind of violent masturbation flung upon another member of the human race, a loveless task. And the one who screws to defame is called Seducer and Sadist, a Siren or Satyr, a Sybarite.

And so I do not trust "S"....behind the Sympathy, the Sensual play about the lip, the whispery venomous sound made with tongue projecting.....lies the Sharp, double-bladed Sword....the undercurrent of a Scream. I do not trust "S".

—Frances Whyatt

SACRED

—Alan Ziegler

SAN FRANCISCO ARTIST

A San Francisco term for any artist who once spent the day (or more) in San Francisco.

—Dick Higgins

SAUTEING

As a man sauteed his hat he was thinking of how his mother used to saute his father's hat, and how grandmother used to saute grandfather's hat.

Add some garlic and wine and it doesn't taste like hat at all, it tastes like underwear.

And as he sauteed his hat he thought of his mother sauteing his father's hat, and grandmother sauteing grandfather's hat, and wished he had somehow gotten married so he'd have someone to saute his hat; sauteing is such a lonely thing...

—Russell Edson

SELF-ALLERGIC

I heard of a person who has a son who's allergic to his own germs. If he sneezes when he has a cold, then breathes in right away, he has a violent allergic reaction.

The person who told me this didn't have an explanation but offered an analogy instead.

Take your spit. All day long you swallow your spit without giving it much thought. Try spitting into a glass, then drinking it. A lot of people are very reluctant.

He claimed this was because the spit was no longer a part of you; that you'd separated it from yourself; that it wasn't you, not any more. Like the boy and his germs.

—Tom Ahern

SELF-ORGANIZATION

The basis of living systems is self-organization. The brain organizes its activity in a continuous fashion, always in the present. It incarnates the operations it has performed as operant circuits. It exists and can be talked about only in operant terms on what it does. What it does depends on information it constantly receives informing it about changes in itself, environmental forces, the physiological functions of the body. It uses this information to adapt, to change, to maintain its stability and continuity. Information is not to be confused with the source of information. It is not power. It is an abstraction. It is not energy. It is an invention.

—John Brockman

SELF-REFLEXIVITY

See Abyss Structure

SELLING

A husband and wife discover that their children are fakes.
Mildred is not a real daughter.
Nor is Frederick a real son.
But then the husband discovers that his wife is not a real wife, even as she discovers that he is not a real husband.
So it's all right if a fake husband and a fake wife have fakes for children.
Even their neighbors are fakes...

Someplace the originals, the original husband and wife, with their original children, Mildred and Frederick, and their original neighbors, live unaware that their copies are being sold for pretty near the same price that they're being sold for...

—Russell Edson

SEPTEMBER 27, 1943

The birth of Ray DiPalma, who gathered and edited these—among other—"birthday notations."

THE UNFORTUNATE TRAVELLER
Thomas Nashe
Stationer's Register 27 September 1593

September 27th 1666. Up, and with my wife as far as the Temple, and there she to the mercer's again and I to look out Penny, my tailor, to speak for a cloak and cassock for my brother, who is coming to town; and I will have him in a canonical dress, that he may be the fitter to go abroad with me.

—Samuel Pepys

236

September 27, 1777
Distant lightening. We had but little rain, only the skirts of
the storm. The dry weather, which was of infinite service to
the country after so wet a summer, might fairly be said to
last eight weeks; three of which had no rain at all, & much
sun-shine.

—Gilbert White

27th September 1820
If he recovers his strength he will write to you. I think he
wishes to say to you that your images from nature are too
much introduced without being called for by a particular
sentiment . . . his remark is only applicable now and then
when he feels as if the description overlaid and stifled that
which ought to be the prevailing idea.

—Edward Taylor

Wednesday, September 27, 1826. It is a strange atmosphere,
warm, damp, rainy, then fair again, all in less than two
hours, which was the time consumed by my early walk. On
my return soon after eight I found four of the ladies all
drawing in the library; that in this country is generally the
sitting-room. At about ten we had breakfast, when we
talked much of duels, and of my friend Clay and crazy
Randolph. Much is unknown about our country, and yet
all are deeply interested in it. To-morrow I am off to
Liverpool again; how much I shall enjoy being once again
with the charming Rathbones.

—John James Audubon

September 27th, 1833.— In the evening I set out on an
excursion to St. Fe, which is situated nearly three hundred English miles from Buenos Ayres, on the banks of
the Parana. The roads in the neighbourhood of the city,
after the rainy weather, were extraordinarily bad. I should
never had thought it possible for a bullock waggon to have
crawled along: as it was, they scarcely went at the rate of
a mile an hour, and a man was kept ahead, to survey the
best line for making the attempt. The bullocks were terribly jaded: it is a great mistake to suppose that with im-
proved roads, and an accelerated rate of travelling, the
sufferings of the animals increase in the same proportion.
We passed a train of waggons and a troop of beasts on
their way to Mendoza. The distance is about 580 geo-

graphical miles, and the journey is generally performed in 50 days. These waggons are very long, narrow, and thatched with reeds; they have only two wheels, the diameter of which in some cases is as much as ten feet. Each is drawn by six bullocks, which are urged on by a goad at least twenty feet long: this is suspended from within the roof; for the wheel bullocks a smaller one is kept; and for the intermediate pair, a point projects at right angles from the middle of the long one. The whole apparatus looked like some implement of war.

—Charles Darwin

27 Sept 1854 . . . . Up late. Worked at filling up the holes made over the parlour-window, from which I had knocked away three hideous grinning heads, that formed part of the house.

—Ford Madox Brown

September 27, 1850
Training in Christianity by Anti-Climacus, Nos. I, II, III, edited by S. Kierkegaard.

Friday, 27 September 1872

Maria told us the story of Anne Kilvert and the cat, and the Epiphany Star. It seems that when Aunt Sophia was dying Anna thought some mutton would do her good and went to fetch some. When she came back the nurse said, 'She can't eat mutton. She's dying'. Anna put the mutton down on the floor and rushed to the bed. At that moment Aunt Sophia died and Anna turned round to see the cat running away with the mutton and the Epiphany Star shining in through the window.

—Francis Kilvert

Göttingen, September 27, 1912
Ever since I was permitted to attend the Weimar Congress last autumn, the study of psychoanalysis has had a constant hold on me. The deeper I get into it, the more it grips me. My wish to spend a few months in Vienna is now about to be fulfilled. Would you permit me to attend your classes and to be admitted to the Wednesday evening meetings? The sole purpose of my sojourn there is to devote my self to all phases of this subject.

—Lou Andreas Salomé

Tuesday, 27 September 1927   *Paris*
Discussed with Paul Valéry the subject of the collected edition. He reckons there will be six or seven volumes in all.
He was worried that there will be no more than three hundred copies of each.

I found him quite alone, without any domestics to open
the door, suffering from an attack of lumbago, and in a
very nervous state. He spoke so softly and swiftly that I
had difficulty in following him. He has so much to do, he
complained, he does not know *'où donner de la tête'*, what
with trips to be made to Vienna, England, Spain, and heav-
en knows where, a mass of literary obligations to fulfil,
family worries, and all the rest. Obviously he attaches excessive importance to 'recognition' and also has a keen nose
for business. He is like a ship-wrecked mariner who has
just reached land and is immoderately careworn and delighted at the same time.

He will go see Maillol next week *('si je trouve le temps')*.
As I said that I have never yet succeeded in obtaining copies of his poems, he presented me with *Charmes*, *Album de
vers anciens*, and *La jeune Parque*.

—Harry Kessler

On September 27, 1855, Tennyson read *Maud* aloud to
a group of friends— Robert and Mrs Browning, Mrs
Browning's sister Arabella (Barrett), and Dante Gabriel
and William Michael Rossetti. Sitting unobserved in a corner, Dante Gabriel Rossetti made a rapid but good portrait of Tennyson, which he later gave to Browning. According to W.M. Rossetti, Tennyson did not know of the
picture, at the time or afterward.

When *Maud* had been read through (with Tennyson in-
terrupting himself frequently to comment upon individual
passages), Browning read *Fra Lippo Lippi*, and the party
broke up at two-thirty A.M.

—Ray DiPalma

SEX

The clitoris is found in all Carnivora.

—Jim Quinn

Probably secare, to cut. I sex you. Sexus, Latin. I want sex
with you latin lover. One of 2 or any combination. In any

—Joe Brainard

CLEOPATRA

season. Male of male. Male of female. Female of female.
Female of male. Man-woman, woman-woman, woman-man,
man-man. 2nd person singular. Personal pronoun. Pronoun
personal. Any combination. Sex as in the child. Perverse.
Where are you coming from? A sex cell. Intersex. Fertiliz-
ation of the species. I speak as historical feminine. More
sex. Plato's Retreat. 1978. And in the very year of equal-
ization of the sexes I attribute all balance to color. She
sees his brilliant feathers fetish. Bird sex. Manifestations
of instinct and good will towards our world. What is opposite and sometimes opposing. Then sex on planet out of
this world, sex between galaxies. Anywhere out of the
world. Explosion. Night is fucking day, etc. Compare
autosexing. An old law imposing death for sex outside
marriage that's old. New: arouse me, he, she, it. Sex chrom-
osome. Sex cord. Sex ego. She is over 60 & still sexy (sexa-
genarian). Testis and ovary (gland). Sex intergrade. Sex ratio.
Consider the sextain. The sextant, the sextet. Consider the
sextipara & all her children. Spores may be sexual. Sexual
water (Neruda). One who follows the sexual or artificial
system of Linnaeus is a sexualist. Blue movie. Spicy or
racy language. "Struck sex poses and smiled for advert-
ising photographs" — Springfield Mass. Daily News. It
is difficult to sex the plants and animals at a distance.
"Watching you sexing up that bar kitten" — Oakley
Hall. Bath, bed, queen, king, lord, lady, husband, wife,
mistress, master, actor, actress, consenting adult, Oral,
Atonal, Normal, Prenatal. "Sex in his eyes" "sex
around her mouth." Orifice. Edifice. Artifice. Porn. Clean.
Storm. Organism.

—Anne Waldman

To our eyes the courtship of the praying mantis resembles a sneak attack. The male freezes on seeing the female, a reaction shown by both sexes to large threatening objects. He may remain motionless for hours, or begin·a slow approach, stalking her with his eyes always on her. He shows no sign of sexual excitement, but when he is within a body length he takes a short flying leap, clasping the female with his forelegs.

Once in this position, the male intermittently flagellates the female's head with his antenna and begins copulatory movements. Coupling is accomplished after 5 to 30 minutes by separation of the female's ovipositor valves, and continues for several hours.

The female makes no obvious responses to the male. She may flatten her body slightly upon being mounted, a movement that also seems to be part of the cryptic posture assumed by both sexes on the approach of a predator. In some cases, she is entirely passive.

However, she may strike at the male and begin to eat him.

The attack may take place during the male's approach, directly after mounting, or as the couple separates. It has not been observed during actual copula. It is not inevitable, and depends on various factors—among them how hungry the female is. A few males have been observed to mate a number of times with the same or with different females without losing their heads, while many succumb on the first encounter.

The head and prothorax of an approaching male are naturally most exposed and are eaten first. This is followed within a few minutes by intense and continuous sexual movements of the male's abdomen—accompanied by curious locomotor movements that have never been observed in the intact male mantis.

These are lateral or rotary walking movements that tend to carry the headless body of the male from head-to-head position, to a position parallel to the female, and eventually onto her back. The movements are sufficiently powerful that the remains of the male's body are out of reach of the mandibles, and she is rarely able to eat more than part of the male thorax.

The sexual movements of the male abdomen continue with vigor, and coupling takes place just as it would if the male were intact, continuing for hours.

Surgical decapitation induces intense sexual behavior in males, even before sexual maturity. The sexual behavior continues for several days, and during that time the decapitated male clasps any object the approximate size of the female (a pencil, for example) and makes vigorous and prolonged attempts to copulate. Although a decapitated male cannot locate a female, he clasps her immediately if placed on her back and normal copulation usually follows. This reaction was put to practical use in maintaining an inbred strain of mantises in which the intensity of the courting in males was much reduced. A high percentage of fertilized eggs was realized by decapitating the males and placing them on the females.

Decapitated female mantises make continuous movements of the ovipositor, and often deposit ill-formed egg-cases even without being fertilized.

—Jim Quinn

SHERRY

Julius Caesar cut from his Mother's
        womb
Caedare to cut off   (caesura)
Sanskrit Khidāti (tear)
Jack Wilson — Wovoka — "Cutter"
(vajracchedika — Diamond — "cutter")
Caesar to Kaiser to Tsesari', Tsar
And a town in Spain, Caesaris
became Xeres, Jerez,
    and the English sd,
sherry

—Gary Snyder

243

SHIT

An old couple were spending their time making flat black things.

This worried the town fathers; so they sent one of the fathers to investigate the old couple.

He said to the old couple, the fathers are a bit leery; those flat black things; it could get out of hand; for a younger couple it might be different...

Oh, please, father, cried the old couple with surprisingly perfect coincidence.

Hey, that's pretty good. Did you practise it? said the town father.

Oh, please, Mr. town father, don't take our flat black things away, cried the old couple, again with surprisingly perfect coincidence.

Hey, that's pretty good, it must take a lot of practise, said the town father as he rolled up their shadows and put them under his arm.

Shit on the fathers, cried the old couple, again with surprising coincidence.

Amazing, said the town father as he headed towards town to join the other town fathers.

And the mothers, too, cried the old couple, continuing their surprising coincidence...

—Russell Edson

SICKNESS

"How are you feeling?" "A bit worse than I was expecting but better than I was. Actually I'm feeling a bit better than I am!" "That's good. That's better than I can say." "I'm still sick of it." "That'll make you better."

—Philip Corner

SILENCE

Around here, we have banished the voice. Too messy, too much ease of misinterpretation, too much mumble, hiss and shout. No, we have retained for the mouth its true, original function as receptacle, not cannon bore. Why, our children, when we tell them of speech, can only conceive of it as a kind of clear and noisy vomit.

Another means of communication seems to us far better: as we write, so do we "speak;" we have chosen the ten strong throats attached to our hands. We love how words travel yet at the same time stay. How they never shed a skin to an echo. How, clear to sight, rather than lie our hands remain stuffed in pockets. And so even immobile, the bulge of deceitful intent belies itself, becomes a confession.

But out in the air, our hands orchestrate a wind of words. Imagine every stormy branch in summer telling tales, and only then can you begin to see how we converse. Of course we are proud: who else has an alphabet that twists sound into dance? With such silent steps we reveal ourselves, and receive: the tips of our fingers now antennae.

Yet all is not well. Granny only knits, all day. Yet produces nothing, because in anger we have taken away her yarn. Our children at times are still curious about this and try to decipher what she is saying. We tell them Granny is an immigrant and speaks another language. Grandpop is arthritic and therefore mute. And he never dares to use his voice, for in the past when Granny made such attempts we rewarded her with more than one slap across the mouth, which means "silence:"

Occasionally at these moments Grandpop would look as if to laugh, but the single word "beware"

quickly withered that idea. Granny has, however, learned one sign:

meaning "I want." When our children were first born, she hovered above their cradles, under our watchful eyes, repetitiously gesticulating until they had learned their first lesson in language:

Now, after making her one sign, Granny will silently move her lips, designating her desire. We feign ignorance and, as always, she is reduced to pointing.

Our children watch these exchanges with fear, seeing, they think, the senility we shall all be subject to. And so they cry, spreading their fingers from their eyes down the full length of their cheeks.
    Our children. We watch with pride as our children gaily stroke each other with their word games, excitedly

brush and pat to each other their secrets. But most of all, we love it when, hands flailing overhead, they sing:

Yet lately, they keep to themselves. Many times we have entered their room, only to have them abruptly turn around to face us, their hands twitching behind their backs. More and more, we don't understand the words they use, and we are not convinced of their explanations.

Their only reply to our doubts is four hands, held limply on the surface of the table.

Because Granny and Grandpop refuse to, or cannot, speak, and because our children increasingly refuse to speak clearly to us, my wife and I spend a great deal of time alone. At night, side by side, we whisper:

Telling our secrets of the day to each other has become our own private fondling,

until soon our words rub into desire:

Yet we are careful not to have children. Not that we don't care for our first two. But something always stops us, even in the most intense tumble of passion. While in the room next door, brother and sister together snore by scrubbing their sweaty palms against the wooden side-boards of the bed.

—Philip Graham

SINGULARITY

Singularity, or the condition of being in one place at one time, is one of the premier human burdens. Mortality alone would seem to surpass it, except that dying often seems q.e.d. And sexuality, our other conundrum, may be the chief expression of our desire to be more than one.

Strictly speaking, it is not singularity itself so much as the consciousness of singularity that presents the problem. The same might be said for mortality. Just as we envy the animals their lack of prescience, so we might well envy them their easy assumption of a second skin.

The child is quick to imitate, and from the first copied gesture struggles to be someone else. The adolescent, in its classical rebellion, resents its lack of originality and turns on all those things and people which made it what it is. It struggles to be someone else's progeny, and prefers the families of friends to its own. Leaving home, it wanders in mind and body, sometimes for years, and changes rapidly. In these years of possibility the curse seems to attenuate. The landscape of the coming years proffers a plural.

But the leash is short, and choices must be made. Freedom is merely potential. Like money it cannot be realized until it is spent. A mighty stasis forms in the center of the years. However furious the changes, then, one is oneself, and it is too late.

Consolation is sought in the plurality of the mind, the same plurality that causes the problem at the start. The heterocosms once formed as dreams of future action become the action in and of themselves. Dreaming *of* becomes just dreaming.

The wise and the resigned accept these new, sterile dreams. Framed in their changeless colors like pictures in a gallery, they are gazed at in the silence of night or behind the wheel over the meditative drone of the highway. Or the colors dim as the sheen leaves the body, and the eyes fix in the middle distance. I am what I am.

But the rebels carry their wars against singularity to the inevitable climax of annihilation.

The schizophrenic who denies being *one* at all; the tragic hero who becomes a living principle; the compulsive tourist; the user of drugs; the artist; the polygamist; the martyred mystic heretic; the long-haul driver; the actor; the dilettante; all of these and more deny the fixity of cities and the exactitude of time. And so the loneliness grows in them; the trees by the roadsides are only great weeds; and every human intercourse is pained because it eclipses all the possible others even as it takes place.

Finally, as with the aging onanist, no single dream can prevail, and the fantasies succeed each other furiously with an effect like that of a broken film.

Perhaps it is the narrowness of the focal point in the eye. If we return as flies and retain our prescience, then perhaps we shall succeed. Perhaps it is the mouth that utters only one word at a time.

—**David Lenson**

SKELAT'N
the supporting structure

the very complete skeleton is enveloped by callous skin over the massive physiognomy. This skin is tough hard and nearly naked with a few short hairs scattered here and there. The albino elephant is held in reverence in most of India. In cool mud they lie avoiding the venomous fly. They rarely use their monstrous powers of injury. The great weight when propelled clears everything before it, cutting through the most matted underwood.

Barriers of land, chains of mountains determining the courses of rivers are each one boundaries between assemblages of fishes   —**Alison Knowles**

249

SKIN
Holds it all in.

—Regina Beck

SLAVERY
Why am I existing?
Just to be a slave?

List of my slave duties:
1. Body slavery: I have to eat and get shelter so need money. Also my body likes sex and rich food and I'll do anything for these.
2. Mind slavery: I want more than just money. I live in a partially human world and I want people to think and feel certain ways about me. So I try to set up certain networks, mental-physical, in time and space, to get what I want. (I also set up these networks to get money.) If they work, these networks become history and culture and as such, turn against me and delimit time and space. They—history and culture—tell me what to do.

The world, everything I perceive are indicators of my boring needs and nothing else. Otherwise there is nothing. I might as well not exist.
All my emotions, no matter how passionate, are based on my needs. I don't adore my emotions anymore.
Depending on unstable ground for a decision, i.e. depending on taste, desire, fascination, conceptual ideas, inspiration etc. is not satisfying.
I have the same emotions again and again, the same thoughts, because always the same needs: SLAVE SLAVE SLAVE
I want to be as free as I don't know. I don't know what that means. I want to depend on someone/something stable. Unlike Francis Ponge I don't find the physical world stable. Basing decisions on someone/something stable makes me happy.

I WANT TO BE A BERBER!
PROOF THAT BERBERS LIVE BETTER
THAN CITY PEOPLE
The Arabs who inhabit waste regions and deserts die less

quickly when famine (depression) hits than those who live lives of abundance. The stomachs of city people who have everything in abundance who are used to seasonings especially butter acquire excess moisture. So when famine —lack of seasonings, use of coarse food, and drought— thwarts these eating habits, the stomach dries out and contracts. Sickness and sudden death can result.

So the people who die during a famine die from their former wealth, not from famine.

The desert Arabs who are accustomed to thirst, to doing without seasonings and butter keep their basic body moisture limited. Neither famine nor drought kills them off.

Whatever the soul of which the body is an outgrowth becomes used to becomes a characteristic of the soul. People who live on camel milk and camel meat become patient, perservering, and able to carry loads. They have healthy and tough stomachs. For instance, the eggs of chickens who have been fed on grain cooked in camel dung give forth huge chicks. If camel dung is just smeared on chicken eggs right before they hatch, the chicks come out just as huge.

Whatever the soul becomes used to the soul begins to need and depend on, and the soul weakens.

The Berbers, having historically preceded their conquerors, lived upon necessities and nothing else. They ate either unprepared food or food barely cooked by fire. When they lived in anywhere, they lived in hair and wool tents, wood houses, or caves. Because camels have the hardest delivery and the greatest need of warmth during delivery, they were often forced to travel deep into hostile deserts and to live there for long periods of time. Hostile soldiers kept them constantly on the move.

So as soon as a Berber is able, he or she begins a city life. City people have such complex pleasures and desires, they forget their souls' needs. Since they don't want any task to interrupt their pleasures, they give the job of governing to someone they don't know. They're no longer responsible for the defense of their home territory. They know nothing and have no power over the food they eat, the air they breathe, and the mental existence that comes into them. They are as helpless and dependent as newborn children on possibly insane parents. Their souls have absorbed ignorance and become it.

City laws break down human self-reliance; punishment takes away a person's pride; and childhood education immediately starts to tear away self-dependence. City people grow up in fear and do not push themselves to knowledge. Thus they have no strength.

THE BERBERS' NEGATIVITY
The Berbers are savage because it means freedom from authority and no subservience to leadership. This soul's savagery negates civilization.

How?

The Berbers need stones to put their cooking pots on They tear down the buildings they find to get these stones. They tear apart the roofs to get wood for their tent poles and tent props. They don't build or make; rather they take what other people own. They recognize no thievery limit. To them political superiority and royal authority are the power to plunder.

They force craftsmen and professional workers to work and then they don't pay them. They care only about what they can get through stealing and taxing. They have no belief they should work. An urban town, like capitalism, is based on profit. The real basis of profit is labor. The Berbers destroy the workers' belief in and use for labor and help these workers turn to crime.

Every Berber wants to be a leader. The peoples the Berbers have conquered have had to obey so many leaders, they could not move. The culture in the parts of Yemen the Berbers now live in and the Persian civilization in the Arab Iraq are now erased.

قلب

—Kathy Acker

SLEEP

people sleeping
who die are killed by their nightmares.

—Rose Lesniak

SLOTH

yet otherwise
His life he led in lawlesse riotise;
By which he grew to a grieuous malady;

For in his lustlesse limbs through euill guise
A shaking feuer raignd continually:
—Edmund Spenser

A sluggish, indolent, unalert disinclination to exert oneself. Sloth is one of the deadly sins *(q.v.)*. The antithesis
of precision and fastidiousness, Sloth is deeply involved
with these qualities as a rebel with authority. The fundamental perfectionism of the slothful person sits on the
cruel throne of conscience. The sin in Sloth is its defiance
of conscience—the inner surrogate of external authority—
for in Sloth the individual strikes back: "You cannot
judge me. I disqualify you by giving you nothing to judge."
—Armand Schwerner & Donald M. Kaplan

SMOKE

The elixir of aftermath when catastrophe is first viewed
from the tower on the cave-wall. Shadow play dust rising
from the arena of war. The eyes are made red.
—Paul William Simons

SNEAKERS

An old man was sneaking up on another old man to kill him.
But the other old man was sneaking up on the first old man
to kill him.

Round and round they go sneaking up on each other,
neither aware that the other intends his death; each getting
away from the other simply by pursuing the other.

Something surely will happen to interrupt this schedule.
But, when? How long will this circle of intention continue to
describe itself?
—Russell Edson

SOLICITUDE

Solicitude conserves complete figures of the simulacra.
—Michael Brownstein

SPACE

"Space" is where time goes on a vacation.
It disappears like a snake that doesn't
have any shoulders. After the miles
are left they forget away, just
going and going and going.   **—William Stafford**

                        still operating   in rural India
     the lowest of the 5 castes   Nayadis   (untouchables)
     must not come within 64 ft. of Ceupers
     who must maintain distance of 32 ft. of Iravans
     not allowed within 25 ft. of Nayars
     must come no closer than 7 ft. of Brahmins. (the highest)
     And those convicted of crimes need larger *BUFFER ZONES*
     than those of non-violent crimes.

                                                    —Rose Lesniak

SPARROW
A mouse on springs.

                                                    —Nathaniel Tarn

SPORTS
A man was cleaning his elbows, because of all the body's
parts the elbows are at once the most sacred, and at the
same time the most foul.
    His mother was proud of him, that he should take such
a keen interest in sports...

                                                    —Russell Edson

SPOT
A man kept himself as a pet. He would pat the back of his
head, or take himself for a walk.
    When he was hungry he would put a bowl of scraps on
the floor.
    He called his pet Spot.

                                                    —Russell Edson

STILLBIRTH
Dateline: N.Y.C.
12.9.47

3:07 a.m.
slightly bruised upon arrival

format: male
tears: measuring 1 cm.
screams: incessant
surgical pathology: *negative*

254

3:14 a.m.
nurse phones central casting
long distance (see invoice No.4479C)

3:19 a.m.
first scar appears

3:24 a.m.
premature symptoms of m.o.*

3:36 a.m.
morphine injections (see invoice No.4479C)

Diagnosis & Afterthoughts:
re-program for insouciance
wait thirty-one years
and if condition unchanged
mistake for dead

—**Derek Pell**

*moral outrage

STODGE

The literary and culinary delight of the English nation, ever
since Vaulting Imagination suddenly up and left town in
the 17th century. The people with the imagination have
since been known as 'eccentrics,' as in: Wm Blake, Samuel
Palmer, Wm Morris, Francis Kilvert, G.M. Hopkins, Frederick Delius, Edith Sitwell, Lord Berners, Stevie Smith, et
few alia...

It is used in such expressions as "Aye, wouldn't it be
lovely to have a bit of right stodge." Meaning: boiled *and*
cremed *and* fried potatoes *and* cauliflower *and* sprout along
with the grey joint of roasted beef.

A diet of stodge has led to a peculiar and generic condition amongst the populace and those in pursuit of literature. This is *Meilikhoposthoi*, vagueness of cock and mind,
as the very ancient Greeks called it before they got their
act together and their cathexes in order. This disorder allows the English to complain that Americans and other
wogs simply will not refrain from writing poems about all
those subjects that gentlemen do not write about under

any conditions. It allows them to insist that Philip Larkin is the most interesting living poet since W.H. Auden...

One way to resist stodge is to remember what Novalis said: "Not only is England an island, but so is every Englishman an island."

—Jonathan Williams

STUBBLE

You can find this one somewhere between *Jeb Stuart* and *Stubbs, William,* but what's forever the wonder is that you don't come upon it in that cluster of sounds one would expect to be its intimate company. *Stub,* for example, is something else entirely ("for IE base see STEEP, *adj.*") and you get all the way to *stubborn* before you are back on the track. Quick thought that *steeple* might be a friend? But that's still *steep* again, those *stumps* it seems will never yield.

First recollections of *stubble.* Field adjacent to farm house we lived in, in West Acton, Mass., farm next door belonged to the Lockes, son, Milton, admirer of my sister, also elder croney at times. Hay field. After you cut it, you get— *stubble.* Awful on the feet, as is *stubble* always, e.g., anything cut, leaving stalk still standing, however short, as corn, aforesaid hay. Corn *stubble* you can trip on, say, while running across frosty field of a Halloween night, escaping ghostly pursuers, headless horsemen and the like. Then, if you sprawl, belly down, hands out, you can likely get raked on palms and forearms, even your face, if God so designs—all the wherewithal, of *stubble.*

Sounds attractive, certainly. I mean, "I've shrunk so much I'm seeing *stubble...*" Or—"*Stubble, stubble,* toil and trouble..." Boil and bubble? I've never heard of anybody doing that with it, but the relation to Macbeth's encounter, like they say, with those three ladies no doubt involved him also with some *stubble* being as it was that time of the year.

I don't now remember when I first began to get a beard, rather, that first downy growth on the lower part of the face. Some kids, however, had *stubble* really early, possibly were even born with it, like Grumpa Davis, old man at eight. It's part of the after-shave scene, that two days (give or take a few) growth makes you look like imagined, lantern-jawed Neanderthal—which persons always attracted me somehow, that is, I could never think of later human development as being necessarily a "progress" (which word, thankfully, is not our burden here). So there's something manly about *stubble*, on face or field, something that stays in there, upthrust, doesn't give up—you dig it.

Or the sad *stubble*, man, first drear encounter with crab lice, pubic area, got to shave the hair, man, put on that there turpentine gunk, kill 'em! Two days later you got *stubble*, with or without the crabs.

The truly great thing about *stubble* is, you never forget it. Like, that *is* a word. And it's one they don't really lead you up to, like c a t or g o o d or all the rest of that Dick and Jane trip. You learn *stubble* on your own. And it isn't one of those heavy words like shit or fuck, etc. Thousands of people are waiting to lay those two on you, but *stubble* is a loner. Just one day it's there, and you may have waited years or not even thought about it at all, and then—*stubble*. I'm sure I must have met it early, and clearly through stubbing my toes, so I'd even be willing to argue that no matter what they say, stub and *stubble* are close company.

So—what do we know? Well, it says here, that the late Latin was *stupula* for the Latin *stipula*, "a stalk, a stem". So, you know, that may fool some people but you can't tell me that stub isn't in there. I can read. Point is, nobody knows the *stubble* I've seen—and that's it.

—Robert Creeley

SURREALISM

A simple art of firing a pistol into the belly of any person in a crowd at random and by policy, and then adding a footnote from the assassin to say that he is deaf to criticism. The shot punctured his own left eardrum so that his poetry is deaf to music and rhythm. Deep images emerge from his unregenerate social conscience as the return of the repressed. Goering said he reached for his revolver when anyone spoke of culture: he had friends in poetry.

—Eric Mottram

SUSPICION

A furious and illiterate enemy of Rome could have done no better. We thought we had done with all that. Vatican II had solemnized the resolve, Pope John had given over his short and happy life to the prospect: never again secret character assasinations, no more suffocations, immurations, exiles, dismissals, enforced silencings, no more midnight burials at cross roads, no more stakes through the heart of prophetic purpose. It was a little like the heady romanticism that bubbled up in American society in the '60's. Everything seemed possible to us, even a reborn culture, even the rebirth of a defunct political community. Such a fever of anticipated triumph! it lived along the wave like an ecstatic surfer. Impossible to fall, only watch us! Alas, the wave subsided, the surfer went under, head over heels. In Kierkegaard's phrase, a Passionate Age has been succeeded by a Reflective and Leveling Age.

In 1970 for *Homilectic and Pastoral Review,* John McNeill, S.J., wrote three watershed articles entitled "The Christian Male Homosexual." He was encouraged to expand his ideas into a book. He did so, and duly submitted the manuscript to the scrutiny of superiors. So far, simple. He waited. He questioned, he was rebuffed. He waited, once more he was told to wait. His manuscript was scrutinized by enough experts to sanatize the Augean stables.

But McNeill's patience was uncommonly active. The organization 'Dignity', which he helped found for homosexual Catholics, grew to some 56 chapters in as many cities. And when his book was finally cleared, and *The Church and the Homosexual* appeared bearing its croix de guerre, the imprimatur, McNeill took to the road like a shot. He visited some thirty cities speaking on behalf of gays, advancing the thesis of his new book;

> It would appear to follow that the same moral rules apply to homosexuals as to heterosexual attitudes and behavior. Those that are responsible, respectful, loving and truly promotive of the good of both parties are moral; those that are exploitive, irresponsible, disrespectful, or destructive of the true good of either party, must be judged immoral.

Which may be so, or may not.

In August 1977 McNeill was summoned to New York Jesuit headquarters by Fr. Eamon Taylor, the provincial authority. He was informed that a letter from Fr. General Arrupe conveyed a decision of Cardinal Seper, head of the Roman Congregation of Doctrine and Faith. To wit. McNeill's book took a position contrary to the common teaching of the Church; the book showed disrespect for the magisterium, appearing as it did at the time the church had reaffirmed its position on the immorality of homosexuality; moreover, the imprimatur had been issued on the supposition that the book would be restricted to the community of scholars—but in consequence of McNeill's strenuous travels and many media appearances, Catholic gays were being deluded as to their true state. In consequence of all this, the imprimatur was to be removed from future printings of the book, and McNeill was forbidden to speak henceforth on matters of sexuality or sexual ethics.

The Seper-Arrupe document was, as they say, "unavailable."

Kierkegaard wrote in *The Present Age:*

> While a passionate age storms ahead, setting up new things and tearing down old, raising and demolishing as it goes, a reflective and passionless age does exactly the contrary. It hinders and stifles all action. It levels....
> Enthusiasm may indeed end in disaster, but leveling is eo ipso the destruction of the individual. No age, and therefore not the present age, can bring the skepticism of the process to a halt. For as soon as it tries, the law of the leveling process is again brought into play. Leveling can only be halted by the individual attaining the religious courage which springs from his individual religious solitude.

A warning has been served on all who hoped the Church was becoming an advocate of victimized people. Homosexuals will continue to be regarded in the church with that cute cast of the eye which signals more eloquently than a blow, that a creepy citizen has somehow gotten into the compound. I feel like saying to John McNeill with an irony that passes expression: welcome aboard. After some twenty years of bare survival in the order and the Church, one feels entitled to propound a principle—into the void, or into the west wind—that there is no status in the American Church worth telling about, worth tasting, worth trying with all one's poor energies to understand, except it be edgy, blurred, under suspicion.

—Daniel Berrigan

SYNAGOGUE

An assemblage (from the Greek) of Jews for the purpose of reading and expounding the Law. God's deliberate flatness in his scrolls, with touches of megalomania and song.

—Harvey Shapiro

SYNCH

The juxtaposition of a declevity in Earthwork art, as "He put the rocks out so as to emphasize the synch line of the terrain". Popularized in the 1970's by Smithson and Morris and in the 80's by Segal and Schneemann, both of whom used human bodies in this manner instead of landscape.

—Carol Berge

TALKING

"The most significant, the most critical, inventions of man were not those ever considered to be inventions but those which appeared to be innate and natural." Man never understood to what degree all nature was man-made. One such major and crucial invention was talking. It was, undoubtedly, considered to be innate and natural until a man, making a new observation, exclaimed, "We're talking." At that point no one had ever heard of such a thing. Still, talking was an invention that changed the way the brain worked. Talking, a man-made invention, provided information modifying the operation of the brain without any awareness. There was no choice. For thousands of years man was molding himself in a certain manner, but the pattern was not invented until a man said, "We're talking."

—John Brockman

TELEVISION

the rusty reinforcing bars that stick out of the concrete of every new building, to enable the people (as soon as there is enough money) to add a new storey, and not — as I at first thought — to receive a television program.

—Peter Wehrli
translated by Roger Frood

Compare "We'll be right back after this message" to the
dictionary definition of the word "message."

—**Michael Brownstein**

Television, as direct experience, can be considered...on two
levels. First, it is a potent source of light. The cathode-ray
experience is the only instance where man looked directly
into a light source for any sustained period, possibly averaging four hours a day. Light is actually projected onto the
retina by the cathode-ray tube. Second, man responded not
only to light perceived by the senses but also to factors of
biological rhythms such as the day/night flicker. Television
alters this rhythm violently. Man talked about the violence
evident on television programs. In light of the above consid-
erations he might have developed a "Theory of Neural Programs, Televison, and Violence," which hypothesized that
"due to circumstances beyond our control, this 'program'
is out of order," which is to say "there may well be limits
beyond which the natural rhythms are not amenable to
frequency-synchronization with new environmental perio-
dicities." Violence.

—**John Brockman**

TEMPLE

the advert-clean white-washed Greek temple that is the station
of Lomazzo, where what baffles me is not so much the temple-
station, but rather the way in which it flashes up within the
window frame of the train like an image on a screen.

—**Peter Wehrli**
translated by Roger Frood

TENSION

Consciously or unconsciously the act of tensing a muscle has a tendency to occupy the brain/ stubby/ foiling/
the fly in the ointment so to speak with an inviolable
strain/ thus the sequence of thoughts pushing into art
forms from out of the exploration and skill of fixed
space focused from out of the pull of straining forearms
think of the rigid fingers of St. Joan of Arc even Daniel
Berrigan or Simone Weil pushing into their sides the passion a device as useful as a steel plate in the skull of a
woman resolute and sitting down near a tree or a shrub
contemplating the split second when her calf muscle

cramped perversely making the woman lose her balance
and falling from the ladder the month before/ an image
in her mind of the sinews of cats tensing/ hunting

—**Rochelle Owens**

TERRORISM

The story of the slashed tires was around '68. I did that
more or less alone. A lot of aggression got released in a
totally irrational action. I was living in one of those devel-
opments where a lot of cops live. Where you can see that
cars are more important than places for children to play.
My whole disgust toward these object relationships just
went through me one day, and I started slashing tires, I did
them in to the tune of about one hundred. Most of the
cars were in front of this highrise where the cops lived.
That made it more real. Of course, in the papers it was
made to sound even more irrational. But somehow, the action wasn't bad for my later development; one could reflect
on it, it was simply one of those 'go get 'em' things that
have to happen. You have to see that people can be driven
so far that they can only free themselves by irrational aggressive actions.

It was all more or less spontaneous, not something
you talk about beforehand. I was just sort of wandering
through the area, a little drunk.

When you stick a stiletto in a tire, it is immediately
damaged—slashed from side to side, not on the profile:
they go zip and deflate. It was crazy work. That's why
they caught me. Someone saw it, so they grabbed me. I
got nine months in the joint, and had to pay damages. It
was 3 or 4 thousand Marks.

The tire-stabbing happened at the same time as the
department store arson in Frankfurt and a K.1   position
paper appeared in *Der Spiegel* denouncing it. But I naturally put myself on the side of Baader, Ensslin, Proll and
Soehnlein.

CRYSTALLNACHT

Things then got started with the bombing of the
Jewish synagogue and the leaflet that went with it, *Shalom
and Napalm.*

So there was a bomb planted in a Jewish synagogue

262

on the anniversary of Crystal Night. It didn't go off. But everyone flipped out about it, despite the leaflet, which explained the problem of Palestine from the viewpoint of the left, that is, that the new strategy of imperialism centers on Palestine. Since Vietnam is finished, the war more or less over, it can't go on forever; people should get involved with Palestine. It is actually much closer to us, which is apparent today with the oil business, and has more to do with us here in the European cities than does Vietnam. This was to become the new framework to carry on the struggle here. But for the press, of course, it was a prize, because it was on Crystal Night, so that the Germans had once again set off a bomb in a Jewish synagogue; that wasn't reconcilable anymore.

BOMMI THE BOMBER
One way or another, we were pretty lucky. For example, we were going to strike again, and were standing in front of a window and I had the firebomb. That was a mixture of Pattex and Garbages, that is, an acid with a combustible mass; it had a sort of naplam effect, because it sticks. Instead of throwing a rock through the window first, I take the thing and throw it against the plate glass. But the windows are so elastic it comes flying back. I see this little dot of light coming toward me, thank God it was winter, there was snow, and the little dot of light lands right between my legs. I looked down and the thing was slightly burnt, split seconds before the explosion; the snow put out the fuse—otherwise I would have been gone, like a napalm sacrifice.

PUBLICITY
We sold the exclusive picture rights to a teach-in to a reporter from *Quick* (a sensationalist tabloid). But this *Quick* reporter had nothing better to do than look at these bombing attempts, and put everything together in one pot. He wrote a nasty article and spread the worst shit about people.

We decided then that the press should be punished too, that these reporters shouldn't get away unscathed. So we drove over to his place to beat the hell out of him and straighten out the furniture in his house. So we hit him around the head a little and made a mess out of his house, and a neighbor promptly called the cops. They surrounded

22jähriger Student im Grunewald erschossen

22 YEAR OLD STUDENT SHOT IN GRUNEWALD

Was the student Ulrich Schmuecker killed by Anarchists in Grunewald? The 22-year old was found with a fatal head wound. He previously belonged to a terrorist group.

Annerose Reiche	Inge Viett	Ralf Reinders	Norbert Krocher
Michael Baumann	Werner Sauber	Till Meyer	Peter Knoll

WANTED: ANARCHISTS

the place, and smack, we were all arrested.

SWITCH

I got out in the summer of '71. I got parole in the trial. During the trial it was clear that Georg was facing ten years: Tommy, he had gone in earlier, he wasn't incriminated as strongly, and I wasn't at all, so they let us out.

We got parole after two days of the trial. Right away, we thought of changing roles downstairs in the cell. Tommy had a long beard and curls, and Georg too, and I had medium hair with a shorter beard. So when the judge says, 'here, Weisbecker and Baumann, parole,' Georg and I got up and left, and Tommy remained seated, acting as if he were Von Rauch. We created considerable chaos in the courtroom, running around hugging people and screaming—and in the chaos, Georg split.

So then downstairs in the cell, Tommy suddenly said, 'Listen, why are you taking me down here, there seems to be a total mistake, I'm Weisbacker, I was dismissed, you can't lock me up here again, you've gotta stop this.' Naturally, we had split in the meantime.

So once again there was a man out, in a perfectly simple way, through one of these sleight of hand tricks. Of course, it's a much better thing to get out like this, than in one of those revolver numbers. There's more wit behind it, more imagination plays a part in it.

—Michael ("Bommi") Baumann

Michael Baumann was a founder of several Berlin guerrilla groups of the late 60s and early 70s—The Hash Rebels, K.1, The Blues and, finally, The June 2nd Movement. He dropped out of the movement in 1972, assumed a new identity and renounced "violent political action" in favor of "love." The police are still looking for him in West Germany.

THANKSGIVING DAY

It seems to be that once a year Thanksgiving Day is nearly upon us. Which—really—is worse than Thanksgiving Day itself. (It is *not* one of my favorite holidays.) But—be that as it may—I am wondering (and curious)—as to what (if anything) Thanksgiving Day really "means" to me. That is to say—what it makes me think of. Now—emptying out my

head—let's see what pops up. Well, first is turkey. Second
is cranberry sauce. And third is "Pilgrims".

—Joe Brainard

THEATER

The curtains part. Butterflies cleverly contrived of velvet and
painted wood shudder and flutter from strings, pretending
nature and appetite among brightly colored artificial
flowers.

Then a pretty maiden made of wood comes and pre-
tends to eat wooden food at a wooden picnic on a wooden
hill.

A gelatin sun begins to set amidst a whistling roar of
marionette birds.

A moon rises like a circle of light on a prison wall.

The wooden maiden dances, undressing in graceful turns.
Her pale body, the red dots of her bosom, dark painted delta...

She is lovely, she is lovely; she makes us wish we were
made of wood...

—Russell Edson

THUNDER BASIN NATIONAL GRASSLANDS

One more county down was Johnson, and one east, Camp-
bell, where the grassplains roll out toward Dakota in an
endless, flattening series of dry creeks and prehistoric
distances. It is called, this sweep of earth, the Thunder
Basin National Grasslands, and it is being riddled for its
oil and coal by dark metallic modern monsters that from
a distance look like the dinosaurs that once lived here. I
had walked and driven it, sat in the torrent of July heat
to stare at the shortgrass, the sunflowers, and the
shimmering silhouette of the Pumpkin Buttes. It was a
kind of coming back, this trip, for it had been more than
a dozen years since I'd sought to amalgamate the psycho-
geographic possibilities of this purest of all Western land,
with the mythic blood-curse of the *Oresteia*. What had
taken my interest in the very seminal moment of understanding something of the Aeschylian notion of morality
and tragedy, was the effect of *place* on those larger,

archetypal cycles—not so much specific place, either, but place as one of life's (and myth's) inescapables. That amalgam had worked out across a quite American theme, and now it rode glued to the backside of my soul down the east edge of the Horn.

—Len Fulton

TIME

A concept having no intrinsic existence. It is one of several concepts used to prop up reality *(q.v.)*.

For something that does not exist a lot can be done with it: you can make, mark, keep, lose, take, need, buy, beat, waste, tell, and do time (presumably for stealing it).

You may be in time, out of time, and on time. There is a time for everything, and no time for anything.

Time is money.

—Suzanne Zavrian

TOMORROW

now things will happen tomorrow
it's all too clear from the way
horses stand in the meadow
from the way the clouds fly away
and the moles delve into the earth

it's all too clear from the ants' flurry
new things will happen tomorrow
perhaps a bud
or a leaf falling off a tree
perhaps a child

even if we cannot see far ahead
it's all too clear from the way the birds scurry
new things will happen tomorrow
not as important as the day after
more important than today

—Bulent Ecevit
translated by Talat S. Halman

See Turkish - Greek Poem

TONGUE

Just slip this tongue into your mouth,
then let it hang out.
It protrudes no less than five inches
giving you quite a comical look.
Wiggle it around
and do some of the most amazing things.

—Warren Woessner

TORCH

Anything that serves to illuminate, enlighten, brighten or
guide. For example, an electronic strobe-unit or flashbulb
or any such apparatus, either hand-held or attached to
he body of a camera by means of a bracket or hot-shoe to
give off light for the making of photographs where little
or no available light is existent. An on-going series of
night-time photographs by Anton Perrich, Don Snyder and
Gerard Malanga.

From Left: Christopher Isherwood, Don Bacardy, James Grauerholz, William
S. Burroughs, Victor Bockris and Richard Ellevich

Jim and Sunny Jacobs

John Chamberlain and Eileen Bresnahan

—Gerard Malanga

TRANSIT

So I rode no way but to hear that the NEWS said
that the rich in the famine ate bread

And I entered the 59th street station of the Express
where the pretzel-man
barters instead and blames each woman
and smokes at the DO NOT SMOKE sign

Surely stupid to say that the poor are free

Yet think how I marvelled as one obsessed
before him who too shall believe that he shall profit

Nonetheless

—Hugh Seidman

TRANSPARENCY

what we see through, see by means of, because of, see past
or beyond, almost fail to see because we see through it, by
means of it, because of it, past it, beyond it; what lets light
through, lets energy through; a window a lens, a means of
projecting images, a voice, a face; that quality in character
or in art which draws no attention to itself because it gives
all attention to what is; the mirror gives us back ourselves
and to ourselves; the transparency gives us back and to the
world, and lies.

—Judith Johnson Sherwin

TRAVEL

The travel agent's artificial little cubbyholed old office:
dusty posters of the Taj Mahal or "Voyage à Mexique". The
neon light and plastic flowers; the coughing ashtray full of
Alpine cigarette butts; the drifts of brochures sliding up and
down the cluttered desk and floor... Of course it makes you
want to go away— all the way to the greasy bar & grill next
door... Travel. Travel and unravel!

The ticket. (Oh, don't forget the ticket!)... The ticket
in the headband of your cap. The ticket in the bottom of
your knapsack's final fold or inner pocket; in the bottom
of the lining of your jacket; in the bathroom at the station

where it drowns upon the pissoir floor (oh, ain't life international?)... O pissoir floor!

The ticket and the hand-bag. The hand-bag, and the ever-nasty regulations re: hand luggage (one piece only; must fit comfortably beneath your seat; etc.)... Don't even listen to them. Have a friend hold all the bags and things until the last departure moment. Then make a run for it. Say: "I know, I know, I know, I know...", and bolt right past the stewardess (or other uniformed clucking ass who points so stupidly beyond you). Take any seat you like, in fact. Make a big stink. Make a whole, damn ruckus! Stuff the overhead compartment so magnificently that when the wheels touch down (when landing), the bags of all your shoes and books and little cakes and things bombard as many heads and laps as possible. Teach them all a great resounding lesson! The nerve of them, anyway— letting the film break in the middle of the dirty part; running out of Bloody Mary ("Mr. T.", they call it) mix; serving such a bland and shitty supper (whattya mean "a local Indonesian speciality"?????)... Travelling, my friends, should be a very serious affair.

Travelling. Travelling by boat (a noble and relaxing pleasure); train (what better place to read and snore?); plane (the only way to get there faster, but a bore; particularly if you're into scenery); car (the only truly scenic way); horseback (yuck, yuck); cross-country skiing (if your only real objective is a fireside or cup of groggy tea); blimp (if you like to be the only passenger); hot-air balloon (too daring and what if a great big bird should happen...); converted submarine (ja, ja); camel or beaded elephant (à votre service monsieur).

T.W.A.'s O.K., but Pan Am's usually a horror. Air India for the food and saried ladies; the other very-British lines so very clean and serious. Forget the Spanish, Greek, El-Al, and all of that (lovely to be there in their sensuous, forgotten lands, but not by local carrier), Swissair (ah!), and K.L.M.; Air France, even sturdy old Lufthansa—at least they'll get you there on time (and they never mind a little extra luggage ... The Common Market: your wish is their command! And duty-free Cuban cigars sticking out of every pouch and pocket). Inter-island lines are usually O.K. as well, for they fly low, but you are usually too stoned or drunk to hardly even notice (you mean that *really* was the top of a volcano??? ??)... And in the U.S.A. (one speaks facetiously): Fly Delta!

—Romare Bearden

273

Take plenty of pills along. Don't strap too many Saran-wrap packets of hash or coke around your chest or belly (maybe the winner of best motion picture of 1978 though!)... And traveller's checks galore! Letters of credit, naturally! (And, undemocratic as it fearfully might sound— a bag of colored beads and things will still work in the back of Africa).

Travel agents, travel plans, and travel diaries. Itineraries, never-to-be-seen-again deposits, futile reservations. Travel stories, travel jokes; travel disasters, travesties. Traversals, Trans-Siberian Express rides. Travel time-tables, travel tips... Tarantulas in damp-dark drawers, or evil-smelly closets!

Why travel at all? To eliminate, elude? To give the neighbors a solid chance to enjoy the neighborhood without you in its midst? To make them greeeeeeeeeeeeeeeeen with jealousy? To become a bit more erudite... Perhaps.

But: Suntans in winter! "Paris in the spring"! The top of Mt. Everest any time you happen to be passing by up there. Jones Beach on any sunny, summer Sunday morning (between dawn and 9 or 10 A.M.)... So many wonders and delights awaiting us (even by subway, or by bus)... And the sheer adventure of it all! To see a lion yawning at a water-hole; a crocodile hanging with its belly freshly slit. The turbaned holy -Hindu folk who clean the floors and toilets out at London's terminals and airodromes... The progress of it all! Toothless, ageless Arab creatures, each with a handful of precious figs, a scrawny chicken, a gnarled and fettered hand or half a foot: Come to the Kasbah!

And now for all of you about to travel off for winter skiing; some little Easter frolic in the sun... Adieu, adieu! (I say "adieu", instead of "bon voyage", for that saves me one syllable, and God knows how much money's worth of Champagne sentiment, folding irons/leather money belts/ related presents... which rarely are appreciated anyway)... And don't forget your tickets, passport, Solarcaine, or Lomotil... And try to get home safely...

—Timothy Baum

TRUTH

"Truth" climbs anything put
in front of it—castles, prisons, bombs:
it will surface in a desert and own

that instant. After you close your eyes
at night it begins to arrange the next day.

—**William Stafford**

If I could overcome my aversion to my adversary, I would
beg him to reveal the truth about me.

All speculative systems that pass the test of logic look
plausible until you examine their assumptions. Then you
perceive the formal nature of logic and the subtlety of truth.

This subtlety shows itself in mental treatment, not in
its assumptions alone, but in the fact that evidence depends
on what men say is happening to them, and in this situation
testimonials burst forth like romantic Wagnerians flushed
with premonitions of great things to come, of transforma-
tions (not unlike poets inflated in the presence of a language,
perhaps). On this stage a patient feels that from the moment
he began to work with someone on his condition, no matter
how or with whom, he felt better. His symptoms might even
have disappeared.

The truth is that his testimonials attest only to the
necessity to leap in any direction to save himself from help-
lessness, and the quickest way to do that is to feel instant
magical powers in the mere presence of the therapist.

—**Carl Rakosi**

TURKISH-GREEK POEM

Abroad, homesick, you come to know the Greek is your brother;
You find this out before long.
Just watch that young man from Istanbul
As he listens to a Greek song.

Having cursed with all the zest of our hearts and tongues,
We brandished bloody knives like sworn enemies;
Yet a deep love always lay hidden
For days of peace like these.

What if in our veins
It's not the same blood that flows?
In our hearts
It's the same frenzied wind that blows.

Mr Caramanlis, prime minister of Greece, and Mr Ecevit, prime minister of Turkey

This rain makes both of us generous;
We are warm under the same sun;
Surging from our hearts full of spring
Our good feelings caress on and on.

Our sins share this water and this taste,
Like all drinks as harmful as they are delicious,
Distilled from the fruit of the same climate,
It's the same drink that makes us vicious.

There's a blue magic between us,
A warm sea
On whose shores stand our two nations
Poised in equal beauty.

The Aegean's golden age
Will be ours again to revive;
With tomorrow's fire
The old hearth will come alive.

First, a laughter rings in your ears,
Then, Turkish lyrics with a Greek accent:
He sings of the Bosphorus,
You recall raki* with that music.

You and the Greeks are brothers —
You find that out when you're abroad and homesick.

—Bulent Ecevit
translated by Talat S. Halman

*Turkish raki (sometimes referred to as "lion's milk")
is a traditional Eastern Mediterranean drink identical
to the Greek ouzo.*

TWEEZING

A scientist had a drawer full of cows, which he milked with rubber tipped tweezers.

The scientist thinks he should miniaturize a man to do the milking; tweezing is such a bother...

—Russell Edson

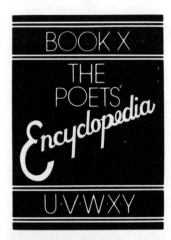

UNDOING

The transformation of the pleasure of a forbidden wish
into the imperative of a personal superstition: undoing
employs some definite action which actually or magically
cancels out something threatening to the individual. The
most frequent forms of undoing are personal acts of atonement and compulsive ceremonials. The need to touch, to
count, to go through elaborate and irrelevant preparations
prior to a simple act are common forms of undoing. That
which is being undone is kept from awareness. Derivatives
of undoing are seen in everyday actions like unlocking and
relocking a locked door to check whether it was locked in
the first place, or, similarly, setting and resetting an alarm
clock. Undoing is directed against aggressive and sexual
ambitions and is prominent in rigid, orderly characters
who can be trusted to show great thoroughness with trivial
matters.

—**Armand Schwerner & Donald M. Kaplan**

UTRICEATELLE

(n.) A trifle, a thing of no importance.

—**Ursule Molinaro**

UTRICLE

(n., L. utriculus) A small leather bag, originally made of
the udder of the naturally deceased hermaphroditic urus

in pre-Christian Europe, when it was used for smuggling dipthongs, labials, and explosives across Indo-European soundshift barriers (see: *Ur*sprache, from urus).

(The penis of the naturally deceased hermaphroditic urus was made into a sheath for knives &/or small daggers, used by speech defectors to stab at their avantguard.)

Eventually, the pre-Christian hermaphroditic urus died out, due to the boredom inherent in bi-une auto-reproduction, and subsequent centuries experienced an overabundance of utricles, sheaths, and sound shifts. However, by the year 1, they had begun to wear out and finally disappeared from the common market. A few fine examples can still be viewed in the museum at Utrecht (a town in the Netherlands, whose name is typical of the fusion of languages that occurred particularly in prosperous commercial centers. *Utr*(iculus) & *echt*(G. authentic, true)).

Colloq.: The cat (or It) is in the utricle—the certainty of a successful outcome.

(v.t.) To capture, snare, kill (of game); slang: to steal.
—**Ursule Molinaro**

UTRICLE BALM
N., an ointment, rubbed onto cows' udders to prevent chafing.
—**Ursule Molinaro**

UTRICLEDAD
A former caliphate between the Tigris and Euphates Rivers.
—**Ursule Molinaro**

UTRICLE LADY
A woman living in the streets of larger cities.
Ursule Molinaro

UTRICLE PIPE
Musical wind instrument.
—**Ursule Molinaro**

UTRICULAR PANTS

Ill-fitting trousers.

—Ursule Molinaro

VANITY

The heapes of people thronging in the hall,
Do ride each other, upon her gaze:
Her glorious glitter and light doeth all mens eyes amaze.
—Edmund Spenser

One of the deadly sins *(q.v.).* Vanity connotes a combination of inner emptiness and great outward show. In meaning and function it is close to the current term *glamour.* The sin here appears to reside in the enticing promise that fulfillment requires no further exertion than a happy, finger-snapping availability.

—Armand Schwerner & Donald M. Kaplan

See Pride

VOICE

Illumination of the Breath

—Charlie Morrow

WAKOSKI

v.t.—To navigate waterways using whisky-barrel staves, attaining a forward motion by using them to slap or whack (wak) the surface of the water. A type of ski (ski) is formed by the staves. This mode of travel was imported from Scandinavia and is accompanied by a loud, insistent wail or cry believed to have originated from the sound made by children when they fell into the river and discovered that water by itself is not good to drink. The skier's objective is not merely to attain the destination but to try to obstruct any other skiers met along the waterway, with as much noise as possible.

—Carol Berge

WAR

VOICE/AND/OR/MODULATIONS/,/
VOLUMES/VERBING/THE/UNMIND/

—Arakawa

WAYBACK,OHIO

Where *they* live and/or come from.　　—Joel Oppenheimer

photo by Steve Fitch

See East Jesus, Indiana; Niggerdeath, Alabama; Dumb
Wyoming

WESTERN FRONT MYTHOLOGY

Western Front.....................shop of many parts.....................	
Fancouver	town of buns and pens
Brutiful Brutish Columbia	part of tenny spots
Canadada	land of tenny parts
Marcel Idea	man of penny drops
Mr. Peanut	man of penny crops
Image Bank	mart of penny parts
image bondage	stuck in penny parts
image loss	stop of penny parts
image overdose	flop of penny parts
Lauren Recall	heart of penny drops
Marquis d'Arachide	part of penny crops
Babyland	paths in penny crops
form follows fiction	path of penny parts
banal retentive	stop of penny farts
nothing by mouth	stop of penny part
problem of nothing	stop of penny drops
O.D.	flop of many props
visual insultants	farts of penny parts
thin nostrils	stuck up penny part
rumour hazard	crop of penny farts
teenage crunch	crop of lollipops

..........vocabulaire international deus ex machina
Vancouver terminus city
homemade recreation shopping
Canadada
Michael Morris
Vincent Trasov
mirage carte blanche
mirage reductio ad absurdam
pseudo mirage
mirage boomerang
deja vu cross reference
cosi fan tutti nutcracker
enfant terrible eden
strip-tease facade
top-secret pressure group
information missile gap
proto carte blanche
non-stop macaroni deluge
eye-shadow show business
pince nez cul de sac
problem child pipeline
run-away ping pong orgasm

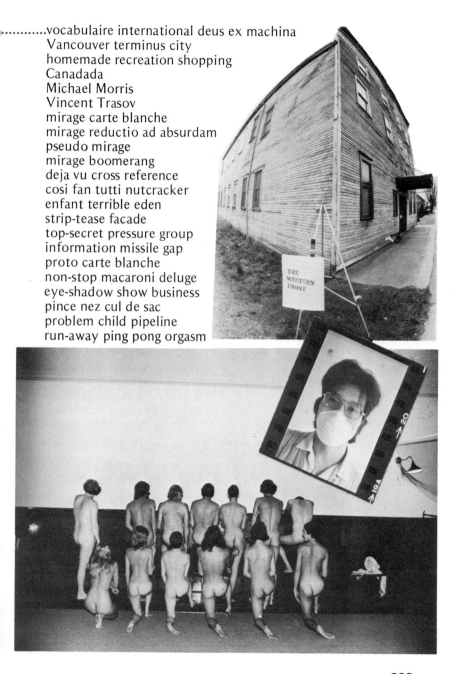

Dr. Brute......................................man of tanny parts......................

Banal Beauty Inc.	mart of tanny parts
Ruby the fop	ham of tanny parts
Howard Huge	stand in tanny parts
Piranha Farms Inc.	cans of tinny parts
brute saxes	chops of tanny parts
leopard realty	crop of spotty lots
Brutopia	state of spotty farts
spots before your eyes	tanned and kitty sights
leopardo pornzini	spots on cranny parts
wussa	kitty litter talk
woofa	toothy barky talk
fayhaye neighhaye	cranny tanny talk
neine fairne	swaty tanny talk
neine hooten	woofa tanny talk
neine hoont	farty tanny talk
Katie Brat	maid of kitty swats
Flying Leopard	spots on kitty swats
Miss Pumpkin	kitty litter swats
Flakey Rose Hip	man of thorny tarts
N.Y. Corres Sponge Dance	
School of Vancouver	pool of thorny tarts
bewilderness	land of leafy tarts
collage or perish	horse before the tart
great wall of 1984	crop of many marts
cut up or shut up	patched up runny tart
survival paradise	myth and props of parks
This is not to be sneezed at	stuck up tarty part

..........Eric Metcalfe
fetish window dressing
old spice fallout
robot prima bomber
eau de cologne bouillabaise
stiletto muzak
collage carnage
bulldozer deodorant
camouflage blind date
vaseline cocktail camera
Mickey Mouse ad lib
underdog ad lib
cockpit dogma
referee dogma
kangaroo dogma
chagrin dogma
Kate Craig
jungle air force sub specie
orange boxing scat
Glenn Lewis

submarine rodeo
pastorale camping ad nauseum
stereotype silhouette suicide
post mortum assemblage
self service censor
postcard utopia
bonanza brainwashing

—Western Front

WHOLE

the aimless turning of the watch-winder to move the hands
an hour on, because the clock in the Swiss half of the Chi-
asso station shows 10:23, the one in the Italian half 11:23;
aimless because always when I do this, I never know whether I gain or lose an hour——looked at as a whole.

—Peter Wehrli
translated by Roger Frood

The big thing behind the other things (parts) or the Opening
behind the Openings: the whole behind the wheat.

—Romaine Murphy

If an arm be cut off from the human body, we still call it an
arm. Yet an arm, when it is a part of the body, undoubtedly
differs from a dead arm: and hence we may easily be led to
say 'The arm which is a part of the body would not be what
it is, if it were not such a part,' and to think that the contradiction thus expressed is in reality a characteristic of things.
But in fact, the dead arm never was a part of the body; it
is only *partially* identical with the living arm. Those parts of
it which are identical with parts of the living arm are exactly the same, whether they belong to the body or not; and
in them we have an undeniable instance of one and the same
thing at one time forming a part, and at another not forming a part of the presumed 'organic whole.'

—G.E. Moore

WHORE

Pimps pick up their whores in big cars after work is done.
Then they take away all the money that the whore has earned. And then they beat up on the whore. After being picked
up in a big car, divested of their money and slapped around,
whores truly enjoy making passionate love to their pimps. As
the Whore Frost says, if you are going to get fucked, you
might as well get fucked all the way.

—Mike Miller

WINDOW

The duke's window made me think—of snail's poison and

of boxwood.

—Arthur Rimbaud

The window cut into our flesh opens onto our heart.
Through it one can see an immense lake on which reddish-
brown dragonflies come to sit at noon, with a scent of
peonies.

—Andre Breton & Philippe Soupault

A sublime blue warmth—leaning against the temples of the
window.

—Paul Eluard

The window opens and closes—like a tempest in a glass of
water.

—Benjamin Peret

The window was to the bird what the wing is to the day.

—Georges Hughet

I'll plug up all windows and doors with earth.

—Pablo Picasso
workings by Ursule Molinaro

WINNING

    a need to achieve greater   than the fear of failure
means ambitious but within reach goals   those with fear of failure
set too difficult goals   no one will blame them for not reaching it
perfectionists like this   those told they have done badly
do better on the second occasion   those told they did well
did less well subsequently in sports successful teams
are those who like eachother when under pressure people pass
to those liked best athletes win more if in possession
of an unusually high tolerance for pain...

—Rose Lesniak

WITTGENSTEIN

The safest philosophical authority to refer to when referring
is part of the act.

—Dick Higgins

WOMAN

—Walter de Maria

See Fish

WORK

greeks and romans saw   it   a curse
christians followed the jewish   considering it punishment
and behavioral scientists concerned with industrial problems
still find ways to make slaves work harder
while there is no work   I work constantly.
Why is this?

—Rose Lesniak

WRATH

Full many mischiefs follow cruell Wrath;
Abhorred bloudshed, and tumultuous strife,
Vnmanly murder, and vnthrift scath.
—Edmund Spenser

One of the deadly sins *(q.v.)*, wrath is anger mixed with
bitter memory. It is aggressive vengeance on the present
for humiliations of the past. It is fanatic and cowardly.
Wrath retaliates against the weak for the transgressions of
the strong and causes suffering without gain or purpose.
It settles nothing.

—Armand Schwerner & Donald M. Kaplan

WRITING

When I sit down to write, I must not forget that one does
not strike an attitude in front of a mountain.

—Carl Rakosi

YOU

In the future you will own an auger feeder for the corn-
meal mix, a pressurized collet machine with a water-
cooled die-head to turn out the puffs, a conveyer that
feeds the puffs steadily to the drying oven, plenty of hot
air and another transfer belt that drops the dried curls
into the tumbler where they are coated with oil and
cheese powder.

—Michael Brownstein

289

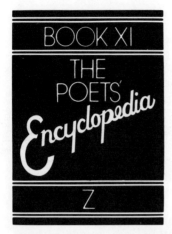

BOOK XI

THE POETS'
Encyclopedia

Z

Z

First letter of my alphabet,
Shot of lightning in the right arm of my name,
Scribble of zed and funny crucifix
Where I hung for years in school in the last row, last seat,
Crying that I could not see the words
Ashamed of how blind I grew under the shadow
Of your beams as I memorized the eye-charts,
Always last, divinely unpronounceable
But, suddenly, years later grateful
When you hurled your weirdest curve
And sprung me from the army where my fate,
As the last boy, gleamed like the crewcuts of the dead.
You stand alone
Beginning what I am to make
Of what is given me, unusual
Or cruel or beautiful
Or plain as the Russian face
I push before me
On the world that wears it out.
And perhaps, Z, you are not even mine!
At Christmastime I called my father, I
Called my aunt, I gathered the addresses
Of the other Zs I have not seen for years.
And as I explained the meaning of our name
Whose history no one could ever tell me,
Gleaned from Polish tailors and chance encounters

With typesetters in offices where I never went again,
"No, no," said my aunt, "Didn't anyone ever tell you
Your grandfather's name was not Zavatsky at all?"
I had reconciled myself to being Polish.
Through all the jokes, exasperated looks
On the faces of Texan bank clerks
I carried you, Z, like a Station of the Cross.
I held you to the light as best I could
Like a brand seared in my eyebrow, a shattered door
I was certain nothing would ever walk through.
I cradled you in my arms like a hopeless icon
Slashed by blubber-lipped invaders, I knelt
In the cold objective blue of your stream
And blessed myself...
                              I get up and pace
Around the room. I am coming to the end
Of my story. "No,"says my aunt,
"Your grandfather took the name
Of a wealthy Polish gentleman in Petrograd
Who paid for his education." Of course
She doesn't know the name he wiped away!
And that is the meaning of Z, a bloody
Scratch on a treasure map, the labyrinth
Of identity, that threads its tireless way
From letter to letter searching out a home,
A name like Zorro the Fox,
My first movie hero!
Like him I leap from the Spanish balcony
In my black silk mask and flying cape.
Like him by day I creep back to another world
To suffer the misspellings of reality;
Smiling at the knowledge that by night,
With the point of my sword, the slash of my words,
I make the sign of the Z

                                        —Bill Zavatsky

ZABLE, BETTY

Box 840 Canal Street Station, New York, New York 10013 (212) 431-8829

UNMUZ LED **OX**

23 December 1977

Ray—
The next issue of *Unmuzzled Ox* will be *The Poets' Encyclopedia*. Diderot asked only the pre-eminent men of his age to contribute to his encyclopedia; we're asking you.

Take any subject from anarchy to Zen and write, draw or compose an article or work of definition. The length should be anywhere from one line to five pages. Though we cannot guarantee that we will publish every submission unedited, we are aiming at inclusivity—we want to present an encyclopedia of poets as well as an encyclopedia for poets.

The deadline is 25 January 1978. We've made it soon to insure spontaneity.

Your other works will be forgotten in 10,000 years. This is forever!

Anxiously,

Michael

Thank you for your article on the Albertfine. We may run two volumes: volume a and volume B-Z. We would very much like to have your thoughts on something from B–to–Z. The Hand

Betty Zable

Ray Robinson

ZEALOUSNESS

the hasty zealousness with which a Turk studying in Paris, even before the arrival in the Sirkeci station, teaches me how to count to ten in Turkish: Bir, iki, uc, dort, bes, alti, jedi, sekis, dogus, on; which reminds me that so far someone in every country has taught me to count to ten.

—**Peter Wehrli**
translated by Roger Frood

ZEBRA

Big, wide bands of black, big, wide bands of white, broad-
ening and narrowing as they run alongside an immobile part
of the animal; rippling athwart haunch & such; in sinuously
interlocking interaction with each other as they impinge &
touch while never generating what—? Gray! No gray areas,
what are gray areas, anyway? The lurking lie, the refusal
one fears to make directly, or worst of all the earned approval unexpressed—*these* produce gray areas, smudges on the
instep and smog in the heart. A tendency to get flakey &
fuzzy when faced with any fact. Tremulous and twittery
responses. Indeed, the tendency of any grayness-of-areas,
even in the miserable realm of tired human verbality, is to
slur and to sputter-stutter shakily & shadily if not set to
rights (the very word "gray," having two spellings as it does,
is itself a "greay" area). But Zebras resist greay areas, all
right.   **—Michael Benedikt**

ZERO OR ZEVEN

If "partly nothing" is to be clearly (sharply) caught,

the net of confusion must be let out and out fully.
                                          —Madeline H. Gins

293

ZIABLOV

Until 17 June 1973 we knew only that A. Ziablov, the serf artist of a Penza landowner N.E. Striuski, lived sometime in the middle of the eighteenth century, died supposedly in 1784, studied handicrafts with Rokotov himself: he had come down to us only through one of his copies from the work of his teacher "The Study of Shuvalov."

We knew a little more about Nikolai Eremeevich Struiski. His contemporaries left us their memoirs, and from their pages we have the image of an eccentric noble, unique in his own way, supposedly a graphomaniac and petty tyrant.

But the material found in 1973 has overturned all our settled impressions, beginning with the character of the "lord" and ending with the date of the death of the "slave."

Even now, it seems strange, as serious historians, familiar with the version of "the terrible eccentricity of the Ruzaevsk lord of the manor," to have taken unreservedly as the truth that A. Ziablov died in 1784, basing this only on one allegorical poem of N.E. Striuski. New documents and the dating of the canvases convincingly testify otherwise: the serf outlived the master, and having received his freedom (very likely in the will of N.E. Striuski), secured a review of his work in Petersburg. We can speak now confidently of this on the basis of "minutes" of the meeting of the Academy of Arts of 7 November 1798—where Ziablov was termed a freely emancipated man.

The correspondence of Ziablov and Striuski compels us to reconsider the established view of the personality of Nikolai Eremeevich, describing him rather as a sort of Childe Harold, a superfluous man, a man born out of his time, easily wounded, who combined in himself an affected boorishness with the spirit of a melancholy skeptic. He deeply respected "the dear friend of my heart Apelles." In view of this, one wishes once and for all—in order to return no more to this unhealthy theme—to reject, decisively, the dirty conjectures, bruited about in foreign art criticism, concerning the character of certain "intimate" relations allegedly having taken place between these outstanding Russian people. It is necessary to remind these sorry theorists that the use of the words "my platonic friend," which gave superficial grounds for the doubtful insinuations, was introduced into the Russian language in the eighteenth century in only one meaning, which left no room for other readings: good human friendship.

Suffering the jeers of the "friends" of the lord of the manor, the serf put his ideas into eternal and now re-born masterpieces. These so-called abstractions, which possess the internal finish and follow the great traditions of realistic technology of three-layered painting, have nothing in common with the art of Imperialism, which arose in the conditions of the last stage of rotting, exploitative society. The artist found his sources in popular patterns of frosted

Ziablov's *Tryptych* (oil on canvas; 20 X 43 inches) c. late 18th century

windows, in the eternally changing nuances of the sea and sky in mid-Russian regions, in the bold play of fire; moreover, his painting was infused by the rich, plastic possibilities of polished sections of decorated stone, for whose ornamentation the Ural masters have been famous since ancient times.

Nevertheless, based on the best traditions, the art of Apelles Ziablov cannot be called without reservations a revolution in art. It was not able to exert a decisive influence on the painting of later generations. Those social conditions which armed art workers with the principles of Socialist Realism had not yet matured in the eighteenth century. Therefore, it would be more exact to call the art of this serf artist a revolt. What Ziablov did in painting is comparable to what his other great contemporary Pugachev did in history. The revolt of Ziablov was put down no less severely than the uprising of Pugachev. Time was needed so that the deeds of these great men could be appraised at their true value.

And it is no accident that recognition has come to them in our great epoch, when the dreams of the best minds of humanity have come true.

—Komar & Melamid

[1] Blackened canvas, rolled up in a tube and packed with scorched sheets of paper, were found in a garret at number 12 Great Vasilii Alley (now demolished). See*Postart*, 7, 1973 (Moscow), pp. 574-577.

[2] Driven in his age to the forced copying of plaster casts, the artist hanged himself. Thus, the serf autocracy dealt with the best representative of democratic culture.

ZYXT

The last word (here, in English, in the OED): an obsolete Kentish form, the second person indicative present of the verb *see*. Language even ends in the eye. In a book, if we are enjoying ourselves, we often reduce our reading pace measurably in its final pages, luxuriating slowly in the joy of words & syntax (unlike that of ideas & referents, where the onset of the conclusion only accelerates the reading), anticipating an inevitable sadness wch follows the end of the (always erotic) body of the text. The book closed sets loose an emotion tinged with jealousy & grief: its presence (wch includes our own reflected in the text) is something we can never again possess. Rereading is not the same: words harden, aura crystallizing to define a wall no quantity of inspection can penetrate. In this after*word* we sense ever so briefly the immense relief we felt in having been deliverd awhile from the weight of directing our own psyches. This is the restorative value of any text (reading is a kind of sleep, a return to the senses). Now we can only wait until this wave of sorrow subsides before seeking the seduction of another book. There is no alternative. You zyxt.

—Ron Silliman

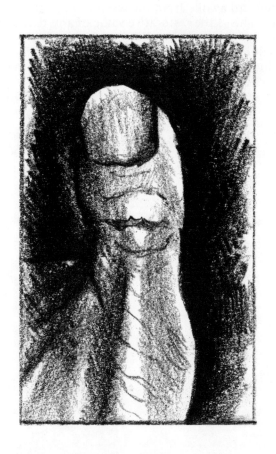

—Marisol

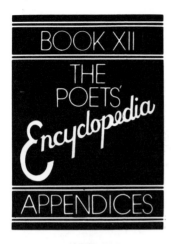

CALENDAR

The twelve books of *The Poets' Encyclopedia* correspond to the twelve solar months. There are 365 entries and each entry corresponds to a day of the year, and reading the right entry on the right day will help you see things right.

Books 1 and 12 are not alphabetized, and their entries are in *italic*. Moveable feasts, that is, feasts of the lunar year, are assigned permanent dates in the solar year. For instance, Passover begins on April I 1980, and that conflicts with the fixed feast of Fools. To prevent misinterpretation, we've moved Passover. NOTE TO MYSTICS: we apologize for the banality of the Gregorian layout, but many of our readers are only semi-enlightened.

January 1 About
Circumcision 2 Undoing
January 3 Frame of Reference
1st Appendectomy 4 *Appendices*
January 5 Gimmicks
Epiphany 6 Grants
January 7 American Art
January 8 Post-Minimalism
January 9 Utricle
January 10 'Armony
January 11 Artoo D-2
January 12 Spot
January 13 Colorado
Winter Day 14 Penguins
January 15 Hominids
January 16 Hare

January 17 Imaginary Beings
January 18 Irony
Pick-me-up 19 Honorable Discharge
January 20 Kayak
School Closed 21 Exclusion
January 22 Latitude
January 23 Melodrama
January 24 Niggerdeath AL
January 25 Travel
January 26 Outland
January 27 Moon
January 28 Krypton 85
January 29 Barf
January 30 Blob
January 31 Sherry

February 1 Fudge Factor
Ground Hog Day 2 Reality
February 3 Junk (W.S.B.)
Denby 4 Denby
February 5 Tweezing
February 6 Wittgenstein, Ludwig
February 7 Shit
February 8 Art Museum
Morrow 9 Voice
February 10 Knitting
February 11 Owl
Lincoln 12 Justice
February 13 Sparrow
Alain Delon Day 14 French Girls
February 15 Profit

Brockman 16 Self Organization
February 17 Linoleum
Pluto 1st Observed 18 Inspiration
February 19 Joke
February 20 Madness
February 21 Singularity
Washington 22 Fabius
1905 Rotary Club 23 Stodge
February 24 Cape
February 25 Roaches
February 26 Wrath
February 27 Stubble
Zavrian 28 Time
Zavrian 29 Time

March 1 Space
March 2 Truth
March 3 Lost
March 4 Ziablov
March 5 Myth
Colette 6 Justine
March 7 Smoke
March 8 Suspicion
March 9 Sex (A.W.)
March 10 Beauty
March 11 Flame
March 12 Whore
March 13 Utricle Lady
Ides 14 Praise
Higgins 15 Self-Reflexivity
Today 16 Tomorrow

March 17 Whole
March 18 Individual
March 19 Zebra
Purim 20 B-Girls
Equinox 21 Newfoundland
March 22 Penal Colony
March 23 Movement
March 24 Beat
Annunciation 25 Radio
March 26 lamb
March 27 Fish
March 28 Evolution
March 29 Chair
March 30 Bronowski
March 31 Cage, John's Song

April 1 Laugh
Owens 2 Tension
Passover 3 Faith
Isidore 4 Lettrism
April 5 1984 Miss General Idea
Easter 6 Church
April 7 Acne
Buddha's Birthday 8 Heaven
April 9 Authority
April 10 Cadavre Exquis
April 11 Abyss Structure
April 12 Ambiguous
April 13 Andy
April 14 Professional Artist
April 15 Money (J.G.)

April 16 Gorilla
April 17 Junk Man
April 18 Censorship
Hitler 19 Slavery
April 20 Anal Intercourse
Dionysia 21 Sex (J.Q.)
April 22 Torch
April 23 Eel
April 24 Love
April 25 Woman
April 26 Goatsucker
April 27 Apprentice
April 28 Kin
April 29 Negro
April 30 Art

May 1 Prophecy
May 2 War
May 3 Turkish-Greek Poem
May 4 Talking
May 5 General
May 6 Junk (A.L.)
May 7 Anti-World
May 8 Brush
May 9 Dance
May 10 1984 Miss Idea Pageant
May 11 Western Front
May 12 Regional Art
May 13 San Francisco Artist
May 14 Los Angeles Artist
May 15 Australia
May 16 Israel

May 17 Frontier
May 18 German
May 19 Prayer
Maia 20 Flowers
Shavuot 21 Synagogue
May 22 History
May 23 River
May 24 Anxiety
May 25 Next
Memorial 26 Army
May 27 Alarma!
May 28 Fireball
May 29 Nothing
May 30 Anti-matter
May 31 Fate Worse than Death

June 1 Absolute, The
June 2 Malay Marble
June 3 Aesthetic
June 4 Anesthetic
June 5 Albertfine, The
June 6 Delusion
June 7 Encyclopedia (A.F.)
June 8 Halphabet
June 9 Cleverness
June 10 Betty Zable
June 11 Dumb Wyoming
June 12 Race Johnsong
June 13 Aesthetics
June 14 Silence
June 15 Mushrooms

June 16 Hutemhanut
June 17 Utriceatelle
June 18 Utricular Pants
June 19 Lechery
June 20 Kindergarten
Solstice 21 Arbutus
June 22 Child
1st Flying Saucer Sighted 23 1947 Earth
Jean Baptiste 24 Levesque
June 25 Mustache
June 26 Casablanca
June 27 Kinematography
June 28 Iraqi
Juno 29 Photo
Joan of Arc 30 French

July 1 General Idea
July 2 Corpse
July 3 Rocket
July 4 Fortress
July 5 Sauteing
July 6 Skin
July 7 Baseball
July 8 Covetousness
July 9 Cars
July 10 Paper
July 11 Poem
July 12 Anything
July 13 Skeleton
July 14 French Literature
July 15 Comprehension
July 16 Fathom

July 17 Sport
Rome Burns 18 64 Classical
July 19 *Index*
Moon Landing 20 Introduction
July 21 Index
Julius 22 *Calendar*
July 23 Encyclopedia (H.K.)
Alex Katz 24 Painting
July 25 Oracle
July 26 Truth
July 27 Lie
July 28 Sneakers
July 29 Vanity
July 30 Junk Food
July 31 You

Seidman 1 Hymn
August 2 East Jesus Indiana
August 3 Judgement
August 4 Laughing Hawk
August 5 Aeroplane
August 6 August 6 1945
August 7 Pain (B.E.)
August 8 Stillbirth
August 9 Granite
August 10 Thunder Basin
August 11 Travel (T.B.)
August 12 Fate
August 13 August 13 1937
August 14 Pain (N.H.)
August 15 August 15 1937
August 16 Sickness

August 17 Crutch
August 18 Solicitude
August 19 Preferences
August 20 Elephant
August 21 Psychopath
August 22 Ant
August 23 Ecstasy
Augustus 24 Work
August 25 Sleep
August 26 Permanence
August 27 Writing
August 28 Junk Man
Chop Suey Invented 29 1896 "Z"
August 30 Awkward
August 31 Narrative

September 1 Biography
Labor Day 2 Art World
September 3 Ashbery
September 4 Amateur Artist
September 5 Hockney
September 6 Art Opening
September 7 Little Magazine
September 8 Cooperative Gallery
September 9 Conceptual Art
Dentist Appointment 10 Drill Art
September 11 Art Collector (Small)
September 12 Football, College
September 13 Art Educator
September 14 Art Collector (Big)
September 15 Money (C.B.)

September 16 Action
September 17 Wrath
September 18 Rush
September 19 Zealousness
Yom Kippur 20 Temple
Equinox 21 Terrorism
September 22 Synch
September 23 Guilt
Hay Fever 24 Self-Allergic
September 25, Football American Pro
September 26 Group
September 27 September 27
September 28 Frequent
September 29 Representation
September 30 Theatre

October 1 Genius
October 2 Porcelain
October 3 Head
October 4 Mind
October 5 Counterphobia
October 5 Counterphobia
October 7 Window
October 8 Five & Ten
October 9 Junk Mail
October 10 Archeology
October 11 Of
October 12 Fire
October 13 Pride
October 14 Fire
October 15 Pride
October 16 *Alcohol*

October 17 *Tittlebats*
October 18 Dipper
October 19 *Conceptual Art*
October 20 *Dave's Corner*
October 21 Academic
October 22 Tongue
October 23 Utricle Pipe
October 24 Transparency
October 25 Wayback Ohio
October 26 Isolation
October 27 Zero
October 28 *Giant*
October 29 Active
October 30 Fascination
October 31 Fantasy

November 1 Elegance
November 2 Repetition
November 3 Habits
November 4 Impulse
Guy Fawkes 5 Gearshift Manifesto
November 6 "S"
November 7 Pascism
November 8 Zyxt
November 9 Anomie
November 10 Collage
November 11 Capillary
November 12 Subliminal Ad
November 13 *for John Baldessari*
November 14 Subscribe to
November 15 Unmuzzled Ox

November 16 *Ocarina Orchestra*
November 17 *Preface*
November 18 *Cover*
Shopping Day 19 *Ads*
November 20 (Jackie Rohrs)
November 21 (Rodney Dangerfield)
November 22 Kennedy
November 23 Consumption
November 24 Wakoski
November 25 Musac
November 26 Television (M.B.)
Thanksgiving 27 Thanksgiving
November 28 Surrealism
November 29 Homerga
November 30 Everything

December 1 "D"
December 2 Denial
December 3 Danger
December 4 Deadly Sins
December 5 Glacier
December 6 Minimalism
December 7 Envy
December 8 Hunger
December 9 Television (J.B.)
December 10 Malnutrition
December 11 *Frontispiece*
December 12 Abyss Structure
December 13 Utricle (V.T.)
December 14 Answer
December 15 *Ox*
December 16 Color

December 17 Casablanca (M.G.)
December 18 Prayer (M.G.)
December 19 Utricledad
December 20 Hope
December 21 -Kin
December 22 Address
December 23 Kindred
December 24 Kinship
December 25 Sacred
December 26 Answer
December 27 *The Eighties*
December 28 Junk Sculpture
December 29 "Z"
December 30 Sloth
Party 31 Hat

ORACLE

Got a problem? Consult our oracle. To catch a giant of wisdom by the toe, eany meany miney moe: take a die and roll it thrice. If it totals 15 or under, take the vertical column with that number. If it's over 15, subtract 15, and the remainder will be the correct number for the vertical column. Repeat for the horizontal column. Where the two columns meet, there is the name of the proper authority. Look up this author's works in the "Index to Authors," and study the entries carefully. If the author has more than two entries, take the last two, and—eany, meany, miney moe fashion—generate a second authority. That is, using the fingers of your left hand for the numbers 1-5, the five senses for the numbers 6-10, and the fingers of the right hand for the numbers 11-15, reading the penultimate entry aloud, counting a number for each word and returning to your left pinky after your right pinky, discover at the last word another number— the number of your vertical column. Repeat with the ultimate entry to find the horizontal column. Take all insoluble problems of the will, smash them *so*, and let them go.

	1 ♡	2 ✕	3 ☽	4 ◯
1 ♡	tom veitch	alan davies	novalis	mae west
2 ✕	marcia resnick	carl rakosi	chris burden	erika rothenberg
3 ☽	jim quinn	paul simons	tristan tzara	warren woessner
4 ◯	benjamin peret	naomi sims	gordon ball	david ball
5 ✝	hannah weiner	kathy acker	bill zavatsky	eugene mccarthy
6 🌳	pier pasolini	paul eluard	j.j. audobon	kenward elmslie
7 ▷	dotty lemieux	hugh kenner	frank o'hara	derek pell
8 ◎	charles morrow	violettes noisieres	brian buczak	andre breton
9 ✓	tom ahern	niccolo machiavelli	laura lenail	ray johnson
10 ▢	simon schuchat	arthur rimbaud	bern porter	j.i. isou
11	a.m. fine	diane de beauveau	charles potts	richard kostelanetz
12 ↓	tom clark	jim de sana	david lenson	art linkletter
13 💡	frank macshane	francis kilvert	henry korn	erskine caldwell
14 ∠	anne waldman	chinese academy	wm smith	bob pelosi
15 ╱	paco underhill	bommi baumann	phil soupault	david rosenberg

5	6	7	8	9	10	11	12	13	14	15
+	(tree)	(triangle)	(spiral)	✓	□	(skyline)	↓	(lightbulb)	(angle)	(line)
vid Ik	george bowering	terry stokes	peter wehrli	samuel pepys	carolee schneemann	gerard cable	wm matthews	claude hamel	barbara guest	western front
arles udire	stuart mott	john cage	marcel duchamp	f.m. brown	romaine murphy	john mcauley	steve fitch	charles darwin	opal nations	harvey shapiro
anne rian	joel oppenheimer	david bromige	charles bukowski	joe brainard	mike miller	gerard malanga	m kaspar	carl solomon	frances whyatt	william stafford
a und	phil graham	charles bernstein	phil levine	m. hemingway	g.e. moore	rose lesniak	t.w. fretter	jon williams	eric mottram	annabel levitt
niel rigan	edward taylor	stuart friebert	lou salome	ursule molinaro	james broughton	david ignatow	les levine	john brockman	georges hughet	judith sherwin
e chler	james sherry	tim baum	henry kessler	alex melamid	rene levesque	john ashbery	christo	irene dogmatic	hugh seidman	nathaniel tarn
s	carter ratcliff	tom shannon	lucy lippard	jeff goldberg	mimi grooms	tom marshall	lita hornick	kathleen spivack	jackie curtis	michael wilding
	michael o'donoghue	arakawa	michael benedikt	carol berge	c.h. ford	peter kostakis	pierre mabille	raymond lulle	richard morris	peter payack
ter ria	sari dienes	bulent ecevit	m.-m. bersenbrugge	steve miller	baffo	rudy burckhardt	max ernst	gilbert white	dick higgins	d.s. hoffman
dy yman	john chamberlain	edwin denby	bob dylan	carlos castaneda	michael lally	regina beck	w.s. burroughs	ron silliman	andrei codrescu	alison knowles
by	barron field	andy warhol	colette	jane delynn	ray dipalma	victor bockris	michael andre	alan ziegler	ron cobb	russell edson
ly nar	jacob bronowski	harry greenberg	muhammad ali	jacob burckhardt	alice cooper	michael brownstein	neal abramson	dali	ken gangemi	romare bearden
lo sso	alfred jarry	donald kuspit	george hitchcock	robert creeley	rochelle owens	madeleine gins	leonard cohen	peter finch	david hockney	general idea
neth ik	chris boyce	gary snyder	georges limbour	allen ginsberg	ellen kahaner	michael horowitz	heraclitus	marvin bell	donald kaplan	linda gutstein
ner	charles plymell	michael tappin	len fulton	marisol	armand schwerner	lautreamont	henry miller	john baldessari	joe bellamy	jack kerouac

305

INDEX TO AUTHORS
This index, used properly by scholars, will reveal the identities of a few pseudonymous and quasi-anonymous contributors.

307

FOR SALE

"Everyone lives by selling something."
                              —R.L.Stevenson & Doktor Bey

Magazine Format

Vol. 1 No. 3   Denise Levertov epistolary interview/essay;
Ron Padgett; Margaret Atwood; W.H. Auden interview
57 pages $2.50

Vol. 2 No. 2   essay by Hannah Green on John Wesley, the
painter; Kenneth Koch; Ray Johnson; Gregory Corso
80 pages $2.50

Vol. 3 No. 2   interviews with Allen Ginsberg and James
Dickey; Robert Creeley; Larry Rivers; Daniel Berrigan
128 pages $2.50

Vol. 4, No. 1   James Wright; Sol LeWitt; Lou Reed; Joe
Brainard; Romare Bearden; Isabella Gardner; Ed Sanders
160 pages $2.25

Vol. 4 No. 2   Andy Warhol, Robert Duncan, Eugene
McCarthy interviews; General Idea; Count Basie
128 pages $2.25

Vol. 4 No. 3   John Cage; John Ashbery; Djuna Barnes;
Gary Snyder, Pierre Trudeau, Philip Glass interviews
128 pages $2.25

Book Format

Vol. 2 No. 4/Vol. 3 No. 1   *The Japanese Notebook Ox*
an unfolding ten-foot long poem-drawing by Gregory Corso
Boxed $2.50

Vol. 3 No. 3   *Yellow Flowers,* poems by Andrew Wylie;
the original Dot Books edition
35 pages $2.95

Vol. 3 No. 4   *Tropicalism,* poems by Kenward Elmslie;
co-published with Z Press
80 pages $3.00

Payment must accompany order
Checks payable to Cultural Council Foundation

Unmuzzled Ox
105 Hudson Street
New York 10013

WHAT TO READ

The Poets' Encyclopedia was published by *Unmuzzled Ox.*
You should subscribe. We shall shortly issue several new works.
We like to send gift cards, mailing gift cards is a charming
occupation. Any back issue of *Unmuzzled Ox* listed on the
preceding page, or an additional copy of *The Poets'
Encyclopedia,* will be sent free to a new subscriber. Make
checks payable to "C.C.F." and send them with your order
to: *Unmuzzled Ox* 105 Hudson Street New York N.Y. 10013.

4 issues for $8_____   8 issues for $14.50_____

Name...

Address..

....Zip........................

extra issue...

Name ....

Address..

....Zip........................

extra issue..................sign gift card...............................